HAWTHORNE

From the portrait by Charles Osgood, 1840

NATHANIEL HAWTHORNE

HAWTHORNE

BY NEWTON ARVIN

. . . . this most deeply planted of American writers, who indicates more than any other the subterranean history of the American character.
—VAN WYCK BROOKS, "AMERICA'S COMING-OF-AGE"

WITH ILLUSTRATIONS

NEW YORK

RUSSELL & RUSSELL

1961

PS
1881
,A7

To

MY MOTHER *and* FATHER

NOTE

I HAVE to express my obligation to the trustees of the Pierpont Morgan Library, and to Miss Belle da Costa Greene, the librarian, for permission to consult the manuscripts of Hawthorne's journals in the possession of the Library, and to make citations from them in this book; to Mr. W. K. Bixby of Saint Louis for permission to quote from the privately printed volume of Hawthorne's love letters based on his collection; and to the Essex Institute of Salem, and Mr. G. G. Wilder of Bowdoin College, for assistance in gathering illustrative material. To the trustees of Yaddo, at Saratoga Springs, and to Mrs. Elizabeth Ames, I am under quite special obligations; and this book owes much, on somewhat different grounds, to Mr. and Mrs. J. W. Ames of Cambridge and Concord.

N. A.

Northampton, Massachusetts
December, 1928

CONTENTS

ILLUSTRATIONS

HAWTHORNE

CHAPTER ONE

Massachusetts, Maine, and Elsewhere

"To insure the greatest efficiency in the dart, the harpooneers of this world must start to their feet from out of idleness, and not from out of toil." — "Moby-Dick."

The thirty-eight New England youths who made up the class of 1825 at Bowdoin College, in the recently admitted State of Maine, uttered their mutual leave-takings in the late summer of that year with probably no more than the usual reminiscent regret, and no more than the usual sanguine inspection of the auguries. A sedate youth from Portland, who was to be known as the chief poet of his time, had just delivered himself of a "commencement part" in the form of an essay on "Our Native Writers." Other parts had been taken by a future Abolitionist and temperance agitator, and by an ill-fated future Congressman; and a young man who was to be Paymaster-general of the navy during the Civil War, and who had failed to qualify for a part, had been one of a club of fourteen formed on the basis of that amiable ignominy. Commencement over, these recent cleavages became as unreal as the more sweeping distinctions of the remote years ahead; and both "ins" and "outs" trudged similarly home to take up, in their various inconspicuous ways, the study of law in New Hampshire attorneys' offices, or the study of theology at Andover, or the pursuit of commerce at Bangor.

None was to be more inconspicuous than the son of a

ship-captain's widow from Salem, who had just distinguished himself in two dubious but characteristic fashions — by paying a fine rather than take a commencement part to which his reasonably high scholarship entitled him, and by refusing to have his silhouette made for the class gallery. Nathaniel Hawthorne had been a shadowy figure even in a small college where shadows could not have been easy to maintain, and he was now to settle down into an obscurity beside which even a law office or a divinity school would have seemed foci of brightness. Yet his companions in college had not been the novices of a monastery, and it was not to any monkish atmosphere that he now returned; his Salem, it is true, was no longer the bustling port of palmy Federalist days, but it was still a busy seaside town, and Hawthorne's classmate, the Reverend George B. Cheever, found it stirring enough, a few years later, when he helped to fire there the opening guns of Abolitionism. There were law offices in Salem from which distinguished jurists had gone and were to go forth; there were East-Indiamen at her wharves to attract the adventurous; and there were pulpits in Salem tabernacles from which both Orthodox and Unitarian could prophesy. If neither the bench nor the sea nor the Spirit had called him, there were already shoe factories near by at Lynn, and textile mills no great distance away at Lowell; even now the new industrialism was making its appeal to the educated youth of Massachusetts. At the very least, there was the Salem Latin School, on Broad Street, where a young graduate of Bowdoin might well have taken his place beside masters from Harvard, the mother college.

At twenty-one, Nathaniel Hawthorne had no such

purposes as these up his sleeve. Indeed, in the eyes of his America, the America of Quincy Adams' administration, he had virtually no serious purposes. On the surface, certainly, nothing could have compared less favorably with the enterprising conduct of his classmates than this sluggish home-coming to his uncle's house on Herbert Street, this settling back into a solitude and inaction no less cloistral than that of his mother, who was still mourning in perfect seclusion for the husband who had died seventeen years before. For a short time, to be sure, there was talk of Hawthorne's entering commercial life through the door of his Uncle Manning's stagecoach business; but of such activities he had had sufficient taste before he had gone off to college four years earlier, and it is doubtful whether either his uncle or Hawthorne himself made more than a ceremonious gesture in this direction. No, he was, in his own eyes, as little fitted for the countinghouse as for the quarter-deck or the bar or the pulpit. These were the scenes for exploiting great talents in the New England of that moment; and, so far as Hawthorne knew, he had no talents of this order — his only well-tested power being a faculty for writing excellent English prose that had been warmly praised at Brunswick by Professor Newman, the author of a famous "Rhetoric." His friend Horatio Bridge had said all along, while they were in college, that "Hath" would turn out to be a writer of fiction; but it was not easy in 1825 to visualize a self-respecting Yankee winning any laurels of that particular growth. The "Sketch Book" and "The Spy", of course, had been read far and wide; but both Washington Irving and Fenimore Cooper were New Yorkers and men of wide

experience; their example could have given little stimulus to Elizabeth Hathorne's son, home again from the
backwoods college on the Androscoggin.

As the cards were stacked in his day and place, everything might seem to have been against Hawthorne's
shutting himself up in his third-story room on Herbert
Street, and certainly against his getting written there a
longish prose romance and "hundreds" of short tales.
No other young man in New England, in the eighteen-
twenties, was doing either of these things, yet Hawthorne did both — and no one who had known him
from the beginning could have been much surprised at
either the solitude or the tales. On the contrary, it
would have been really amazing if he had done the
writing in anything but loneliness and with anything
but the most jealously guarded secrecy. To such an end
all the forces of his childhood and adolescence had
converged.

To begin with, there had been the mere memory of
those "stern and black-bearded" Puritan ancestors of his
who had led such useful — such terribly useful — lives
in the Salem of the seventeenth century. For better or
worse, nothing here need be attributed to strict "hered-
ity"; too many other strains — Gardners and Phelpses
and Mannings and so on — had diluted or sweetened
the blood of William and John Hathorne[1] before Nathaniel was born. But there can be no doubt that Major
Hathorne and his son Colonel Hathorne had survived
actively in the imaginations of their descendants, and
that their shadowy figures, in the eyes of such a child as

[1] The spelling of the name was changed by Hawthorne himself at the end
of his college career.

Nathaniel Hawthorne certainly was, must have been, for more reasons than one, dimly and duskily oppressive. The fact that their hands had been stained with blood, the blood of Quakers and witches, was bad enough, and the tradition of a curse laid upon their line by one of those witches was no doubt still gloomier. All that, however, lay well over a century behind, and might be supposed to have been mollified, if not expiated, by the sheer passage of time. It would have been much harder to forget what great men those Hathornes had been in their day, what expeditions they had led against the Indians, what courts they had presided over, what speeches they had delivered in the colonial assembly, what correspondence they had carried on with the second Charles's secretaries, and even what sermons they had had the authority to preach. To a Salem boy, in the very early nineteenth century, whose first two American ancestors had been men of this mark — soldiers, judges, lay preachers, legislators, all in a lifetime — it might well have seemed that there was but one true path to glory, but one serious ''mode of glorifying God or being serviceable to mankind in his day and generation''; that it was an ill thing to have a poetic imagination, and, in short, that to be a writer of storybooks was little better, little less degenerate, than to be a fiddler.

No Hathorne, to be sure, since the austere Colonel, had been a man of so great consideration as he. The condition into which the race fell in the eighteenth century was to be described by our own Hawthorne as ''dreary and unprosperous''; and certainly the little house on Union Street where he was born in 1804 argues no very brilliant culmination to the genealogical tale. But what-

ever else the intervening Hathornes may have been, they
were realistic men of action such as colonial and Federalist Massachusetts was happy to produce — men who
got things done, served the State, and held their peace.
No calling could have been more honorable in the old
colony than the calling of the sea; and had they not
been, for three or four generations, not only seamen but
ship captains, commanders of merchantmen and privateers? Captain Daniel Hathorne, Nathaniel's grandfather, had been commander of a Revolutionary brig, the
Fair American — a bluff mariner whose gallant encounter with a British transport some leagues off the coast
of Portugal had won him the title of "Bold Daniel"
and the immortality of enshrinement in a ship-surgeon's
ballad. The boy's father, Captain Nathaniel Hathorne,
"a silent, reserved, severe man, of an athletic and rather
slender build, and habitually of a rather melancholy
cast of thought", had, in the very sunniest days of
Salem's glory as a port, commanded a merchant vessel in
the Guiana trade, and had died of yellow fever at Surinam when Nathaniel was but four years old. And if we
are not to forget what were the lordliest claims to honor
in the Salem of that generation, we must recall that one
of Hawthorne's paternal aunts had married a Crowninshield, and that another was the wife of Simon Forrester: two of the great merchant princes of Essex County
— two of the grandees of Derby Street — were thus
among the uncles of the silent captain's children. What
a soil for a scribbler of romances to spring from!

It must have been clear fairly early that the only son
and second child of Captain Hathorne was not cut from
quite the same stout fabric. We hear little of his boy-

hood, but that little is not what we should predict of the
offspring of soldiers and seafarers. Certainly he would
have realized soon enough that his own path was not
going to lead him to the warehouse or the quarter-deck,
or to any of the stages on which those other Hathornes
and Hathorne "in-laws" had played out their virile
rôles. Within a stone's throw of the Manning house on
Herbert Street, whither the bereaved family removed in
1808, were Derby Wharf and Crowninshield Wharf,
which even after Jefferson's Embargo must have been
crowded with shipping; but we hear nothing of Captain
Daniel's grandson haunting the waterside to watch the
stately incoming vessels as they docked, paid their duties,
and discharged their romantic cargoes. The boy was
eight years old when the War of 1812 broke out, and
many an embryonic "man of action" among his young
contemporaries would have been hovering about the
docks in a feverish state of excitement as the privateers
of Salem set sail for their booty of British frigates;
but we detect no echo of these noisy realities in the
anecdotes of Hawthorne's boyhood. His forebears had
come to terms easily, or at least decisively, with the life
about them. He himself was to be granted no such
grace.

It was a queer changeling, to judge from the records,
that these pragmatic Hathornes and Mannings and
Forresters must have been bewildered to discover in their
family circle. None of them, for example, ever forgot
that funny outburst of his when, at a very early age, he
was being treated with too officious friendliness by a
middle-aged woman: "Take her away! She is ugly and
fat, and has a loud voice!" As a promise of Hawthorn-

esque achievements to come, this "squeamish love of
the beautiful" was a singular trait to crop out thus
precociously. We cannot but speculate what his Aunt
Rachel and Uncle Simon Forrester may have thought
of a six-year-old who memorized passages from Shakespeare merely from hearing them read, and went about,
in and out of season, declaiming a favorite line from
"Richard III":

"My Lord, stand back, and let the coffin pass !"

Instead of making models of schooners with the other
Salem boys and sailing them in the North River, young
Hawthorne preferred to go off on long walks by himself
out toward Legg's Hill, and heaven knows what other
remote and unfrequented places. As if this were not
escape enough, he would tell Elizabeth and Louisa, his
sisters, long and fantastic tales of trips he would make
to distant spots, sailing easily through the air — tales
that always ended, so Elizabeth remembered, with the
threat, "And I'll never come back again !" All this was
perhaps not inexplicable in a boy who had pored over
the "Faerie Queene" and "The Castle of Indolence" and
"The Pilgrim's Progress" almost from the time he could
read anything, and whose own tenuous connection with
the prose world about him was little short of Spenserian.
He had been only nine when an accident to his foot in
ballplaying threatened him with permanent disability,
and did actually keep him incarcerated at home for weeks
and months that finally mounted up to well over two
years. But this disaster Hawthorne was to remember
chiefly as a blessing: "Providence favoring" him in his
"grievous disinclination to go to school", as he was to
put it, he could lie for hours on the floor, his bandaged

foot on a pillow, and read — shades of Colonel John Hathorne! — the works of Rousseau.

Commonly, of course, there is no great harm in Spenser and Thomson at any age, and at the age of ten there is probably not much harm even in Rousseau; certainly if these ideal and moonshiny writers are taken along with the proper infusion of reality in the form of baseball games, snowball fights, and marbles. But here was a boy who had already, as it certainly appeared, a more natural connection with the world of the Red Cross Knight and the Enchanter Indolence than with the world of Simon Forrester and Robert Manning, and whose premature love of solitude was being abetted by a virtual invalidism from the age of nine to the age of twelve. It was a real question what was to keep him, at so crucial an age, from living in that fantastic fairy world more hours of the day than were quite wholesome for a boy whose life was to be led in maritime and industrial Massachusetts. What was to keep Essex Street from seeming more remote to him, imaginatively at least, than that voluptuous Bower of Bliss into which the young Guyon penetrated so hardily? What was to help him make the right adjustment between the excellent Thomson's "pleasing land of drowsy hed . . . of dreams that wave before the half-shut eye" and the grimy actualities of Salem Common? Nathaniel Hawthorne had given signs enough already of a resourceful fancy; he was never to be hard pressed to find a fictitious world in which to take refuge from the here and now: what he needed at this age was experiences that would make a provincial seaport also seem a natural home for the imagination. Such experiences he was never to have, and it was the

fault of many things: among others, of the ball that
struck his foot when he was nine years old.

His love of solitude was coöperating with his introspective habits, and the progress of both was to be fortified by circumstance. For that matter, he could not
remember the day when intense solitude had not been
preserved by the most important member of his family.
Five years had passed, at the time of the accident, since
Captain Hathorne's ship had come back from Guiana
without him, and Nathaniel's mother had eaten no
meals with the rest of them in all that period. What had
begun as the expression of violent grief — Elizabeth
Hathorne was in her early thirties in 1808 — had taken
a turn not at all uncommon in New England, and had
settled into the dreary rite of a monotonous sorrow: if
the shadow of that ancestral curse was to assume substance and depth, it could hardly have borne more heavily than this. "A forlorn widow" Hawthorne was to
describe, many years later, as a fiction, "whose grief out-
lasted even its vitality, and grew to be merely a torpid
habit, and was saddest then." "A torpid habit!" —
That was what his own temper was going to make
only too fatally easy for him to acquire: was not the mal-
ediction of the poor witch, Rebekah Nurse, doing its
work at last in setting him this early model of torpidity?

Nor was this all. A generation ago his Grandfather
Manning had bought a considerable property down in
Maine, which was even yet a frontier State in the strictest sense; and here his Uncle Richard Manning, the very
year of the accident, had built a house quite like a hundred houses in Salem, but so much too grand for the
shores of Sebago Lake that the natives had dubbed it

"Manning's Folly." To Raymond, Maine, then, as if Herbert Street were not lonely enough, Elizabeth Hathorne, almost as soon as Nathaniel was really well again, set off with the three children; and there she settled down in the house which her brother Robert had built for her on the opposite side of Dingley Brook from Richard's house. It was, in truth, a fine, wild, solitary place. Here there was no need of walking half the forenoon to find a spot like Legg's Hill; Dingley Bay was retired enough for any one, even Nathaniel Hawthorne, and for such tastes what could be better than the great flat rock on the edge of Thomas Pond, not a mile away, where Dingley Brook had its rise, and where he could lie stretched out for as many hours as the sun was warm, fishing for perch and minnows, or trying his skill at making pebbles skip across the water? All summer long, if he chose, he could wander in the woods with an old fowling-piece shooting hen hawks and partridges; or, in one of the little coves and bays of the lake, strip and bathe alone, as he was to do in other waters so many times in later life. In the winter, when the lake froze over, and when there was a full moon, he could skate by himself until midnight — "with the deep shadows of the icy hills on either hand." If it grew too late, and he could not easily get home, he could take refuge in some log cabin near the shore, with ten chances to one of finding a great log burning on the hearth, where he could "sit in the ample chimney, and look at the stars through the great aperture through which the flames went roaring up."

"If the Indians were very fond of this part of the country, it is easy to see why," he wrote in the diary his

Uncle Richard had given him; and added, "I should have
made a good Indian if I had been born in a wigwam."
Why could he not stay on forever in Raymond, hunting,
fishing, skating, swimming, walking — always walking
— as free as a bird in the air? He was to remember that
happy existence to his last days, to remember it with
sharp nostalgia; yet it was there, he was to say, that he
first got his "cursed habits of solitude." And unhappily
it was not the life of an Indian that he was going to live,
or the virtues of an Indian that he was going to need;
already, after only a year or two in Raymond his Uncle
Richard, back in Salem, was protesting that it was high
time Nathaniel was coming home and getting some
preparation for college instead of living on like a young
savage in Maine. These were the kinds of facts he would
now have to deal with: college and the stagecoach business, or college and the ministry, or college and the law
— college, at all events, and some useful rôle beyond it
that all the lonely pine forests in the world would never
help him for one minute to play. So back to Salem it
was — back to Salem and his Uncle William's ledgers,
the "five-dollar school", and the salty smells of Herbert
Street. No more of Dingley Bay, and the flat rock by
Thomas Pond, and the sun setting in streams of fiery
light over the crags of Rattlesnake Mountain. Nathaniel
Hawthorne was the descendant of State builders, and the
sooner he should come to know it, the better.

Compared with Raymond, Salem was a tiresome place
indeed, and it was an irksome three years that he was
now to spend there. "I do not know what to do with
myself here," he wrote to Louisa. "I shall never be
contented here, I am sure." No wonder he had no idea

what to do with himself: to be fifteen years old, shy, self-contained, proud, a good deal given to daydreaming, was not to have the best equipment in the world for catching up with the other Salem adolescents from whom for five or six years he had been, in one way or another, separated. In Raymond, though there had been William Symmes, a colored boy, for him to go fishing with, to say nothing of Robinson Cook and Jacob Dingley, it had been natural enough to be alone when he chose to. In Salem, if he kept by himself, it had to be in defiance of the boys across the street and around the corner and at the five-dollar school: boys who could not have had much respect for solitude. As a Hathorne, moreover, with aristocratic connections, he could not mingle with the sons of common laborers; and he was too poor to go the way of the young Pickerings and Olivers and Salton-stalls.

It was only through his Uncle Richard Manning's bounty, in fact, that college was to be possible for him; and this meant making himself useful in his Uncle William's coach offices several hours a day, keeping books and learning the value of a dollar. This was dull work, to be sure, but it was better after all than going to school; and sooner or later it meant that he could have a tutor and recite his Latin and Greek lessons at home every morning — leaving the rest of the day for the office and the preparation of his lessons and walks to Gallows Hill and his own reading. What was now, in this last direc-tion, taking the place of Spenser and "The Pilgrim's Progress", which he knew so well? Would his new favorites carry him on the same fantastic journeys away from Salem and into the Arthurian landscape or to the

Delectable Mountains? Well, he had now discovered the "Arabian Nights" and the city of Bagdad under the Caliphate of Harun-al-Rashid. He read "The Mysteries of Udolpho." He read "St. Leon" and "Caleb Williams", and was not soon to forget Godwin's grandiose heroes. "I admire Godwin's novels," he wrote, "and intend to read them all." He discovered, most momentously of all, the "Author of 'Waverley'." Here was the enchantment of distance in all earnest; and the spell was cast, not by an Elizabethan or by a Restoration Puritan, themselves as good as legendary, but by a nineteenth-century advocate, a subject of King George the Fourth, who was even now producing one marvelous book a year, and showing how a contemporary could create romance. In 1820, the year of "Ivanhoe", Nathaniel wrote, "I shall read the 'Abbot' . . . as soon as I can hire it. I have read all Scott's novels except that. I wish I had not, that I might have the pleasure of reading them again." The romantic movement was in full flower; were its seeds to be scattered even here on the rocky ledges of the North Shore? Was Salem to have a Scott, when perhaps she needed a Fielding, if not a Smollett?

It was a question of some importance, for young Nathaniel Hawthorne, reading his Godwin, his Radcliffe, his Scott, was coming to some conclusions about the stagecoach business as he figured out his columns of debits and credits; was trying out his wings, unknown to his realistic uncles, in quite a different element. Up in Raymond, his Uncle Richard had given him a blank book to keep a diary in, feeling no doubt that there was no better way for a boy who had some profession ahead of him, of forming systematic habits of observation and record. But system was not all that Nathaniel had learned in keeping a diary; he had tasted the heady joys of composition for its own sake, and he was not easily to recover his sobriety. The truth was, he had gone so far as to write poetry — a set of stanzas on the tragic death by drowning of Mr. Nathaniel Knight's wife and infant; and these he had read to William Symmes, adding that "he would not have his Uncle Richard see the poetry on any account, for he would be sure to laugh." And if he now went on writing verses between Latin lessons, it was not to show them to his Uncle William; at the most, it was to copy them out in letters to Louisa, with injunctions to her to burn them as soon as they were read. At one time, indeed, it looked as if the fury had spent itself. "I have almost given up writing poetry," he wrote, the year before he went to college — with a protest that was to recur more than once in later years: "No man can be a Poet and a book-keeper at the same time." Certainly it was not easy to manage two horses at once, when one of them was a hackney and the other Pegasus. Certainly it was hard to make peace between the Muses and the stagecoach business. The same perplexity was to beset him, later on, in many guises.

College, meanwhile, was only around the corner; and what problems did that not raise?

I have not yet concluded what profession I shall have, he wrote to his mother in Raymond, the winter before he was to enter college. The being a minister is of course out of the question. I should not think that even you could desire me to choose so dull a way of

life. Oh, no, mother, I was not born to vegetate forever in one place, and to live and die as calm and tran-
quil as — a puddle of water. As to lawyers, there are
so many of them already that one half of them (upon a
moderate calculation) are in a state of actual starvation.
A physician, then, seems to be "Hobson's choice";
but yet I should not like to live by the diseases and infirmities of my fellow-creatures. . . . Oh, that I was
rich enough to live without a profession! What do
you think of my becoming an author, and relying for
support upon my pen? Indeed, I think the illegibility
of my hand-writing is very author-like. How proud
you would feel to see my works praised by the review-
ers as equal to the proudest productions of the scribbling sons of John Bull. But authors are always poor
devils, and therefore may Satan take them.

This was no doubt the right tone of banter for a
Hathorne to take when he spoke of a career in literature,
but we need not for a moment be deceived by it: the diary
and the Knight tragedy and the author of "Waverley"
had done their work; Nathaniel Hawthorne at sixteen
knew that he could turn his experiences into good verse
and even into good strong prose when he put his mind
to it, and, come what might, he was going to follow in
other footsteps than those of the Hathornes and Mannings. The stagecoach business was doomed, and how
many other sensible occupations along with it!

He had, in spite of his Uncle William and his Uncle
Richard, no desire to go to college. Nothing of this,
naturally, was allowed to come to their ears, but he
could not keep it from leaking out in letters to his
mother and Louisa. "Four years of the best part of my
life," he wrote, "is a great deal to throw away." True
enough, this reluctance veiled itself under an unwilling-

ness to be a burden on his uncles for that prodigious period; but we need not doubt that there were stronger motives than this beneath the surface. What could college mean but more Latin and Greek, more contact with unfledged lawyers and doctors and divines, more of the hated duties of the classroom? And what had these to do with authorship?

Yet college it was inevitably to be; happily, not Harvard, however, but Bowdoin, which was at any rate in Maine, and not too far from Raymond. Harvard was the place for sons of the Salem baronage, for the aforementioned Pickerings and Olivers and Saltonstalls; but not for the dependent nephew of Richard Manning. Nevertheless, the young college in Brunswick, still in its first quarter-century, was largely conducted by Harvard graduates; its president, moreover, was the author of a biographical dictionary, and the great Parker Cleaveland was on its faculty. If its tuition was low, and living cheap within its walls, so much the better for Nathaniel Hawthorne. He would have liked to escape college altogether; but he was not sorry to leave Salem behind him, and there was doubtless some gaiety in his heart, one September morning in 1821, as he clambered into the stagecoach that ran from Boston to Portland, and said good-by to Massachusetts for the better part of the next four years. At Portsmouth he was joined by three other collegians, two other freshmen and a sophomore; and at last college had for him virtually begun. Before Portland was reached he was friends with Alfred Mason, who was to be his roommate; with Jonathan Cilley, whom he was to celebrate in prose after an untimely death; and with Franklin

Pierce, who was to be with him, quite literally, until the end.

It was a question now what Bowdoin College was prepared to do, during these bright years of the glorious young Republic, for a youth with a creative imagination that had found its proper aliment in Spenser and Bunyan and Scott — a youth who was telling himself that the writing of such romance might not be too high a task for him, and who was but looking, all unconsciously no doubt, for the masters and the mates who would help him to perform it well. Could Bowdoin do for him what Salem had not done? Could it somehow make the creative life seem a natural and likely destiny for a young American? Could it welcome his adolescent poetry and romance along with the talents of a Franklin Pierce, and lead him into a world where both would seem necessary and honorable? How unfair such questions are! No college since the world began has been prepared to go very far in that direction, and Bowdoin College in the Era of Good Feeling was not Christ Church in the sixteenth century or Edinburgh in the eighteenth. It was on the edge of the New England frontier; it had but just been taken over by the legislature of the State of Maine; it was not being run in the spirit of the Renaissance, but in the spirit of the pioneer; what the citizens of Maine expected of it was clear enough, and that was anything but poetry. If President Allen had been asked whether it was poets that Bowdoin hoped to turn out, the good man would scarcely have known what the question meant. He could only have said that the dozen men on his faculty were equipped to furnish their students with the essentials of a traditional "liberal" discipline, a discipline that aimed at the learned professions; that Latin, Greek, Roman history, mathematics, moral philosophy, rhetoric, and a discreet modicum of "natural philosophy" were the paths to usefulness in society. He could have said that Bowdoin, like Harvard, was prepared to turn out — as it did ! — Congregational ministers, professors of modern languages, senators and governors, allopathic physicians, and presidents. It was not the imagination that Bowdoin could hope to cultivate, but the intellect and the will. In 1821, with less than two hundred students and a handful of professors, with a chapel building and two dormitories and a recitation hall, without elms or gravel walks or memorial fountains, Bowdoin was doing its work with unimpeachable success. Nathaniel Hawthorne might shift for himself.

It was exactly what he was used to doing and prepared to continue to do. Nothing he encountered at Bowdoin was to work any revolution in that respect. Neither his professors nor his provincial companions were the sort of men who could have been expected to search out that shy creative impulse in him, speak the right word to it, and set it to work in a free and proud and natural way. What might have happened if there had been a Hallam in the class of '25, or a Jowett at Bowdoin, who now can say? As it was, Professor Packard and Professor Newman and the rest did what they had to do, said what they had to say, and slept with easy consciences. Giving instruction in the classics and in rhetoric was one thing, and nourishing the literature of the Republic was another; it would have been a kind of miracle if the two rôles had coincided in one man. And who could have expected that the sons of Maine deacons and justices of the peace and lumber magnates would have known a great writer in the bud if they had seen one? Particularly since this Nathaniel Hawthorne had none of the expansive virtues anyway, and was not very responsive to influence.

Not that he gave no signs of the virtue that was in him, or went entirely unmarked by his teachers and fellows. He was no great student, it is true, as his classmate Henry Longfellow was; he did a good deal of unauthorized and certainly desultory reading; there were some branches — metaphysics and mathematics — that he neglected shamelessly and stubbornly; and he would not, under any circumstances, declaim. But Professor Packard remembered his Latin prose exercises for the rest of a long lifetime; and it is said that Professor Newman had so high a regard for his talents in English composition that he fell into the habit of reading Hawthorne's themes aloud to his assembled family. "The recollection is very distinct of Hawthorne's reluctant step and averted look, when he presented himself at the Professor's study, and with girlish diffidence submitted a composition which no man in his class could equal." His style, in fact, must already have achieved its firm and fine Augustan texture, and Professor Newman might well have been moved to give thanks for that. But a glance through the pages of the professor's "Rhetoric" will make it manifest why his influence remained a formal one. The word was not Professor Newman's to speak, and indeed it went unspoken.

There was, of course, young Henry Longfellow, three years his junior, who already had to his credit poems that had seen print, and who so infallibly recited in his quiet, confident, studious, gentlemanly way. This might have been Longfellow's moment with Hawthorne: the word might now have passed between them. If it failed to do so, was it only because of the difference in their ages? Was it only because Longfellow belonged to the Peucinian, the conservative literary society, and Hawthorne belonged to the Athenean, the more advanced? Was it the difference between a background of Portland's best society and the background of solitude at Raymond? But Stephen Longfellow, Henry's elder brother, had Portland society behind him too, and there was no great silence between Hawthorne and him. No, it could only have been that Hawthorne's perception was more acute than he could have known; that in some obscure, unconscious way he knew that Longfellow and he spoke a different vernacular and could establish no real communication; that Longfellow's world was a cultivated, charming, bookish, sunny world, pleasing to look at from a distance, perhaps, but not a home for the imagination. In later years they could speak even across the gap between them, even across Longfellow's uncertain comprehension and rather vague sympathy; but in Brunswick it was too early for that, and both undergraduates went their separate ways without a sign of recognition. If, as they came and went to Professor Packard's Latin class, or listened to declamations in chapel on Wednesday mornings, Longfellow exemplified the literary life in Hawthorne's eyes, it was for reasons that could have heartened him but little;

if he himself was to be a writer, clearly it would have
to be on a very dissimilar tenure.

What he looked for in friends, indeed, seemed to be,
on a curious compensatory principle, not imaginative
companionship or common literary tastes, but something that should stand at a polar distance from just
that, something coarse, prosaic, matter-of-fact, muscular; something set inertly on the common earth and as
little volatile as possible. Perhaps to be with Frank
Pierce or Horatio Bridge gave him a warm sense of the
tough objective fact, the fact untouched by fancy, the
letter without the spirit. Perhaps some instinct told
him that these unimaginative youths, with their cards,
and their light wines, and their campus games, their
easily achieved high spirits and easily defined practical
purposes, had something for him that the Longfellows
of the earth could never give him, something he would
neglect at his peril. If there was no connection between
his dusky inner world and the bright outer world in
which Pierce lived, at least he could take both worlds
straight; he could drink both wine and water, but he
need not dilute the one with the other. At any rate, it
was men like Pierce and Bridge and Cilley whom he
clove to most tenaciously; it was their hilarities that he
enjoyed partaking in, and their confidences that he enjoyed hearing. Undoubtedly, too, there was something
about him that exercised a strong sway over them;
something in his shyness, his taciturnity, his grave
smile, his marvelous eyes, that told them what order
he belonged to, whose man he was. But he remained
always a little puzzling even to his intimates. "I love
Hathorne," said Cilley; "I admire him: but I do not

know him. He lives in a mysterious world of thought and imagination which he never permits me to enter." That, perhaps, was Hawthorne's problem too, the problem of how to admit Cilley into that mysterious world, how to bridge the chasm between them. What was the clue? What was the password? Was there, indeed, a route that he could chart?

His four years at Brunswick were an attempt to solve that problem, and they were not very successful. At the end, as at the beginning, and in spite of all the fellowship that came between, he had that unhappy sense of estrangement from the ordinary concerns of men which had been growing upon him for so many years. He could play cards for small stakes and rejoice over getting fined for the misdemeanor along with the rest. He could take his place in the ranks of the college military company that Frank Pierce organized and helped to officer; this kind of drilling was to be preferred to certain others. He could participate in the discreet revelries at Ward's Tavern, and in a spirit that made him always a desired guest. Yet "he never told a story or sang a song. His voice was never heard in any shout of merriment; but the silent, beaming smile would testify to his keen appreciation of the scene and to his enjoyment of the wit. He would sit for a whole evening with head gently inclined to one side, hearing every word, seeing every gesture, and yet scarcely a word would pass his lips." To any of these convivialities, Hawthorne preferred his wanderings about the backwoods country in and around Brunswick, made on one unsocial pretext or another — gathering blackberries under the pines, or going bat-fowling in the twilight, or standing on the

brink of the Androscoggin to watch the great logs as
they tumbled down its current, or fishing for trout in
the clear little stream that emptied into it, or walking
the two or three miles over sandy roads to Maquoit Bay,
where one could have a glimpse of salt water if not of
the open sea itself. These were the things Hawthorne
was to remember longest and most fondly, and all the
rest was to fade rapidly from his mind; or, if it did not
actually fade, was to take on, once college was over, the
air of something encountered in a dream, something
alien, spectral, remote. He had come to care deeply for
Pierce and Cilley and Bridge, to care for them more
deeply than he would ever have supposed possible: but
how many things there were he could not say to them!
With what portentous finality he had to recognize, at
the last, that the more resolutely they should go their
ways, the farther their paths would diverge from his.
How hard it was to believe in their aspirations, or communicate his own to them! As the end of his senior
year drew on, it must have looked as if Bowdoin, far
from undoing the work of Salem and Raymond, had
but added its own item to the bad total. Instead of
facing buoyantly the broad world that lay beyond its
ceremonies, Hawthorne was shrinking with acute apprehension from all that the others were so eager to
confront.

That apprehension his well-meaning Cousin Dike
had made articulate the very month before commencement, having dropped in on Hawthorne at Brunswick
on his way home from somewhere in Maine, and having then, when he got back to Salem and was ques-
tioned by the family, given a magnanimous report on

the young man. What could they not all expect of Nat; what great things was he not almost certain to achieve? — So ran the burden of his testimony. Probably none of them therefore was prepared for the retort that came back from Bowdoin in a letter to Louisa.

I am not very well pleased with Mr. Dike's report of me. The family had before conceived much too high an opinion of my talents, and had probably formed expectations which I shall never realize. I have thought much upon the subject, and have finally come to the conclusion that I shall never make a distinguished figure in the world, and all I hope or wish is to plod along with the multitude.

What Louisa may have made of this protest, we cannot know; she could hardly have taken it at its face value. Hawthorne had won golden opinions from others besides the members of his family — from his teachers and classmates, and from President Allen himself. His present achievements had taken no very tangible form, but nothing about him seemed to predict a future of plodding along with the multitude. If Louisa read between the lines she no doubt perceived the state of mind from which her brother's words arose — the anxiety lest he be credited with talents he did not have, with aspirations he did not cherish; the eagerness, if that was the alternative, to disclaim all talents and aspirations whatever. It was as if he preferred to make no promises at all rather than make promises he could not hope to keep.

Meanwhile he was not telling any one the whole truth, and perhaps it was but obscurely evident to himself. It was to come out in disguise when it did

come out; but for the discerning eye there was, in the
romance Hawthorne was soon to write, a paragraph
that showed clearly enough what fire he had put his
irons in. Did the family read between the lines? "Fanshawe," we are told of the hero, "had hitherto deemed
himself unconnected with the world, unconcerned in
its feelings, and uninfluenced by it in any of his pur-
suits. In this respect he probably deceived himself. If
his inmost heart could have been laid open, there would
have been discovered that dream of undying fame,
which, dream as it is, is more powerful than a thousand
realities. But, at any rate, he had seemed, to others
and to himself, a solitary being, upon whom the hopes
and fears of ordinary men were ineffectual." Here, in
a few pregnant words, was an account of what happened in the late summer and fall of 1825, an emblematic
description of that return from Brunswick to Salem
which was to seem so inglorious in every retrospect.
No less than the Pierces and Bridges and Cilleys, Hawthorne had his eye on a far and difficult goal, but unlike
them he could envisage his journey toward it only as a
journey in solitude. In the world that he knew there
were broad, pervious, well-trodden paths to fame of the
kind they were to win; there were no paths at all to his
kind of fame, no guides, no blazes, no charts; if a man
was to set out in that direction, he must be prepared
for the fatigues of the wilderness and the perils of solitude — prepared too, perhaps, for the discovery that
the goal itself was a flickering mirage.

Some sense of this, indeterminate enough, no doubt,
must have been present to him as he installed himself
languidly in the little third-story southwest room

under the eaves of the house on Herbert Street, and gazed out at the bustle of the waterside streets below him, and listened abstractedly to the distant shouts of teamsters. Here he was with a bachelor's diploma from Bowdoin in his pocket, and the high hopes of the whole family on his shoulders, and the excellent examples before him of all those industrious relatives and friends — and what was he himself on fire to do? Nothing less than to try his hand at storybook writing, at making up plots and imagining men and women enacting them, at polishing and perfecting his prose style — to see, in short, whether that vivid inner world in which he found it so delightful to live might be brought into some fruitful relation with the authentic outer world of Salem, of Massachusetts, of New England, even of the dimly outlined background of all America. Fortunately he did not guess how much was at stake — for America, if not for himself — in the outcome of his so wayward, so obscure, so small and private undertaking. Fortunately, too, he did not guess how much of his life was to be passed in that "dismal chamber" or what dangers he was to run before he should emerge from it at last.

CHAPTER TWO

THE HILL DIFFICULTY

"Thought you greatness was to ripen for you like a pear?" —
Whitman, "Democratic Vistas."

"SINCE we last met, which you remember was in Saw-
tell's room, where you read a farewell poem to the relics
of the class," Hawthorne was to write, twelve years
later, to Longfellow — "ever since that time I have
secluded myself from society; and yet I never meant
any such thing, nor dreamed what sort of life I was
going to lead." It had indeed been a singular affair,
this spectacle of a young man — a young man who
aimed, not at the spiritual peace of an anchorite, but at
the literary fame of a prose romancer — isolating himself from the common human life where all his materials should have lain, and shutting himself up in
his room to brood like a monk over human destiny, to
read books *about* the real world, and to write inter-
minably — but about what? Was this the right discipline for a Balzac, a Dickens, even a Scott? Was a
"Heart of Midlothian", to say nothing of a "Cousin
Pons" or a "Martin Chuzzlewit", to be sent forth from
the dim cell of a recluse? No wonder Hawthorne never
intended such a thing: his cool judgment would have
told him, even at the outset, what hazards he was running, as a creative artist, in taking up such a mode of
life. Unhappily, his cool judgment was not called into
play at the outset, or for many years to come; and mean-

while he did the only thing he would have been likely, under the circumstances, to do.

For the forces of his own temperament, of his youthful reading, and of contemporary America, were, as we have already partly seen, at war with Hawthorne's aspirations as a writer, or at the best not in alliance with them. Whatever produced it — the Hathorne austerity and his mother's morbid sensibility in his blood, or the lonely years of his boyhood, or the social bleakness of Brunswick — certainly the diffidence, the shyness, the aloofness that had become his most salient qualities were an obstacle to the formation of those humane and cordial habits that would have brought him into relation with real men and women, in whom he had, after all, so deep and curious an interest. If meditative poetry had been the vein he most desired to strike, he could no doubt have cultivated his solitude with impunity; as it was, he was in the position of a man capitulating without a struggle to his most malignant enemy. Here he was, on the threshold of his journey, setting up a dualism that was to molest him to the end, shunning the ordinary occupations, the grand typical experiences of human life, when what he most wanted to do was to translate them into art. And is it fanciful to see in this surrender to a misanthropic habit the outcome in part of his earliest contacts with literature — of that boyish and youthful poring over the works of the great Puritans and the great romantics; of that taste for Spenser, Milton, and Bunyan, and the later taste for Rousseau and Godwin and Scott? Had not all these cultivated in him, by one delicate pressure or another, a moral or an imaginative distrust of experience, a "fine inhumanity", an impulse to deny the world, or to escape from it? Denial and escape! — those were the alternatives that Bunyan and Rousseau had to offer him; and small wonder if he tended to view his environment as a repellent compound of Vanity Fair and "civilized society." Small wonder if he had come to think of greatness as the product of loneliness — not, as it is, of symbolic solitude, but of literal isolation, which is only the path to sainthood.

At all events, there were in truth, for a young man aspiring to literature, excuses enough for regarding the American scene, the New England scene certainly, with diffidence and distrust. Not that there had not been, as there continued to be, high talk in official and quasi-official quarters about the Future of American Letters; not that eminent personages had not enjoined the American Poet to arise and sing. But in 1825 this eloquence had not yet lost its prevailingly political ring: it was still distinctly forensic, republican, even consular. And it retained the color of a rather abstract hopefulness, a somewhat Israelitish aspiration. Concrete proposals for the fostering of literary talent were still notably wanting; and meanwhile American publishers, in the happy absence of an international copyright, made hay in the sunshine of European fecundity. Ten years later, Hawthorne was to record, with resentful resignation, his discovery, confirmed by more than one experience, that "no American publisher will meddle with an American work — seldom if by a known writer, and never if by a new one — unless at the writer's risk." The American author, in consequence, had pretty inevitably to be either a man of means and leisure or, as

MAINE HALL, BOWDOIN, WHERE HAWTHORNE
LIVED AS A SOPHOMORE

76 FEDERAL STREET, BRUNSWICK, WHERE
HAWTHORNE LIVED AS A JUNIOR AND SENIOR

Bryant and Emerson and Bancroft were demonstrating, a man with a practical profession. Less than a year before the college commencement we began with, Henry Longfellow's father had written to him the soundest of advice on just this score. "A literary life, to one who has the means of support, must be very pleasant. But there is not wealth enough in this country to afford encouragement and patronage to merely literary men." When Erie canals had to be built and Cumberland roads to be laid out, where, as Stephen Longfellow observed, was the money to pay young poets for their odes and young novelists for their romances? And the works of Scott and Byron, on this side of the Atlantic, were as free as the public lands.

The chillness of a writer's economic prospects was bad enough, but there were deterrents at once more serious and more impalpable than this. In the New England of that decade, Hawthorne would scarcely have known whither to turn for companionship with men as interested as he in the creative life regarded as an autonomy, as something more than a handmaid to politics. Literally nowhere, in that tight little Yankee world, was there a Leigh Hunt to publish a young man's sonnets, to write sonnets in competition with him, or to introduce him to the Italian poets. Nowhere was there even a minor Goethe to perform the laying on of hands, or a minor Victor Hugo to administer the accolade. There were people of cultivation in Boston, of course; scholarly men like George Ticknor, who had studied in German universities and who were prepared to lecture on modern European literatures; but one can too easily imagine what the conversation

of these men would have been like. There were the
"cultivated old clergymen", as Poe was to call them, of
the *North American Review*, with their austere imitations
of Edinburgh journalism; the last thing these powers
were likely to do was to print any sketches that might
come to them out of Salem. Boston, in those days, had
no poets living in cheap lodgings, eating in second-rate
chophouses, quarreling in seedy cenacles over the
problems of versification; no intransigeant little sheets
like Leigh Hunt's to print the work of any unknown
and unconventional young Keats. If there was an intellectual "atmosphere" in Boston, it was a dry, thin,
delicately provincial element; and it had collected with
the greatest density it could yet attain, not in any
book-printer's sanctum or poet-haunted basement café,
but in the shadowy and shelf-lined recesses of the
Athenæum. Certainly there was never a moment when
Boston, as a setting for the literary life, could have
beckoned to Hawthorne with a touch of the seductive-
ness of London or Paris; and if New York came a little
nearer to making a home for cliques of young writers
— well, what an extraordinary set those Pauldings and
Hallecks and Verplancks were! The highway from
Brunswick or Salem to their haunts had simply never
been mapped. Nathaniel Hawthorne would have stayed
shut up in his room in Salem for the rest of his mortal
life before he would have ventured into that urbane
and dandified region.

He was to do, in the sequel, neither of these things;
but he was to make experiment of the dismal chamber
with deadly thoroughness before describing himself to
Longfellow, now Professor of Modern Languages at

Harvard, as "dwelling in an owl's nest." How noise-
lessly and imperceptibly that owlishness had crept upon
him! How easy and natural it had seemed to postpone
from month to month the plunge into Uncle William's
business, and meanwhile to sit at his own pine table
day after day, scribbling pages and pages of manuscript,
or reading Cotton Mather's "Magnalia", or merely gazing into the coal fire and meditating! Solitude, in those
months following commencement, was becoming for
him an insistent, an almost physical necessity, like
bathing in cold water; and nowhere in the world was it
easier to be by oneself than here on Herbert Street. No
other family in the world would have made so few
demands on one's sociability as this family in which
seclusion, now that Elizabeth and Louisa had fallen into
their mother's ways, was the very principle of household ritual — this family in which meals were rarely
eaten in common, and most frequently served in the
privacy of separate bedrooms. Here one could believe,
almost without effort, that the realities of the nineteenth century were no realities at all, but vague and
dubious rumors, less substantial than the presences of
one's Puritan forebears, less credible than the men and
women of romance, less urgent than the voices of one's
own quixotic dreaming. There would, at last, be no
classes for Hawthorne to attend, no accounts for him
to keep, no tiresome and unintelligible people for him
to adapt himself to at the cost of his own integrity.
One day would be very much like another; his outer
life would take on a drowsy, mesmeric monotony; all
the little adjustments of animal existence would be
made once for all, fixed in unresisting patterns like the

daily movement of sunlight across the carpet, unob-
structive to the operations of the fancy. Inactive as
such a life might seem from the outside, for how much
strenuous activity it would nevertheless leave time!

For it was not mere indolence that made this torpid
habit so easy to adopt and sustain, so difficult to throw
off when it had become constitutional and worn.
Hawthorne knew — no one better! — that life could
have its intensity, its vividness, its depth, as truly in
this solitary room of his as in the forum and the market-
place where his contemporaries were even now astir.
He knew what could be made of the hours one spent
brooding over the strange inexplicable facts of human
fate, facts that had come to him partly from his books,
of course, but partly, too, fresh and first-hand. He was
never weary of speculating what, in either case, they
could mean. He was never weary of considering the
destiny of the human beings who stalked through the
pages of literature with a gait so lofty and heroic, who
rose up out of the fogs of the past with a port so haughty,
and who scurried about, in Brunswick and Salem, so
meanly and ignobly. There was nothing about them
that did not interest and even fascinate him, and the
fascination grew the more he pondered over them. It
was endlessly absorbing to guess why greatness and pet-
tiness elbow each other so crowdingly in men's affairs;
why sordidness and beauty are, as it seems, so meaning-
lessly mingled; and, in particular, why there is so in-
scrutable an alternation of gaiety and gloom in what
men do, so dark an undercurrent in the stream that glit-
ters so brightly on the surface. What, in all this going
and coming, we may imagine him asking, what is real

and what is merely spectral? — For certainly, as he ruminated here winter and summer in silence, there was much in the world outside, remembered or distantly regarded, that seemed more illusory than his own night-mares. Perhaps, he may have thought, perhaps it is only the gloom that is tangible! Perhaps the dark undercurrent is the stream itself! About that, at all events, there was something that he could feel sure of, something that, unlike much else, did not evaporate, no matter how long he pondered on it; and Hawthorne found himself, during those eventless years that would have seemed to all other men alive so tame, so poor, so frosty, entertaining angels — fallen angels, if you will — whose presence was intolerant of boredom.

In such terms would the real history of those years have to be written; but the materials for it, so far as they exist, must be looked for in the tales that were their palpable result, and these must wait for their place. Meanwhile, let us see what externalities made up the count of days he was to speak of as "very tran-quil and not unhappy" when he looked back upon them from the vantage point of forty-seven.

It is true that they were outwardly very tranquil; true too that they were spent, as he said, very much as an owl would spend them. "His habits were as regu-lar as possible," said his sister Elizabeth years later. "In the evening after tea he went out for about one hour, whatever the weather was; and in winter, after his return, he ate a pint bowl of thick chocolate (not cocoa, but the old-fashioned chocolate) crumbled full of bread: eating never hurt him then, and he liked good things. In summer he ate something equivalent, finishing with fruit in the season of it. In the evening, we discussed political affairs, upon which we differed in opinion, he being a Democrat, and I of the opposite party. In reality, his interest in such things was so slight that I think nothing would have kept it alive but my contentious spirit. Sometimes, when he had a book that he particularly liked, he would not talk." Indeed, if this was true, he must have been frequently taciturn.

Another witness who remembered him at this time testified that "he was even then a most noticeable person, never going into society, and deeply engaged in reading everything he could lay his hands on. It was said in those days that he had read everything in the Athenæum Library in Salem." To the scholarly Longfellow, to be sure, he disclaimed any credit as a student — "I have indeed turned over a good many books, but in so desultory a way that it cannot be called study, nor has it left me the fruit of study" — but perhaps this meant only that he was not ready to give lectures on what he had so uncalculatingly read. Such an attitude toward books he was never to adopt or even to understand; he was never, in the literary sense, to be interested in literature. But in a deeper sense Hawthorne had always drawn sustenance from books, and he now fell back upon them with the slightly desperate zest of a prisoner in a well-stocked library. There were few types of reading that he left quite untasted; he is known to have gone through the works of Voltaire, and it is on record that in the year 1830 he drew from the Salem Athenæum such works as Hitt on fruit trees and a three-volume English botany. But so far as he preferred one type of reading to another, it was

history and the literature of travel that he reverted to
most faithfully. He discovered what wealth there was
in such unpromising tomes as Vertol's "History of
Sweden" and the Massachusetts Historical Collection.
All history, he found, has juice in it, even the history
of the Reformation; but naturally the early records of
his own country — Felt's "Annals of Salem", Cotton
Mather, the "History of Haverhill" — had claims
upon him that no other chronicles could make. Was
it not out of stuff such as this, stuff not always indeed
so fertile or so fine, imaginatively viewed, that the
European romancers had spun their fiction? It had,
like all history that had got into books, the charm of
facts at once human and distant, as Hawthorne on one
side liked facts to be; and it cast over him, with its
ancestral, its even pious connotations, a curiously irre-
sistible spell. The travelers, on very similar grounds,
engaged him endlessly: Pausanias, Herodotus, Mandeville, Hakluyt, Tournefort, Bartram, Madden, Chrishull
— with what an alluring combination of the vivid and
the remote they conjured up for him those Mediterranean, those Asiatic, those Australasian lands where
the imagination found it so easy to be at home! Inert
as he might seem physically, Hawthorne had in him
the blood of emigrants and sea captains, of men who
had found one spot, one village, too cramped a stage for
the actions they had to perform; and whether it was this,
or merely the tenuity of his connections with the Salem
about him, his unconquerable sense of estrangement
from it, true it is that the recluse was also a wanderer,
a wanderer in time and place, a native of a hundred
far countries more congenial than Massachusetts, a

coeval of countless men less alien to him than Webster or Calhoun.

Even in the flesh, though for a young American he was solitary and sluggish enough, he was not literally inert. There was never a time, except in cold weather, when the somber pleasure of being shut up in his room was great enough to keep him from escaping, in the cool of the early morning, to some cove or inlet of the bay where he could bathe in tingling salt water, and get a breath of the sea into his lungs, and stand dreaming for a moment with his eye on the curved horizon. For a long time he disliked to be abroad except at such hours and after nightfall. Indeed, if he ventured out in the evening, it was more likely than not to be on a wet and murky night, when there was no disconcerting full moon, and the poorly lighted streets of the town were as deserted as they could be, and he could go and come without encountering anybody but the night-watch and a luckless reveller or two. In the winter, especially, it is true, when the pine table and his sheets of blank paper held him most absorbingly at the labor of composition, there would be days on end when he would not stir beyond the threshold of his chamber. But even for Hawthorne this complete immurement could not last forever; even for him there would come times — after a few years, would come more and more frequently — when the shadows in the midst of which he lived seemed to deprive him of all credence in the reality of human life, all confidence in the truth of the visible world; and he would be driven forth to mingle, however close to its margin, with the current that flowed so steadily beyond his four walls. If he could

not participate in the movement, if he shrank from
elbowing Tom, Dick, and Harry, at least he could be
a spectator; he could administer a kind of pinch to
himself by climbing up into the steeple of the South
Church and gazing over the town that clustered about
its foot, animated in the warm summer sunshine; or he
could take up his station on the bench before the toll-
gatherer's house in the middle of the Beverly Bridge
and watch the teamsters and carters and coach drivers
pass and repass through a long and sultry day. He discovered that it was better than nothing, as a means of
reassuring himself about this slippery world, to spend
the whole day walking along the seashore — on Salem
Neck or so relatively far away as Nahant — where he
could be alone and yet not quite secluded; where he
might see a group of girls sitting on the edge of a rocky
basin and paddling their feet in its water, or a small
boat riding at anchor a few rods off the shore with a
party of fishers in roundabout jackets; where, in short,
there would be a few other human beings to remind
him that his own existence was not a mere illusion. At
one time the fishing village of Swampscott, over beyond
Marblehead, knew him well; the old salts in Mr. Bart-
lett's store, spinning their yarns about cruises against
the French and expeditions against the cod, smelling
strongly of rum and tar, were images of an unmistakable substantiality; a certain fresh-visaged maiden
behind the counter of a little notion store, whom he
had first seen on the bridge near King's Beach, is said to
have made Hawthorne's heart flutter for a few days
with a quite terrestrial excitement. But he exchanged
no words with either the tars or the maiden.

On two or three occasions, so difficult was it to maintain a yearlong isolation, Hawthorne went still farther afield; took advantage of his nominal connection with a stagecoach line to make excursions into other parts of New England — northern Vermont and the New Hampshire mountains — and once, finding himself as far away as Albany, and deciding to be a real Mandeville, went the whole length of the Erie Canal to Buffalo and saw Niagara. These were lands, unmistakably, in which one could journey forever and be in no danger of getting one's feet off the earth. An unkempt, unsmoothed, raw-boned, nasalized country — humanly speaking — this America assuredly was. How far away, how positively astronomic, seemed, in contrast, the China of Marco Polo, the Constantinople of Gibbon, even the Scotland of Scott! Here there were no pompous and fantastic cities; no echoes, no fragrances of the Middle Ages; no costumed figures with the air of having stepped from a tapestry or an illumination. Here were only the gaunt little cities of the New England interior, the backwoods villages of New Hampshire, the new brick and muddy streets and bustling markets of the Canal cities in central New York State. Here were freshly painted stagecoaches with their sharp-featured drivers; flat, rectangular, crowded, slowly moving canal boats, and canal freighters laden with lumber, salt from Syracuse, or Genesee flour; the covered wagons of itinerant showmen; the sleighing teams of Burlington dealers on their way through the Crawford Notch to Portland. Here were taverns, inns, even "hotels", of every variety, from Ethan Crawford's

mountain lodge with the antlers of a deer over the door-
way, to the stylish Maverick House in East Boston, its
landlord fashionably dressed, its barroom crowded with
Sunday gentlemen ("clerks" on week days) from the
city, its bill of fare for the day stuck up beside the
door. And what a seedy, uncouth, lank, miscellaneous
population it was that came and went restlessly in
these stagecoaches, canal boats, sleighing teams! What
manner of folk were these countrymen of his? What language must he learn to communicate with them? As he
wandered about New England and New York on these
(for him) adventurous excursions, Hawthorne felt growing up in him an odd, aloof affection for these tobacco-
chewing mountaineers, these ruddy Irish emigrants,
these flashily dressed city swells, these sharp-eyed trad-
ers from Detroit, all these strenuous, alert, pragmatic,
unimaginative Yankees, going about their prosy business as if Rochester or Hartford were the center of the
universe, and 1830 the very summer of the Golden Age.
But how aloof that affection was! With what essential
solitude he felt himself, he the "unoccupied", the
"idle", the merely speculative one, invested!

Then the renewed, intensified loneliness, when he was
back in it, of his chamber under the eaves, and the
attempt, rendered (if anything) more onerous by these
interludes, to "open an intercourse with the world" by
means of the tales and sketches he would go on writing. For he had not been only a reader and a dreamer in
those months and years that ensued upon college; his
aspiration to be a writer had not remained a mere untenanted Castle in Spain. So coercive, indeed, had his

ambition been, and so tenacious his purpose, that with no external incitement, and no sense of a responsive audience, he had fallen to work, perhaps during the last year at Bowdoin, on a series of "Seven Tales of My Native Land"; and during the following year he had had the industry to write a whole book — the romance he entitled "Fanshawe." The fate of neither the tales nor the book, to be sure, had been anything but disheartening. The "Seven Tales", after reading them to his sister Elizabeth, he had sent to one publisher after another, only to have them returned without ceremony; and when finally a venturesome printer had been found to undertake their issuance, this worthy had procrastinated so unconscionably that at last Hawthorne demanded their return and, with a temporary sense that his great expectations were a fraud, burned them to gray ashes. "Fanshawe" had had somewhat better luck: no publisher had been willing to take any risk with it, but Messrs. Marsh and Capen in Boston had agreed to print it at Hawthorne's expense, and no doubt it was worth the hundred dollars it cost when the thin little volume with the quotation from Southey on the title page ("Wilt thou go with me?") found its way into the young author's hands. Unhappily there was no resounding European name on that title page; there was, in fact, no name at all; and the readers who might have greeted Hawthorne on the threshold of a great career had turned away from "Fanshawe" apathetically if by chance they had observed it on bookstalls. Perhaps a score of copies had been sold in six months; certainly the little book had been as good as still-born; and in a second outburst of impatience and vexation,

Hawthorne had summoned in all the copies he was able to find, and warmed his benumbed fingers as well as he could at another bonfire.

The effect of these reverses was chilling in the extreme. It was like setting forth on a fine spring morning with a high adventuresome zeal, only to be overtaken by a bleak and driving snowstorm, and sent scurrying back to one's quarters in discomfiture and chagrin. What if it was the wildest folly in the world for an unheard-of Salem youth to aim at authorship! What if there was not a soul in all New England who had any desire to read the kind of stories he was able to write! Possibly, after all, his Uncle William was right, and the family business was the only path to usefulness for a young man with his economic prospects and the education he had had. Could even a young man go on forever writing tales that no one would read? Could one shout forever, without becoming mad, to an empty hall? After four years of apparently fruitless labor at this arduous art, Hawthorne seemed to himself not to have gained an inch of ground, and possibly, in a certain sense, to have lost ground — to have lost, at all events, that shy and secret confidence in himself with which he had set to his work at starting. There was a moment when he was on the point of abandoning all his grandiose aims entirely — for what other aims, how could he have said? — and then a god came down in a machine, a god in the person of Samuel Griswold Goodrich, and the day was saved. This Goodrich, himself a writer of sorts and also an editor and publisher, had unaccountably come upon "Fanshawe", had been impressed with its qualities, and had made inquiries

about its authorship of Messrs. Marsh and Capen. The
result was a correspondence with "N. Hawthorne"
and an invitation to him to write for the new annual
gift book which, under the name of "The Token", this
same Goodrich was about to publish. Here at last was
recognition of a kind. Here was one listener at least in
that echoing hall. Did not Goodrich go so far as to
say that "had 'Fanshawe' been in the hands of more
extensive dealers, I do believe it would have paid you
a profit?" Was he not willing to pay Hawthorne
thirty-five dollars for the story of "The Gentle Boy?"
A fresh start could now be taken — it was the year
1830 — and Hawthorne could see whether "The Token"
might not be the channel by which an intercourse with
the world might be opened.

"The world," alas, however, was the American
Republic under the consulship of Jackson; and it was
not mainly concerned with making communication
easy between itself and a young romance writer like
Nathaniel Hawthorne. The next five or six years were
to be a demonstration of that gloomy truth — a demonstration also that it takes two to make a communication, that the listener must go through a discipline as
athletic and achieve a temper as mellowed as his who
speaks, and that otherwise only mutual perplexity will
ensue. Hawthorne discovered with prompt and vivid
certainty that the American mind had passed through
no such discipline; that, willing as it might be to listen,
it heard a false and flashy voice with as much delight as
a pure one, and hearkened to neither with more than
half its attention. He learned what a creative artist
has to suffer from the want of a vigilant and punctilious

criticism, and the lesson was not lost upon him. But he
came dreadfully close to taking the American public at
its word.

Goodrich, all honor to him, did what he could do.
"The Token" did what lay in its power. Year after
year, in time for the Christmas trade, those ornate little
red or purple morocco volumes would appear with
their sentimental engravings full of Byronesque ruins,
figures from pastoral or military life, and weeping wil-
lows; with their facetious sketches by N. P. Willis,
their elegant lyrics by Mrs. Sigourney, and their dusky
tales by Nathaniel Hawthorne — or rather, since the
veil was not yet lifted, by "The Author of 'The Gentle
Boy'" or "Oberon" or "Ashley A. Royce." And what,
for Hawthorne, was the outcome? "He wrote numerous
articles," said Goodrich later, "which appeared in the
'Token'; occasionally an astute critic seemed to see
through them, and to discover the soul that was in
them; but in general they passed without notice. Such
articles as 'Sights from a Steeple', 'Night Sketches',
'The Wives of the Dead', 'The Prophetic Pictures', now
universally acknowledged to be productions of extraordinary depth, meaning, and power, extorted hardly a
word of either praise or blame, while columns were
given to pieces since totally forgotten."

Hawthorne himself, after many years, was to record
what had happened, with cool reminiscent irony:

These stories were published in Magazines and Annu-
als, extending over a period of ten or twelve years, and
comprising the whole of the writer's young manhood,
without making (so far as he has ever been aware) the
slightest impression on the public. . . . Throughout

48 HAWTHORNE

the time above specified, he had no incitement to literary effort in a reasonable prospect of reputation or profit: nothing but the pleasure itself of composition, — an enjoyment not at all amiss in its way, and perhaps essential to the merit of the work in hand, but which, in the long run, will hardly keep the chill out of a writer's heart, or the numbness out of his fingers. To this total lack of sympathy, at the age when his mind would naturally have been most effervescent, the Public owe it (and it is certainly an effect not to be regretted, on either part), that the Author can show nothing for the thought and industry of that portion of his life, save the forty sketches, or thereabouts, included in these volumes.

If the mere limitation of output had been the only effect of this disheartening deafness on the part of his audience, there would perhaps have been no grounds for the bitterest regret. But the worst effects, both temporary and permanent, were to go far deeper than this. "It is not good for man," Hawthorne noted, in "The Prophetic Pictures", "to cherish a solitary ambition": and certainly it is not good for a creative artist to conceive or be allowed to conceive of his work as irrelevant to the great purposes of the society about him, as frivolous, peripheral, and vain. On what does the health of his soul depend if not on pride? And how can he feel pride in work that must be done furtively, apologetically, anonymously, as Hawthorne felt himself forced to do his? How can his imagination function freely and naturally in an atmosphere in which he is encouraged to distrust its validity and to discredit its real significance? How can greatness be expected to ripen, with merely spontaneous vitality, "like a pear?"

Hawthorne's experience, during the decade and a half of his young manhood, was an answer to these questions. In spite of the encouragement of Goodrich's cordiality, of being published in "The Token" and later in one or two other periodicals, and of occasional recognition by a writer like Park Benjamin, he found himself, with growing and paralyzing thoroughness, losing his essential respect for his art and, with it, his respect for himself as a valuable member of society. In all that he wrote at this time there is the mark of this unhappy sense of alienation, oftenest disguised by an allegory, but allowed, in two or three pieces, to take explicit form. Consider that sketch of "The Devil in Manuscript", in which, under a transparent veil, he records his bitter conviction that a writer of tales is a kind of vagabond.

You cannot conceive — says Oberon in this piece — what an effect the composition of these tales has had on me. I have become ambitious of a bubble, and careless of solid reputation. I am surrounding myself with shadows, which bewilder me, by aping the realities of life. They have drawn me aside from the beaten path of the world, and led me into a strange sort of solitude — a solitude in the midst of men — where nobody wishes for what I do, nor thinks nor feels as I do. The tales have done all this.

A sorry affair is the intellectual life of a nation in which literary fame seems, even to its most splendidly endowed geniuses, "a bubble." How much is rotten in the State when an author can write as Hawthorne wrote, still under the guise of Oberon, in "My Home Return":

"He shall be taught," said I, "by my life, and by my death, that the world is a sad one for him who shrinks from its sober duties. My experience shall warn him to adopt some great and serious aim, such as manhood will cling to, that he may not feel himself, too late, a cumberer of this overladen earth, but a man among men. I will beseech him not to follow an eccentric path, nor, by stepping aside from the highway of human affairs, to relinquish his claim upon human sympathy. *And often, as a text of deep and varied meaning, I will remind him that he is an American.*"

As time went on the feeling grew upon Hawthorne that the practice of literature could not, if he was to preserve his sanity, be persevered in for its own sake; that the mere writing of tales was carrying him farther and farther from the main current of life, instead of nearer and nearer to it; and that, at any cost, he must strive to "get back" into the center of human affairs. But, alas, how was this to be done? Was it possible that his long solitude had unfitted him permanently for the world's "sober duties?" Was it possible that, like the hero of "Wakefield", he had exposed himself to the risk of losing his place forever when he had taken the first step aside from the common path? "I have gone too far astray," exclaims the young man in "Little Annie's Ramble", "for the town crier to call me back"; and there were times when he despaired of ever being anything but an owl. Writing to Bridge in a typical mood of dejection, he compared himself to one drifting helplessly toward a cataract, and ended, "I'm a doomed man, and over I must go." At one time he seems to have considered, at least half seriously, isolating himself among the Canterbury Shakers, whom he had visited on one of his trips in New Hampshire: but even this proved too decisive a step for his enfeebled will to take. The idea of a doom too inexorable to be struggled against had possession of his mind, at least in his blacker moments; and his notebooks for the year 1835 are full of suggestions for tales in which an arbitrary and meaningless destiny holds fantastic sway in human lives.

A well-concerted train of events — reads one of these — to be thrown into confusion by some misplaced circumstance, unsuspected till the catastrophe, yet exerting its influence from beginning to end.

A person to be writing a tale — runs another — and to find that it shapes itself against his intentions; that the characters act otherwise than he thought; that unforeseen events occur; and a catastrophe comes which he strives in vain to avert. It might shadow forth his own fate, — he having made himself one of the personages.

A person to consider himself — runs a third — as the prime mover of certain remarkable events, but to discover that his actions have not contributed in the least thereto. Another person to be the cause, without suspecting it.

In these, and a dozen other notes, his oppressive sense of powerlessness to shape his own circumstances found, with something of the distortion of a dream, symbolic utterance.

What might have happened at this juncture, but for the providential agency of Goodrich and Bridge, it is not pleasant to speculate. Probably American literature came closer than any one has ever realized to the loss of one of its cardinal figures. Probably another year of the same loneliness, the same sense of unrecognition, would have made it impossible for Hawthorne to fend off any longer the strain of pure morbidity in what he wrote, or perhaps to go on writing at all; three tales that belong to 1835 — "The Minister's Black Veil", "The Prophetic Pictures", and "Fancy's Show-Box" — showed, as we shall see, in what direction the wind was blowing. Luckily a stimulus from without was to turn the tide, and set in motion forces that with the lapse of time were to coöperate with Hawthorne's own impotent desire for "activity." Late in 1835, Goodrich obtained for him the editorship of a periodical known as the *American Magazine of Useful and Entertaining Knowledge*, which had been published since the previous year in Boston. With no real impulse to do this kind of work, but with a desperate sense that this outlet to the real world was better than none, Hawthorne moved to Boston early in 1836, and spent the next six months reading proof, writing quasi-encyclopaedic fillers to accompany the engravings that were the magazine's special pride, and dunning the Bewick Company for his salary. The situation, for the author of "The Gray Champion", was by no means an ideal one; the opportunities for exercising his peculiar gifts were slight or non-existent; and the parlous state of the magazine, which failed soon after Hawthorne left it, could have given him little enthusiasm for his duties. By June, indeed, he was sufficiently weary of writing brief biographies of American statesmen and summary histories of great nations — and of not being paid his salary — to throw up the job decisively and withdraw to Salem in dudgeon. But disconcerting as the experience proved, it was after all a breaking of the ice; for six months he had been, no matter how ingloriously, a participator in the daily prose of ordinary life, and his disappointment at the end had the substantial blackness of a shadow cast by a visible, not an imaginary, cloud. His desire to escape from the owl's nest had been reënforced rather than weakened, and though it was still far from clear how escape was to be effected, he was never again to be in the same doubts about its possibility.

The next move was to be Bridge's, with the ambiguous coöperation of Goodrich. Hawthorne had now contributed to "The Token" and to one or two other periodicals more than thirty tales and sketches — enough, as it seemed to Bridge, for a selection to be republished in a volume, with the author's name, at last, on the title page. Had not an English critic, in a notice of "The Token" for the previous year, made special remark of tales by "The Author of 'Sights from a Steeple'?" Had not Park Benjamin done the same thing in the *New England Magazine*, and was he not, in the fall of the present year, to take advantage of his editorial prerogatives, in his new *American Monthly Magazine*, by announcing to the world the real name of "Ashley A. Royce" and enjoining him to collect his sketches in a book? Now or never, said Bridge, was the moment for Hawthorne to come before the public on his own merits, and little as Hawthorne, in the low spirits that ensued upon his Boston adventure, was inclined to make any such effort, the friendly pressure from Bridge, and Goodrich's less disinterested encouragement, were too much for his inertia. Unknown to Hawthorne, Bridge had undertaken to bear the financial responsibility that no publisher would assume, and early in 1837 appeared the "Twice-Told Tales" over the imprint of the American Stationers' Company of Boston. Longfellow's cordial if somewhat florid review in the *North American* was to follow in June, and Hawthorne could regard himself at last as, however obscurely, one of the men of letters of America.

Now neither Longfellow nor any one else in 1837 could have been expected to read very searchingly between the lines of so unassuming a volume, or to have seen in it a document of the first importance in the history of the American literary consciousness. Yet at this distance we can see that "Twice-Told Tales" (with a few pieces postponed to other collections) is nothing less than that. Here were the first fruits of a career that had been unique, at that period, in its devotion to the literary life; and is it not memorable that the tales should betray so intense a preoccupation with the problem of the individual, especially the exceptional individual, in relation to his environment? Is it not striking that our first writer of genius whose concern was with the heart of man and not merely with his actions should have come so close to the center of this problem? Hawthorne himself, writing of the tales many years later, showed that he was aware of what he had been about:

They have none of the abstruseness of idea — he said — or obscurity of expression, which mark the written communications of a solitary mind with itself. They never need translation. . . . They are not the talk of a secluded man with his own mind and heart,

. . . but his attempts, and very imperfectly successful ones, to open an intercourse with the world.

Need we be surprised then, if, through the translating processes of creative writing, his own predicament reappears in the situations of his imaginary figures?

"Fanshawe" itself, indeed, had been the first chapter in the record. No doubt the hand of Godwin and perhaps the hand of Byron can be detected in this unsteady little portrait of a proud and lonely individual sacrificing himself, through exaggerated delicacy of feeling, on the altar of another man's happiness. But it is the hand of young Hawthorne himself, and not of his masters, that is at work in the analysis of Fanshawe's passion for Ellen Langton: "He read her character with accuracy, and had seen how fit she was to love, and to be loved, by a man who could find his happiness in the common occupations of the world; and Fanshawe never deceived himself so far as to suppose that this would be the case with him." He saw that his love for Ellen "was the yearning of a soul, formed by Nature in a peculiar mould, for communion with those to whom it bore a resemblance, yet of whom it was not." Once in his short life Fanshawe is moved by a purely human emotion, and it incites him to uncharacteristic energy in the search for the abducted Ellen and the rescue of her from her captor; but he is punished for his pride in holding himself aloof from other men by the knowledge that she really loves the entirely normal Edward Walcott, and for her own sake he rejects the hand that, more out of gratitude than affection, she offers him. An early grave is Fanshawe's reward for cherishing a solitary ambition, and the happiness of Ellen and Edward is their reward for taking no step aside from the common path. Such was Hawthorne's first tentative answer to the problem of isolation and its fruits.

That answer was to undergo expansion and enrichment with everything that he now went on to write. The most various materials, presenting themselves to his imagination for a dozen superficial reasons, were drawn by a resistless centripetal movement to that common center, and drew from it their essential energy.

Steeping himself in the history of Puritan Massachusetts, and brooding over the wrongs done to the early Quakers by his own ancestors and others, he put this material to use in "The Gentle Boy", the pathetic tale of the Quaker child Ilbrahim separated from his mother by the harsh decree of the Puritans and brought to a premature death by his sufferings, despite the protection of the man and woman who risk everything, in that cruel setting, by adopting him. The Puritans are the ostensible villains of the tale: but how can we evade the "moral" implicit in the misery of which Ilbrahim's mother, clinging fanatically to her spiritual loneliness, is in another sense the cause? Observe the contrast between the Quakeress and Dorothy Pearson, Ilbrahim's foster-mother: Dorothy's "very aspect proved that she was blameless, so far as mortal could be so, in respect to God and man; while the enthusiast, in her robe of sackcloth and girdle of knotted cord, had as evidently violated the duties of the present life and the future, by fixing her attention wholly on the latter." And the moral sufferings of Tobias Pearson, who cuts himself

off from the rest of the community by adopting Ilbrahim, round out the parable.

How richly emblematic, too, is that tale of "Peter
Goldthwaite's Treasure!" Nowhere is the specific
"Hawthornesque" touch more unmistakable than in
this study of poor cracked old Peter Goldthwaite living
with only an old crone in that vast ancient barn of a
house in which, as he confidently believes, an ancestral
treasure is concealed, and which he at length sets to
work to tear down, beam by beam, joint by joint, from
the inside, in the conviction that in some secret cranny
he will come upon his grandfather's chest of gold. How
little does he realize the freakishness of his ways until
that moment when his old partner, John Brown, shouts
to him from the street outside, and Peter, peering out
from his window on the normal life of the world, has
a sudden chilling sense of his own madness. "For a
while he doubted whether there were any hidden chest
of gold, and, in that case, whether it was so exceedingly
wise to tear the house down, only to be convinced of
its non-existence." And indeed the chest of gold proves
in sober truth to be only a box of worthless old paper
money, and Peter's real estate, the only thing of value
about the property, falls into the hands of the realistic
John Brown. Not unlike his is the strange fate of
Wakefield, the London citizen who, in response to a
momentary whim, and on the pretext of going a long
journey, leaves his home one evening, takes up his lodg-
ing a street or two away, and then finds that the lapsing
years leave him powerless to make the return which at
the outset seemed so easy a matter. Wakefield is the
prototype of all those who, without appreciating the

full gravity of the step, turn aside from the normal system of things and condemn themselves to irrevocable outlawry. He gets back home at last, to be sure, but at what a price! "Stay, Wakefield! Would you go to the sole home that is left you? Then step into your grave!"

In such translucent symbols did Hawthorne, even as he clung to his own solitude and shrank from contact with practical life, embody his perception of the punishment that is visited upon the solitary. His imagination, instead of playing freely and flexibly over the intricate facts of human existence — "seeing the thing as in itself it really is" — was entangling itself in the briars of a special and abnormal experience; was looking at the world from a distorted angle and through colored lenses. Was this the penalty he had himself to pay? Was he too looking for a treasure where it did not lie, and neglecting the substantial riches beneath his feet? Certainly the process was to go even farther and bear even darker fruits; was to overcast the play of his imagination with a cloudy and obfuscating sense of the presence of guilt at the heart of all human relations, and hide from him those sources of spiritual joy that lie beyond the springs of spiritual confusion. Guilt was to become, out of all right proportion, his monotonous theme. It was to stain his whole view of human personality. And was this but the consequence of his having Puritan blood in his veins and the gloomy dogmas of the Puritans in his hereditary memory? The explanation holds water no better than a sieve. He had no more Puritan blood than Emerson and hundreds of other New Englanders of his time: and who will say that they were obsessed with the spectral presence of guilt? No: there are more things to sunder Hawthorne from the Puritans than to link him with them; and if, like them, he brooded on the black fatalities of human error and vice, it was the result not of any Calvinist theology, but of his own somber consciousness of separation from the ways of his fellow men — a consciousness in which the sense of guilt luxuriates like noisome growths in a swamp. Mark the form that guiltiness habitually takes in his representation of it, and you will be in no doubt of its origin. The essential sin, he would seem to say, lies in whatever shuts up the spirit in a dungeon where it is alone, beyond the reach of common sympathies and the general sunlight. All that isolates, damns; all that associates, saves.

No theme, from the beginning, had seemed to plumb greater depths in Hawthorne's imagination than that of the dark connection between guilt and secrecy. Crime itself, no matter how monstrous, seemed to him less hideous than its concealment; and a comparatively trifling misdeed became to his vision the deadliest of evils if it remained hidden and unconfessed. In one of the earliest tales, "Roger Malvin's Burial", he treated this theme with intense anticipatory vividness. Reuben Bourne, who after an Indian battle leaves Roger Malvin, at his own injunction, to die of his mortal wounds in the wilderness, is made to suffer out of all proportion to that quite venial wrong because he lacks the moral courage to tell Malvin's daughter, his betrothed, what he has done. "Concealment had imparted to a justifiable act much of the secret effect of guilt," and Reuben Bourne's life with Dorcas is poisoned at its very center by that knowledge: something like penance is exacted, in the end, by Reuben's accidental murder of their son on the spot where, years before, Roger Malvin had died in solitude. But the story of Reuben Bourne might seem an exceptional one if Hawthorne had not gone on to find the allegories for his growing conviction that every human breast, even the holiest, is the repository of at least some one germ of unmanifested culpability. None of these tales has greater force, in its sinister singleness of tone, than that story of the pious clergyman, the Reverend Mr. Hooper, who suddenly astonishes his parishioners, one Sunday morning, by appearing at church with a heavy black veil over his face, and who persistently refuses to remove it through the rest of a long life. Is "the minister's black veil" the symbol of some unique evil? We are not allowed to suppose so. As he lies on his deathbed Mr. Hooper, still grimly clutching the folds of crape to his features, gasps out the terrible truth:

When the friend shows his inmost heart to his friend; the lover to his best beloved; when man does not vainly shrink from the eye of his Creator, loathesomely treasuring up the secret of his sin; then deem me a monster, for the symbol beneath which I have lived, and die! I look around me, and, lo! on every visage a Black Veil!

Looking back upon this period Hawthorne once told Elizabeth Peabody that among the writings he had burned in a fit of despair were perhaps the most powerful things he had written, but that these were objectionable to him on account of their morbidity. "He remarked that, when he found, on re-reading anything, that it had not the healthiness of nature, he felt as if he had been guilty of a lie. He was not sure that he had burnt all that deserved that fate." And indeed it is not easy to exonerate from the charge of morbidity two or three of the pieces that escaped the flames — pieces in which his unhealthy preoccupation with guilt assumes the form of a misanthropy that far out-Puritans the Puritans. Take that sketch, one of the least skilful in execution, which he called "Fancy's Show-Box", and in which he speculates on the problem "whether the soul may contract" the stains of guilt "in all their depth and flagrancy, from deeds which may have been plotted and resolved upon, but which, physically, have never had existence." Here is the secrecy of guilt, with a vengeance! How far had Hawthorne wandered from imaginative sanity when he became capable of viewing all human personality as tainted and corrupt because all men have unuttered and unacted impulses to crime! And can one doubt for a moment that this unwholesome creative mood was the product of his own unnaturally prolonged silence, his own abnormal inaction? Out of the very depths of that mood, and lit up by it with as lurid an imaginative glare as Hawthorne was ever again to light, sprang that beautiful evil fancy, "Young Goodman Brown." In the heart of a midnight forest, and in the red radiance of an infernal altar, Young Goodman Brown of Salem makes the horrid discovery that all that he has honored and respected — in the persons of his most virtuous fellow townsmen and even of his pure wife, Faith — is but the cloak for intrinsic wickedness of every atrocious and debasing kind. Worse yet, he learns from the lips of his Satanic guide that the insight and sympathy he has thus so terribly gained are but insight into guilt and sympathy with sin; that the larger fellowship he is to enter into is a fellowship of hypocrites and knaves. "It shall be yours to penetrate in every bosom," he is told, "the deep mystery of sin, the fountain of all wicked arts, and which inexhaustibly supplies more evil impulses than human power — than my power at its utmost — can make manifest in deeds." So far as this, then, had estrangement gone, and only on such dark terms, for one moment at least, could Hawthorne envisage the resumption of human sympathies.

The moment passed, and a mood that had in it the seeds of more than imaginative disease was robbed of its worst maleficence by finding utterance in these impersonal symbols. It is evidence at once of Hawthorne's fundamental soundness of intellect and of the verdict he was capable of passing on himself, that he came closer than this to the real truth about the nature of evil in the human heart. We have seen how his own experience led him to scrutinize from every angle the predicament of the isolated individual, and to dramatize in a dozen ways the sense of guilt that is the product of solitude. From his own experience too, and his pitiless introspections, arose that doctrine — if the stiff word may be used! — that the worst of all sins is pride, that he who holds himself aloof from ordinary men and arrogates to himself more than ordinary prerogatives is the least forgivable of sinners. This "doctrine" was to lie at the base of his greatest work in literature at his ripest period, and we need not pause too long upon it at this point. Here we need only observe how searching a judgment it was of his own most dangerous impulses, and with what vitality of symbolic representation it was, even in his first acknowledged volume, translated into literary speech.

From this point of view a sketch called "The Man of Adamant", published in "The Token" for 1837, is doubly significant. Under the guise of an allegorical satire on Puritanism, Hawthorne veiled a still more indirect satire on himself, or at least on the temperamental type to which he felt himself in danger of belonging. It was, to be sure, the spiritual pride of the Puritan at his worst, that he was consciously lampooning in the figure of Richard Digby — that most incredible of bigots who, finding even the Pilgrim community too imperfect spiritually for his grandiose self-righteousness, withdraws to a gloomy cavern in the wilderness and declares that only through its narrow entrance does the road to salvation lead. But something more intimate than an intellectual judgment lay behind this portrait of a man whose heart turns slowly to stone with the progress of a radical disease, and who is himself, in his self-imposed solitude, turned into adamant by the damps that drip coldly from the ceiling of his cavern. An intensity made possible by something more than vicarious experience animated the concluding words:

Friendship, and Love, and Piety, all human and celestial sympathies, should keep aloof from that hidden cave; for there still sits, and, unless an earthquake crumble down the roof upon his head, shall sit forever, the shape of Richard Digby, in the attitude of repelling the whole race of mortals, — not from heaven, — but from the horrible loneliness of his dark, cold sepulchre!

On a higher artistic level than "The Man of Adamant", "Lady Eleanore's Mantle", the third of the Province House series, is a still more telling parable of pride. Who that has read it can forget the picture of the haughty Lady Eleanore Rochcliffe standing in the midst of the aristocratic guests at the ball given by her uncle, the provincial governor, and holding herself invincibly aloof? "She beheld the spectacle, not with vulgar ridicule, as disdaining to be pleased with the provincial mockery of a court festival, but with the deeper scorn of one whose spirit held itself too high to participate in the enjoyment of other human souls." The mad youth, Jervase Helwyse, who interrupts the gaiety of the ball by suddenly appearing, kneeling at Lady Eleanore's feet, and begging her to take one sip of holy wine from the goblet he holds up to her, finds the right words for her own madness: "This shall be the symbol that you have not sought to withdraw yourself from the chain of human sympathies, — which whoso would shake off must keep company with fallen angels." Lady Eleanore, of course, not in anger, but with a melancholy contempt, rejects the proffered drink; and on the same night there breaks out in Boston a gruesome plague of which, after it has spread far and wide, the source is discovered to have been the rich mantle she had worn on the night of the ball. Lady Eleanore herself falls a victim to the general malady, and dies horribly, in the presence of Jervase Helwyse, with these words on her lips:

The curse of Heaven hath stricken me, because I would not call man my brother, nor woman sister. I wrapped myself in PRIDE as in a MANTLE, and scorned the sympathies of nature; and therefore has nature made this wretched body the medium of a dreadful sympathy.

Thus vividly did Hawthorne perceive what are the fruits of that arrogance which is at the heart of the Puritan temper, and thus fearfully, we may be sure, did he represent to himself the pitfalls he had peculiarly to avoid. It would have been well for him, both as a man and as an artist, if he had perceived with equal clarity the brighter or at any rate the nobler side of Puritanism, and criticized himself, in its light, with equal severity. For if the abstract dogmas of Calvinism are as harshly deterministic as the philosophy of modern science, Calvinism in practice was the most strenuous of creeds; the greatest of the Puritans, far from yielding fatalistically to some superior will, asserted their own wills at every turn with the resoluteness and vehemence of men for whom freedom is an unchallenged reality. Now the unhappiest product of that play of forces which molded Hawthorne's personality, the circumstances of his time and the obscure facts of his innate constitution, was a dusky fatalism in the shadow of which all action seemed, or tended to seem, vain and profitless, and the will became the victim of a deadly creeping paralysis. We have seen, so far as explanation is possible, how this was the result of his long solitude; and we shall see later what were its reverberations in his subsequent years. At this point we need but observe how, like that kindred sense of guilt, this fatalism discolored his view of human life and distorted his representation of it in literature.

How few of the personages in the "Twice-Told Tales"

seem to be the agents of their own destiny! How generally are they the playthings of occult and whimsical powers! With how little struggle, on the whole, they yield to the strange pressures upon them! Wakefield is typical, and Wakefield, we are told, "had contrived, *or rather he had happened*, to dissever himself from the world." "Would that I had a folio to write, instead of an article of a dozen pages!" exclaims Hawthorne in that tale. "Then might I exemplify how an influence, beyond our control, lays its strong hand on every deed which we do, and weaves its consequences into an iron tissue of necessity." And so Wakefield lets the years slip by him without a gesture of protest; and Roger Malvin accepts his fate sullenly and hopelessly; and Lady Eleanore Rochcliffe wears to the ball, as indifferent to its effects as if she were hypnotized, the mantle that she knows to be laden with disease. Doctor Heidigger's decrepit guests, with all their sad knowledge of what folly brings in its train, drink the rejuvenating potion which he offers to them, and when they find their youth apparently restored, relapse into the same follies that had made them the bad examples they were. Adam Colburn and Martha Pierson, in "The Shaker Bridal", accept with stern resignation the fate that keeps them apart for so many years and makes a mockery of their marriage ceremony when at last it becomes possible. And what is the moral of "The Prophetic Pictures"? Why are not Walter and Elinor, in that tale, effectively warned in their youth by the premonitory portraits which the great artist paints for them? Is it not because, dreadful as is the fate which these portraits foreshadow, they themselves are impotent to affect the course of their lives? Resignation, inertness, passivity — these take the place of conflict in all but a few of the tales: and how false, in consequence, is the picture of human life that emerges from them! How false, at least, if we are to think like philosophers, and recognize that the will, being merely the expression of natural demands, is as potent as any other power in nature, and that frustration is but the penalty of ignorance. The greatest literature is in this sense philosophical and provides for a certain balance, not capriciously weighted in one of its scales, between the energies of the hero and the forces of the universe; and if the "Twice-Told Tales" are not great literature it is largely because of the factitious fatalism that pervades them.

Yet if it does not survive the application of such a test, this earliest work of Hawthorne's must be recognized as coming nearer to greatness than anything that had preceded and very much that was to follow it in American letters; and this because it sprang, after all, from a deeper psychological experience than any other American writer had shown the capacity for. It is not true that the will is merely impotent; yet neither is it true that the will is all-powerful, that the universe is consciously beneficent to mankind, and that conflict infallibly issues in victory for the hero. These assumptions were the basis of conduct in Hawthorne's day, if no later, and had inspired, as they were to continue to inspire, most of American literature. Hawthorne was the first of American writers to go in his own person to the very center of human experience, and demonstrate this facile optimism a myth. Unlike most of his contemporaries, he was not interested in the kind of effort in which victory is easy and predictable, and this enabled him to discover how tragically real, on a certain level, are the possibilities of defeat. So his Wakefields, his Peter Goldthwaites, his Goodman Browns, imperfectly realistic as they are, have the elements of a genuine humanity in them, a deeper humanity than Cooper's men of action or Poe's all-capable mechanisms ever attain. No doubt, in creating them, Hawthorne was seeking obscurely to indemnify himself for his own failure to mold his environment to his will: some such motive is at the root of all creation, and here, because the theme issues from so deep a source, it is peculiarly and inexpugnably valid.

To "The Token" for 1833 Hawthorne had contributed a tale entitled "The Canterbury Pilgrims" (not reprinted until the issuance of "The Snow Image" volume) in which the sanest if not the deepest mood of his early period found utterance, and which forecast with peculiar relevance the course his life was to take in the years following the appearance of "Twice-Told Tales." A young man and woman, members of the Shaker community at Canterbury, who have decided to forsake it and throw themselves into the busy life of the world, fall in at twilight with a group of pilgrims on their way, in just the opposite direction, to join the brethren at Canterbury in the hope of leaving all worldly cares and disappointments behind them. In the gathering darkness, seated about a wayside spring not far from the community, these fugitives from reality — an unsuccessful poet, a bankrupted merchant, a poverty-stricken

farmer with his family — expound one by one the motives that have led them to this capitulation, and seek
to deter Josiah and Miriam from pursuing their sanguine and courageous purpose. The young Shakers
listen gravely to these disheartening admonitions, and
then — "after one instant's hesitation, they opened
their arms, and sealed their resolve with as pure and
fond an embrace as ever youthful love had hallowed.
'We will not go back,' said they. 'The world never can
be dark to us, for we will always love one another.'"
It was Hawthorne's own decision, made thus in the
sphere of the imagination four or five years before it
was to take overt effect. Like Josiah and Miriam, he
was effectually forewarned; he was under no illusions
about the possibilities of easy "success" and easy happiness; but like them he had had, for the moment, his
taste of reclusion; like them, he was determined to
exchange it, come what might, for participation. And
in the experience of falling in love at last, he was to
find an assurance that the darkness of the world need
never be complete or incorrigible.

CHAPTER THREE

"THE WORLD CALLED ME FORTH"

"Lord! a man should have the fine point of his soul taken off to become fit for this world." — Keats, Letter to Reynolds.

No CHAPTER ended abruptly in Hawthorne's life as a writer on the spring day in 1837 when "Twice-Told Tales" came fresh from the printer's in Boston. During the autumns and winters of the following two years he continued to apply himself for hours at a time to composition at the pine table in his old chamber, and the results of his application enriched the pages of the last "Token" (the issue for 1838), of the new *Democratic Review*, and of one or two other periodicals. But it was clear to Hawthorne, if to no one else, that he was making drafts on old deposits, working old veins, exploiting sources of inspiration that could no longer go on renewing themselves from within; that only some refreshment of his own experience, some spiritual change of air, could keep his work as a writer from losing all its vitality and pith. His interest in writing, indeed, regarded as an end in itself, was increasingly, for the time being, diminishing; in the letter to Longfellow on the occasion so often alluded to, he even pretended that it had only been in default of more important concerns that he had ever set pen to paper at all, and that if he now continued to do so, it was because "I see little prospect but that I shall have to scribble for a living." No words could have done less justice to Hawthorne's permanent desires, but they were faithful enough to his mood in the late summer and fall of 1837 — to the mood in which he protested to Elizabeth Peabody, "I am tired of being an ornament. I want a little piece of land that I can call my own, big enough to stand upon, big enough to be buried in. I want to have something to do with this material world." He is said at this point to have struck his hand vigorously on a table near by. "If I could only make tables, I should feel myself more of a man."

In such a frame of mind literature could scarcely have engaged his best exertions; and, though in the least creative period that followed he "scribbled" something or other "for a living", it was not until the autumn of 1842 that Hawthorne, withdrawn again from the central current, returned with the old inventive ardor to composition. Had he, in the meantime, established relations with the "material world" on a more significant basis than either he or that world conceded his writing to be? Had his participation in human affairs been of a sort to change the whole habit of his work in literature? Had the old insubstantiality of materials that he so bitterly lamented given way to a new apprehension of the dense facts of human life? Or had participation been postponed too long? Had it been too late for him to begin, as a creative writer, his most essential discipline? Only the pieces in the "Mosses from an Old Manse" were to answer these questions. Meanwhile we must see how he responded to the world when it called him forth.

As Hawthorne, a married man settling down in the Old Manse in the summer of 1842, looked back over

the preceding five years, what was present to him as a
summary impression must have been the radical incon-
gruities of the kinds of life he had observed and shared,
their clumsy stratification of desires, their flat lowlands
and bleak heights of personality, without mutual communication. It must have seemed to him that he had
been moving not in one world, but in two: that one of
these worlds was warm, gross, sweaty, muscular, unilluminated, crass; that the other was a thin-aired upland, strewn with tenuous and evanescent growths,
blown upon by faint and chilly breezes, and shimmering
in a tepid sunlight. Somehow not quite at home in
either, he observed that his experience had been divided
between the two. In the one dwelt Franklin Pierce and
Bridge and Jonathan Cilley, the yeomen at North
Adams, the shipmasters at Long Wharf, and the cattle
dealers at Brighton Fair; in the other dwelt Sophia
Peabody and her sisters, Miss Burley, Jones Very, the
cranks and theorists at Brook Farm, and Waldo Emerson.
He had felt himself drawn strongly, by every impulse
of his under-nourished imagination, to the brisk and
noisy facts of the coarser world. How thoroughly it
filled in all outlines! How rich it was in stimuli to a
mind bent on comprehending all aspects of conduct,
all gradations of character! Yet certainly something
had been amiss in his contact with that world. He
had turned from it in impatience or weariness again
and again — turned from it precisely to find refuge in
the cooler and purer air of Sophia Peabody's world.
And here he was at last in the half-Emersonian Manse,
surrounded by evidences of Sophia's taste in decoration,
living on vegetables, and blessed with poets and philos-

ophers for neighbors! But did he "belong" in this any more than in that other setting?

At all events, they had made their appeals to him with almost simultaneous urgency in the year of the "Twice-Told Tales." While the book was in press, indeed, he had had his first glimpse into that gross though benevolent Jacksonian system in which the usufructs of democratic polity were made the reward of democratic triumph, and of which he himself was to be at three periods in his life a minor part. Both Pierce and Cilley had recently become members of Congress on the Democratic side, and both of them, like good dispensers of patronage, were disposed to use what influence they had with Van Buren's cabinet to the advantage of their college friend and fellow Democrat. An exploring expedition with the South Seas as its goal was being organized by the Navy Department, and it was thought that Hawthorne, as a probably adaptable man of letters, would do admirably for its historian; certainly his pen would have been no less well employed on such a task than on Goodrich's informative books for children. Fortunately the project came to nothing, and Hawthorne's sharing in the spoils was to be postponed for more than a year; but there had been opened up to him one economic resource that he was never again to ignore. There is something not encouraging to sentimentality in the simple cynicism with which Hawthorne accepted in practice the political morality of his day.

During the ensuing summer Hawthorne so far abandoned all his unsociable habits as to pay an extended visit to Horatio Bridge, living a bachelor life in his paternal mansion just outside of Augusta, Maine. The visit was an adventure in the pedestrian. Bridge, with a small inherited fortune, was engaged in an industrial enterprise, the construction of a milldam across the Kennebec, which made him for the moment one of the barons of that still half-frontier community. Gangs of Irish immigrants and French Canadians, workers on the dam, were encamped with their families in shanties along the river banks, where they lived an alternately jovial and quarrelsome existence painted crudely in the primary colors. But Hawthorne was in a mood for observing just such facts as these; and every evening in his notebook he recorded the reportorial profits of the day — "hints for characters", as he sometimes called them, or "remarkables", or merely unqualified data. A middle-aged Irishwoman completing her toilet in the open before her shanty; pretty if unkempt young mothers lugging their inevitable infants; a Yankee quarreling with a Canadian whom he declared to have struck one of his oxen; the black-eyed servant girl Nancy who made beds for Bridge and lived with his tenants in another part of the house; the Governor of Maine and his council striding about the barroom of a tavern after a session at the Mansion House — here were men and women who had never got into literature, who bore about them none of the prerogatives of romance, who were unmistakable flesh and blood, and were waiting — could he fail to speculate? — for the Balzac who should apprehend and dramatize their "comedy."

For there can be no doubt that such an intention, and not merely a naïve curiosity, was prompting Hawthorne to observe Bridge's neighbors with so searching an eye. One day as they sat with others on the stoop of a tavern in the town, Hawthorne was witness to the good-natured taunting by his companions of a somewhat simple-minded fellow who was inquiring, without suspicion of the dubious ways into which she had fallen, for his absconded wife. "I would have given considerable to witness his meeting with his wife," commented Hawthorne, after recording that the poor cuckold had been led off to find her by a well-informed guide. And he continued, "There was a moral pictur-esqueness in the contrasts of the scene, — a man moved as deeply as his nature would admit, in the midst of hard-ened, gibing spectators, heartless towards him. *It is worth thinking over and studying out.* [The italics are not his.] He seemed rather hurt and pricked by the jests thrown at him, yet bore it patiently, and sometimes al-most joined in the laugh. He was cowed by his situation, being of an easy, unenergetic temper." Now why should Hawthorne not have made imaginative use even out of stuff so unlovely, so meager in surface graces, so uncouth and bedraggled as this? It is in the sum of just such petty miseries, he must have reflected, that half the pathos of human life can be said to lie; and why should one hope to improve upon it by conjuring up imaginary situations, simplified to conform to an arbitrary moral pattern? A pattern, of course, there must be in the end; but all its truth and beauty will depend on its allegiance to the preliminary fact.

So at least Hawthorne doubtless felt as he drove about the countryside with Bridge, or dined with him in the tavern at Hallowell, or sat up nights talking with him and his eccentric house guest and French

tutor, the mercurial M. Schaeffer, or studied his fellow
passengers in the stagecoach from Augusta to Thomas-
ton, whither he finally went for a brief visit with
Cilley. He felt less sure of the general principle — or
perhaps, rather, of his own capacity for adhering to
it — after he was back in Salem in August, and began
again to make the other kind of entry in his notebook,
the kind of entry in which he attempted to find an
objective formula for some passage in his inner experience, to phrase some "allegory of the heart." Now he
was a metaphysician, an introspective poet, not — as
in Maine — a Chaucerian observer of men. "A young
man and girl meet together, each in search of a person
to be known by some particular sign. They watch and
wait a great while for that person to pass. At last some
casual circumstance discloses that each is the one that
the other is waiting for. Moral — what we need for
our happiness is often close at hand, if we knew but
how to seek for it." Could any pattern be more aprio-
ristic than this? Could any fable bear less resemblance
to the unsymmetrical facts of life? Yet so imperfectly
as this had Hawthorne at the present juncture reconciled the diverging demands of his creative power.

There was to be, none the less, a strangely anticipatory truth, for Hawthorne's own future, in the entry
just quoted. What he needed most acutely for his own
happiness at this restive and dissatisfied period was
no farther away than the Peabody house at the edge
of the burying ground on Charter Street. The conviction had for some time been growing upon him that
what seemed the incurable emptiness of his life was due
largely to his ignorance of so deep a human experience

as the love between the sexes. In the tales and sketches he was writing at about this period a singular note of wistfulness recurs in his allusions to women and young girls — allusions that, except for something sharp and painful in them, would bear the ear-marks of eighteen rather than of thirty-three. It was during this very fall that he wrote that prose ode on solitude, "Foot-prints on the Sea-shore", representing himself wandering alone (as indeed he had been doing) on the weed-strewn beach, playing games with his own tracks in the sand, and now and then throwing himself at length to bask and dream in the sunlight. "Here, should I will it, I can summon up a single shade, and be myself her lover. Yes, dreamer, — but your lonely heart will be the colder for such fancies." And at the end of the day, when a fishing party, cooking their supper on the beach, signal to him to join them, one appeal moves him more than the rest. "The ladies wave their hand-kerchiefs. Can I decline? No; and be it owned, after all my solitary joys, that this is the sweetest moment of a Day by the Sea-shore."

Elizabeth Peabody, then, determined woman though she was, was working better than she knew in laying siege to the well-garrisoned Manning house with her lionizing designs on the author of "Twice-Told Tales." Hawthorne was not to be budged by appeals to his literary vanity; but Elizabeth's great show of friendliness, partly disguised by solicitude for his sisters, was too much for his resistance, and once the interchange of calls between Charter Street and Herbert Street had begun, his heart was in a more effectual net than the one she cast. No woman so full of energy, so

resolutely executive, so companionable with men of the
world as Elizabeth Peabody was could have made, on
any but a friendly level, the slightest progress against
Hawthorne's diffidence in the presence of all women,
bred of a dozen years of the strictest celibacy. But indeed it was Hawthorne the rising author that Elizabeth
was content to deal with, and on such terms their
friendship was sturdy enough. With Elizabeth's younger
sister Sophia it would have been very different. "At
length, a certain Dove was revealed to me," he was
later to write to her, "in the shadow of a seclusion as
deep as my own had been." If there was a touch of
hyperbole in this, if the Peabody family could scarcely
compete with the Hawthornes for systematic solitude,
it was true that Sophia, unlike her sisters Elizabeth and
Mary, had been a prisoner in her room for a larger portion of her days than Hawthorne himself could boast.
She had been for years, in fact, as a result of early medical mistreatment, virtually an invalid, the prey to
almost constant headaches of varying intensity and pro-
traction. Her temperament being what it was, all this
had given her the mildness and patient cheerfulness, not
the acerbity, of the chronic sufferer; and there must
have been something not quite earthly in her fragile,
white-wrapped, soft-voiced presence on that afternoon when Hawthorne first saw her and, with an impulsive emphasis unaccustomed in him, urged her to
accompany Elizabeth and himself that evening to Miss
Burley's. Within a few months they were lovers, only
just unacknowledged to each other, and within a year
they were secretly engaged.

How could it have fallen out otherwise? It was not

SOPHIA PEABODY HAWTHORNE

only that Hawthorne, with a deeply if not intensely emotional nature, was consciously and articulately ready for just such an experience; it was also that Sophia Peabody was, in his possible sphere of acquaintance, the one woman who could have overcome the special reluctances he would have felt. How fearfully he would have shrunk from intimate relations with a woman of large physical vitality and robust emotional needs! How difficult it would have been to turn from the shadowy feminine figures of his lonely fantasies to a woman with a vigor comparable at every point with his own! And how intolerant he would have been — he who had been worshiped with strange silent devotion by his mother and two sisters — of an assertive intellect, a temper capable of disequilibrium, a tough and independent will! Sophia threatened him in none of these disastrous ways. She was, physically, of an extreme tenuity, and shivered in every wind from the east. Her sensibility was infinite; she had, among other powers, considerable talent in draughtsmanship and painting with water colors, but her ardors were delicate, melodious, and a little thin; "unwilling as my body was" (to leave the house on a fine day), she once wrote, "Ideality led me out." On one early occasion, after Hawthorne had called, she felt the next morning, she said, "quite lark-like, or like John of Bologna's Mercury." And lark-like, to judge from everything she said and did, she evidently was: there was nothing of the nightingale and as little of the bluejay in her makeup. Like the lark she belonged to the early morning, and like the lark she was constitutionally devotional, and even idolatrous. Before Hawthorne came,

she had magnified lyrically and with some effusiveness
the two or three great men of her acquaintanceship —
Washington Allston, Doctor Channing, Emerson —
and she was prepared, she was even dedicated, to sing
lauds with the same fervor to him. "He has a celestial
expression," was one of her first descriptions of him;
and her last words on the subject were to be in a similar
vein. What wonder if Hawthorne felt no painful inadequacy in himself when she was in question! The fate
of his daydream mistresses was sealed.

The Peabody family were to lead him into other
paths as well as the path of love. Through them he
was initiated into a world he would otherwise have
known only from the outside, a world of high thoughts
and large aspirations and beautiful desires. Elizabeth
herself was an associate of Bronson Alcott at his exper-
imental Temple School in Boston, and one of that loosely
organized group of the tender-minded who were beginning to meet at George Ripley's house and elsewhere in
the city to discuss German metaphysics and the errors
of contemporary society. Largely under her ægis a
similar if less distinguished group in Salem had taken
to meeting weekly at Miss Susan Burley's, and these
Saturday nights were essential episodes in the first winter of Hawthorne's acquaintanceship with Sophia,
whose headaches just now were mercifully intermit-
tent. How different from anything else in his experience
was this transcendental atmosphere! What human
being, for example, could have been less like Jonathan
Cilley than that mystical sonneteer, Jones Very? After
a year or two in a Greek tutorship at Harvard, Very
had come back to his native Salem, and was at just this

time passing through a religious experience so intense and, in some of its expressions, so untoward, that he was in many quarters reputed to be stark mad. The suspicion, if not wholly unfounded, was exaggerated; Very had indeed said that he felt it an honor to wash his face — "being, as it were, the temple of the Spirit" — but a slight knowledge of mystical literature would have helped his enemies to understand such a metaphor, and if they had read his sonnets they would have seen that he was capable of utterance sedate and "sane" enough. Yet he preached an abnegation of the will that was Asiatic rather than Jacksonian; and was so little a product of his strenuous age that, once his great ecstasy was over, he was content to live on idly in its receding luster, and accept with quiet simplicity whatever homage was paid to him as a *schöne Seele.*

Sophia, inevitably, was second to none of Jones Very's admirers either in time or in unction. In a letter written late in 1838 to Elizabeth in Boston she recorded a visit from him paid chiefly for the sake of seeing their brother George, just then lying mortally ill in bed. "His conversation with George was divine," she wrote, "and such level rays of celestial light as beamed from his face upon George, every time he looked up at him, were lovely to behold." This very marked predilection of Sophia's for the supermundane was gratified by another of Very's admirers, a person to whom, in fact, Elizabeth Peabody had introduced the Salem mystic. This was no less a figure than Waldo Emerson, the author of "Nature," who thought Elizabeth one of the most remarkable women of her time, and who had praised Sophia's own line drawings. Visits from him

in Salem were, it appears, like angels' visits not merely
in respect of being few and far between. "We had an
exquisite visit from Waldo," wrote Sophia early that
summer. "It was the warbling of the Attic bird . . .
I told Mary, that night after he had gone, that I felt
like a *gem;* that was the only way I could express it."
On another occasion she told Mary that she thought
Emerson was "the Word again," and after a different
visit from the one mentioned she wrote, "I think Mr.
Emerson is the greatest man that ever lived. *As a
whole* he is satisfactory . . . He is indeed a 'Supernal
Vision.' . . . Mr. Emerson is Pure Tone." It is prob-
able that Sophia had the essential talents of the acolyte.
The precincts into which she conducted Hawthorne, at
all events, were definitely priestlike.

What difficulty he may have had at the outset in
breathing this high air there is no means of being sure.
Certainly he enjoyed his absence from it in the summer
of this year with peculiar zest. Just before he set out
for the western part of the State late in July, he called
on the Peabodys to say his good-bys, and while there
was urged by Mary to keep a journal of his excursion.
"He at first said he should not write anything," said
Sophia in a letter, "but finally concluded it would suit
very well for hints for future stories." In fact, as at
Augusta, he did keep a journal and with great assidu-
ity. During those weeks at North Adams he appears
to have been under bond with himself not to miss any
contour, any shade, any gesture in the life of man or of
nature as he should observe it; no purple shadow thrown
by a passing cloud on Greylock, no drollery of Berkshire speech or dress or custom, no attitude of dogs or

pigs or horses even, were to escape his scrutiny. "There
is something of the hawk-eye about you too," said a
one-armed soap-maker to him one morning on the steps
of the tavern, after remarking that "my study is man";
and his intuition was so far right that Hawthorne
found the amateur psychologist himself worth three or
four pages of analysis. And with what gusto, what
perspicacity in the detection of motive, what tireless-
ness in the elaboration of stroke, what love of the
third dimension, analyses like this of the soap-maker
Haynes are managed! How studious Hawthorne is of
the individualizing detail — the incongruous elevation of the man's talk, a survival of more respectable
days; his manner of describing the anguish of amputa-
tion; the familiarity with which his great dog mouthed
the edge of his trousers and licked his bare foot, also
maimed; his half-defiant, half-humorous response to
condescension! It is as if Hawthorne's long removal
from the world, instead of dulling his clairvoyance, had
but sharpened it preternaturally, sharpened it by making him attentive to even microscopic phenomena.

So, as he lounged about the tavern at North Adams
or tramped over the upland roads or visited Williams-
town for a day at commencement time, he kept his
eye out for "remarkable characters" and discovered
them in the most unlikely guises — in a mirthful,
loud-voiced, broad-breeched blacksmith; in an under-
witted old man walking about the hills with an um-
brella; in the maidservants at the tavern; in a traveling
young surgeon-dentist who was also a licensed Baptist
preacher. All was grist that came to his mill. And the
hours he was able to spend bathing in solitude in a pool

below Hudson's falls were not the first he was to forget after the summer was over and he journeyed in a leisurely way down the Connecticut valley to Hartford and Lichfield and other towns in that vicinity, and then by slow stages back to Boston. "I have been rambling about since the middle of July till within a week or two past," he wrote to Longfellow in October, "and have had such a pleasant time as seldom happens to a man of my age and experience." His thirst for impressions of actuality had been generously slaked among the Berkshires; his memory was enriched with types and incidents; and he was now determined to find some rôle to play that should be more than spectatorial.

His opportunity, according to the legend, came to him again through the agency of Elizabeth Peabody. At one of the gatherings in Boston at which she was always a salient figure, Elizabeth overheard George Bancroft, recently appointed collector of the Port of Boston, boasting that the Democratic Party was the political friend of all American literary men. "But there's Hawthorne," she interposed. "You've done nothing for him." And in answer to Bancroft's plea that Hawthorne had refused political office (as to be sure he once had), she rejoined, "I happen to know that he would be very glad of employment." The arrow struck its mark, and within a few weeks Hawthorne had received an appointment as measurer at the Boston Customhouse, and during the first few days of 1839 entered upon his duties there.

If what he most desired was to have something to do with the material world, he now had his wish, and with a vengeance. Few occupations even in the gift of the Washington bureaucrats could have been dingier, more earth-and-watery, less enlivened with ideas, than this. Hawthorne's duties took him, in the language of the service, "outside", and seem to have consisted largely in supervising the measurement of cargoes of coal and salt as they were brought into the port by British and Canadian schooners. A man so unaccustomed as Hawthorne to the handling of commodities of any tangible sort might have been excused for adjusting himself slowly and painfully to such a routine: it is eloquent of a paradoxical capacity in him for superficial adaptation that he mastered his responsibilities quickly and executed them with an odd, unassuming efficiency. It was in the following June that Bancroft spoke to Emerson of Hawthorne as "the most efficient and best of the Custom House officers"; and it is on record that, because the wages of his subordinate workmen depended on the number of hours they spent daily at the wharves, he made it a point in all weathers to be on hand as early and to remain as late as possible. Almost from the beginning Hawthorne found his occupations, in themselves, irksome and unprofitable — how could a man with an active mind have had any other feeling? — but to the very end of his service in the Customhouse, two years later, he was able to buoy himself up, temporarily at least, by reminding himself that he was doing what the world regarded as a man's work.

My life only is a burden — he wrote to Sophia during his first summer at Long Wharf — in the same way that it is to every toilsome man; and mine is a healthy weariness, such as needs only a night's sleep to remove it. But from henceforth forever I shall be entitled to call the sons of toil my brethren, and shall know how to sympathize with them, seeing that I likewise have risen at the dawn, and borne the fervor of the midday sun, nor turned my heavy footsteps homeward till eventide. Years hence, perhaps, the experience that my heart is acquiring now will flow out in truth and wisdom.

Early the next spring, when he was beginning to write with growing impatience of "this unblest Custom House" as "a very grievous thralldom", he could yet find it possible to say:

It is good for me, on many accounts, that my life has had this passage in it. Thou canst not think how much more I know than I did a year ago — what a stronger sense I have of power to act as a man among men — what worldly wisdom I have gained, and wisdom also that is not altogether of this world. And, when I quit this earthly cavern where I am now buried, nothing will cling to me that ought to be left behind.

And after still another year, a year of recurrent and passionate revulsions from the grime and soot of his duties, he could write, after a busy day, and one of his last days, in the harbor:

It was exhilarating to see the vessels, how they bounded over the waves, while a sheet of foam broke out around them. I found a good deal of enjoyment, too, in the busy scene around me; for several vessels were disgorging themselves . . . on the wharf, and everybody seemed to be working with might and main. It pleased thy husband to think that he also had a part to act in the material and tangible business of this life, and that a part of all this industry could not have gone on without his presence.

In such utterances, and in the states of mind that lay behind them, Hawthorne gave evidence that in all this eagerness for participation he had surrendered — happily on but one level and only for the present moment — to the ideals of Jacksonian America; had half conceded to the proposition that literature is no serious activity for a healthy man, as compared, for instance, with the measuring of coal and salt; had come close to making the fatal mistake of supposing that participation was itself an end, a vindication of his status as a citizen, and not merely a means to the enrichment of his experience and the deepening of his art. An unconditional surrender to such falsities he could never make: too much already lay behind him for that to be conceivable; but for many months, subconscious as the issues were, he was being divided between two incompatible loyalties, and it was doubtless the strain of that confusion, even more than the dinginess of his tasks, that underlay his almost chronic mood of rebellion and discontent. Again and again the fatigue, the low spirits, that were the price he paid for his dutifulness, betrayed him into outbursts of resentment and even petulance. During the second February, he wrote to Sophia describing a typical day spent in a dismal dock at the north end of the city. Across the water, he said, he could see the white shaft of the Bunker Hill Monument:

. . . and what interested me considerably more, a church-steeple, with the dial of a clock upon it, whereby I was enabled to measure the march of the weary hours . . . At last came the sunset, with delicate clouds, and a purple light upon the islands; and your husband blessed it, because it was the signal of his release, and so came home to talk with his dearest wife.

"I do think that it is the doom laid upon me," he complained a little later, "of murdering so many of the brightest hours of the day at that unblest Custom-House, that makes such havoc with my wits." Reassure himself as he might that he was exercising the functions of a public servant, his sense of being a prisoner to tasks that made no demands on his real powers was too acute and too insistent to allow him to stay indefinitely at the Customhouse; and when, in 1841, a Whig administration came into office, Hawthorne did not even wait for the ejectment that would probably have followed, but handed in his resignation to Bancroft, and with the exuberance of a captive freed from his dungeon, turned his face in quite a different direction.

The two years in Boston Harbor, however, had not been quite fruitlessly spent in an angry dissatisfaction with his labors mitigated by a misapprehension as to what they might be worth. In his moments of deepest wisdom Hawthorne remembered that he was an imaginative writer far more truly than he was a measurer, and that the Customhouse would have justified its draughts upon his energies if in the long run it should equip him to write with a new truth and a new richness of reference. Writing and the measuring of coal — like writing and the bookkeeping of his boyhood — were clearly not to be carried on at the same time: but the future might be another matter!

Belovedest — he wrote to Sophia in the spring of 1840 — I sometimes wish that thou couldst be with me on board my salt-vessels and colliers, because there are many things of which thou mightst make such pretty descriptions; and in future years, when thy husband is again busy at the loom of fiction, he would weave in these little pictures. My fancy is rendered so torpid by my ungenial way of life, that I cannot sketch off the scenes and portraits that interest me; and I am forced to trust them to my memory, with the hope of recalling them at some more favorable period.

Then, as if to insure himself against at least one loss, he proceeded to describe a little Mediterranean boy from Malaga whom he had been observing for some days past on the deck and in the hold of a Yankee coal vessel. "Do thou remember this little boy, dearest," he concluded, "and perhaps I may make something more beautiful of him than thou wouldst think from these rough and imperfect touches." Two years before he might have doubted whether he could ever again feel the original zest for composition; as his second year at the Customhouse wore on, and he continued perforce to give the old muscles no exercise, he began to feel the promptings of insuppressible instincts.

I do not get intolerably tired any longer — he wrote in November — and my thoughts sometimes wander back to literature, and I have momentary impulses to write stories. But this will not be at present. The utmost that I can hope to do will be to portray some of the characteristics of the life which I am now living, and of the people with whom I am brought into contact, for future use.

Had Hawthorne always perceived so clearly as this the terms on which the creative life is most profitably led, his history as a man and a writer would have been a happier one than, with all its victories, it actually was. How much better than the old estrangement, the old introspection, was this nascent power of forming direct relations, imaginatively, with the involved drama of human experience. But this power, as if it had been slighted too long, was never to receive its full development. Too perfectly, for that, had Hawthorne developed the technique of escape; and even now — from the very outset of his Customhouse life indeed — he was allowing it to dominate his thinking and feeling about the most important relationship into which he had yet entered.

In the early months of 1839, if not before, Hawthorne and Sophia Peabody were definitely though secretly engaged to be married. Was not this in an even weightier sense than his assumption of public responsibilities a step toward participation? Was not this approach to the deepest of experiences — the experience for which he had, in his cold solitude, so long yearned — emblematic of a new attitude toward all experience, a new seriousness in his adjustment to reality? What personal status could be, in most of its implications, more social than marriage, and was not his marriage with Sophia a matter, at this point, merely of time? We might expect that something like this would have been the theme of his letters to her, that their exuberance would have been partly the fruit of his sense that Sophia's destiny and his were now involved in the general destiny of men and women. In fact, however, their language is anything but the language of participation. It is true that Hawthorne felt and expressed a

new substantiality, a new significance, in the fabric
of his personal life.

Thou only hast taught me that I have a heart — he
wrote to Sophia once during a short stay in Salem —
thou only hast thrown a light deep downward, and upward, into my soul. Thou only hast revealed me to
myself; for without thy aid, my best knowledge of
myself would have been merely to know my own
shadow — to watch it flickering on the wall, and
mistake its fantasies for my own real actions. Indeed, we are but shadows — we are not endowed with
real life, and all that seems most real about us is but
the thinnest substance of a dream — till the heart is
touched. That touch creates us — then we begin to
be — thereby we are beings of reality, and inheritors
of eternity. Now, dearest, dost thou comprehend what
thou hast done for me?

Yet in this same letter he gave utterance to his belief
that it was their long, separate solitude that had made
them fit for each other, and particularly that he would
have been less worthy of her if he had held himself
less austerely aloof from the world.

Now I begin to understand — he wrote — why I
was imprisoned so many years in this lonely chamber,
and why I could never break through the viewless bolts
and bars; for if I had sooner made my escape into the
world, I should have grown hard and rough, and been
covered with earthly dust, and my heart would have
become callous by rude encounters with the multitude; so that I should have been all unfit to shelter a
heavenly Dove in my arms. But living in solitude till
the fullness of time was come, I still kept the dew of
my youth and the freshness of my heart, and had these
to offer to my Dove.

But what sort of philosophy is this that makes love a product not of the rich central soil where all experiences flourish, but of a removed and special earth? Did Hawthorne really want to live, even now, in two unrelated worlds, the world in which tables are made and coal is measured, and a world in which love should be the only reality?

There is much in the letters of his courtship to suggest that he yielded to this emotional dualism. No doubt it was the coincidence of his new, unaccustomed, uncongenial duties and the great happiness of his engagement that made it peculiarly difficult to bring both into the focus of a single regard. Certainly he wrote to Sophia like a man turning in relief from one quarter of the skies to another rather than like a man facing confidently in one fixed direction. The evening hours he could spend in fancy with her, he seemed to say, were what made his long days on the waterfront tolerable: they did not give those days an enhanced significance.

I have a mind, some day, to send my dearest a journal of all my doings and sufferings, my whole external life, from the time I awake at dawn till I close my eyes at night. What a dry, dull history would it be! But then, apart from this, I would write another journal, of my inward life throughout the self-same day, — my fits of pleasant thought, and those likewise which are shadowed by passing clouds, — the yearnings of my heart towards my Dove, — my pictures of what we are to enjoy together. Nobody would think that the same man could live two such different lives simultaneously. But then . . . the grosser life is a dream, and the spiritual life a reality.

Hawthorne had forgotten his Canterbury pilgrims when he wrote this: he was refusing to allow the woman he loved to share the "grosser life" with him, and insisting that she maintain a sphere apart for their irrelevant relations.

At times this demand for isolation *with* Sophia was given even more explicit statement.

Dearest wife, thy husband is sometimes driven — he wrote during his second spring at the Customhouse — to wish that thou and he could mount upon a cloud (as we used to fancy in those heavenly walks of ours), and be borne quite out of sight and hearing of all the world; but now, all the people in the world seem to come between us. How happy were Adam and Eve! There was no third person to come between them, and all the infinity around them only served to press their hearts closer together. We love one another as well as they; but there is no silent and lovely garden of Eden for us.

The very next day he wrote to tell her of an "immense misfortune" that had befallen him, the receiving of an invitation to a party the following Friday evening, and to protest that he wanted no such social intercourse but only to be left alone with her — or rather, a perhaps essential proviso, with his thoughts of her. "How strange it is, tender and fragile little Sophie," he once wrote, "that your protection should have become absolutely necessary to such a great, rough, burly, broad-shouldered personage as I! I need your support as much as you need mine."

Now the idiom of love letters is no doubt an incommensurable one, and cannot be translated by the ordinary rules. None the less, an idiom it is, not a jargon;

and, with all allowances made for playfulness and exaggeration, it is disconcerting to find Hawthorne recurring so insistently, in his outpourings to Sophia, to the theme of their joint isolation from the rest of humanity. It is disconcerting to find him exulting, not over the expansion and enrichment of his world, but over the "protection" and "repose" his marriage is to bring him. "I never, till now," he wrote during the first spring of their engagement, "had a friend who could give me repose; all have disturbed me, and, whether for pleasure or pain, it was still disturbance. But peace overflows from your heart into mine." . . . "All have disturbed me"! So that was what love and marriage were to mean — freedom from disturbance, insulation from experience. The work wrought by the years in the dismal chamber was not, then, by this agency, to be undone. "Between him and the outer world," said an observer many years later, "came only his wife. There was something at once comical and pathetic in the dismayed appeal with which he turned to her when the ordinary business of life bewildered and jarred on him, and the alertness and bright gentleness with which she served as his shield and shelter." For Hawthorne the private individual — since he was thus spared one cannot say how much distress — it is perhaps possible to rejoice that this was true. For Hawthorne the literary artist, it is impossible not to regret that it was true in just these terms.

So deep, at all events, was his present need of refreshment and repose, after the thankless and weary months at the Customhouse, and so much stronger than even he suspected was his desire for marriage with Sophia and

the seclusion it might make possible, that we cannot
be much surprised at the eventual failure of his next
experiment in adjustment. This was the Brook Farm
adventure, which he was later to describe as ''certainly
the most romantic episode of his own life'' — and
romantic it undeniably was, if only in the quixotism
that led Hawthorne to engage serious hopes in an enterprise so little calculated to hold him permanently.
Neither repose nor solitude was to be achievable in
this direction; and with nothing less than these would
Hawthorne now have been long content. Yet if his
decision to throw in his lot with the Brook Farmers
was quixotic, it was not, in the spring of 1841, an unnatural one for him to come to. Marriage with Sophia
had, by a mutual agreement, been postponed until her
health should be completely recovered; and though
she was now steadily gaining ground, her invalidism
was not yet a thing of the past. With his resignation
from the measurership therefore, Hawthorne was as
footloose as before, and eager to make some arrange-
ment which would enable him to return to literary
work, and at the same time to husband the little capital he had accumulated.

At this juncture he was approached by the Reverend
George Ripley, a member of the so-called Transcendental Club, to the meetings of which, through his friendship with Elizabeth Peabody, Hawthorne had now and
then been admitted. Ripley, dissatisfied with the Christian ministry as he then found it, had recently resigned
from his pastorate at a Unitarian church in Boston, and
was proposing to his fellow Transcendentalists a practical application of some of their social theories — in

brief, a quasi-communistic experiment on the banks of
the Charles River in West Roxbury. Not many of the
more authoritative idealists had taken kindly to the
project; but Hawthorne, distinctly a marginal figure
among them, was attracted, in his present mood, by
Ripley's professed aspiration to "insure a more natural
union between intellectual and manual labor than
now exists; to combine the thinker and the worker,
as far as possible, in the same individual." The duties
of a customhouse official had not proved compatible
with creative activity: perhaps the labors of a plough-
man and a stable-boy would turn out to be more pro-
pitious. Certainly, to a man still torn between two
theories of the good life, it was a seductive possibility.
"We are striving," Ripley once wrote to a correspond-
ent, "to establish a mode of life which shall combine
the enchantments of poetry with the facts of daily
experience." Not for one hour of his life was Hawthorne a reformer, but as a creative writer he might
have phrased his intentions in some such words as
these. He responded without long hesitation, then,
to Ripley's overtures; and speculated seriously on the
possibility of making a home at Brook Farm for Sophia
and himself, once they should be married.

Sudden as his immersion was, during the early days at
the farm, in "the facts of daily experience", Hawthorne
found it easy enough to view them in a pleasantly
poetic light. In contrast with the lonely passages
in city life as he had known it, there was a warmth
and charm, even for an unsociable man, in the friendly
domestic informality with which the handful of pio-
neers spent those first snowy April days in the kitchen

and living-room of the West Roxbury farmhouse. In contrast with the dull routine on the colliers and salt vessels, there was an exhilaration in the robuster, more Virgilian tasks to which, when the bad weather was over, he set himself. Compared with Boston and the docks, the meadowlands along the Charles seemed idyllically retired and solitary. Over the whole enterprise — I had almost said, escapade — lay the glamor of generous purposes, fresh possibilities in the conduct of human relations, novel expressions of capacity; and for many weeks this glamor intervened between Hawthorne and a far-sighted estimate of his position. His letters are, for him, unprecedentedly buoyant and almost youthfully humorous.

This is one of the most beautiful places I ever saw in my life — he wrote to Louisa early in May — and as secluded as if it were a hundred miles from any city or village. There are woods in which we can ramble all day without meeting anybody or scarcely seeing a house. Our house stands apart from the main road, so that we are not troubled even with passengers looking at us. Once in a while we have a transcendental visitor, such as Mr. Alcott; but generally we pass whole days without seeing a single face, save those of the brethren. The whole fraternity eat together; and such a delectable way of life has never been seen on earth since the days of the early Christians. We get up at half-past four, breakfast at half-past six, dine at half-past twelve, and go to bed at nine.

Stimulated by all these elements of adventure, Hawthorne threw himself into the little community's arduous occupations with all the zeal he had shown at the Customhouse and with far greater zest. Bancroft had praised him for his industry, and Ripley in his turn testified that Hawthorne "worked like a dragon." He himself boasted of his exertions with jocose fullness of detail.

Before breakfast — he wrote to Sophia on the second day — I went out to the barn and began to chop hay for the cattle, and with such 'righteous vehemence' (as Mr. Ripley says) did I labor, that in the space of ten minutes I broke the machine. Then I brought wood and replenished the fires; and finally sat down to breakfast, and ate up a huge mound of buckwheat cakes. After breakfast, Mr. Ripley put a four-pronged instrument into my hands, which he gave me to understand was called a pitchfork; and he and Mr. Farley being armed with similar weapons, we all three commenced a gallant attack upon a heap of manure.

As time went on, other husbandman's labors engaged him — milking, cutting straw and hay for the cattle, planting potatoes and pease, carting loads of oak — but it was the dungheap that occupied him most steadily. Throughout April and May, in spite of this dull restriction, his spirits remained high, and he was able to joke sincerely enough about his "gold-mine." "There is nothing so unseemly and disagreeable in this sort of toil as thou wouldst think," he wrote. "It defiles the hands, indeed, but not the soul."

But if Ripley congratulated himself in these first weeks on the accession of a perfect coworker, he was reckoning only on the surface of Hawthorne's current state of spirit. In fact, the enthusiasms of April and May were almost purely illusory — the final flare-up of an old ardor, an old eagerness for worldly activity, not the symptoms of a new impulse. The psychic fatigue of the two years in Boston was not to be recovered from by so superficial a change as this; it was at least as likely to be intensified; and it was by no very gradual process that, as the novelty of the experience dimmed, Hawthorne's discontent reasserted itself, and the days of his application to the dungheap began to be numbered. So early as the first day of June he confessed to Sophia:

I have been too busy to write a long letter by this opportunity, for I think this present life of mine gives me an antipathy to pen and ink, even more than my Custom-House experience did . . . In the midst of toil, or after a hard day's work in the gold-mine, my soul obstinately refuses to be poured out on paper. That abominable gold-mine! Thank God, we anticipate getting rid of its treasures in the course of two or three days! Of all hateful places that is the worst, and I shall never comfort myself for having spent so many days of blessed sunshine there. It is my opinion, dearest, that a man's soul may be buried and perish under a dung-heap, or in a furrow of the field, just as well as under a pile of money.

With that final sentence went the last flicker of Hawthorne's hope that he might here combine physical and intellectual activity in any lasting alliance; but he did not yet abandon all expectation of settling at Brook Farm, on some terms, if the experiment should flourish. For the next two or three months, indeed, he continued to labor in the woodshed and the bean field and the dungheap, though with growing resentment at their tediousness and squalor.

Belovedest, I am very well — he wrote in the second week of August — and not at all weary, for yesterday's

rain gave us a holiday; and, moreover, the labors of the
farm are not so pressing as they have been. And, joy-
ful thought! in a little more than a fortnight thy husband will be free from his bondage, — free to think of
his Dove, — free to enjoy Nature, — free to think and
feel! I do think that a greater weight will then be
removed from me than when Christian's burden fell
off at the foot of the Cross. Even my Custom House
experience was not such a thralldom and weariness;
my mind and heart were freer. Oh, belovedest, labor
is the curse of the world, and nobody can meddle with
it without becoming proportionably brutified! Dost
thou think it a praiseworthy matter that I have spent
five golden months in providing food for cows and
horses? Dearest, it is not so.

The freedom thus joyfully anticipated was not a
departure from the farm for good, but a visit of two or
three weeks in Salem, made partly in response to appeals from his mother and sisters, partly for the sake
of an imperatively needed respite. And how vividly
it became clear, once he was back in Salem, that his
first enthusiasm for life at Brook Farm — for any life
in a group — was, as I have said, illusory! How powerfully, and how revealingly, the old associations swept
over him! With what sudden certainty of conviction
did he realize that, as he wrote to Sophia, if it had
not been for her, he would have relapsed "immediately
and irrecoverably" into the way of life in which he
had spent his youth! The yearning of three years
earlier for a rôle to play in the midst of men was at
last decisively stilled; and a yearning for the shared
solitude of some unlikely Eden had assumed its place.
"If, in the interval since I quitted this lonely old chamber," he confessed, "I had found no woman (and thou

wast the only possible one) to impart reality and significance to life, I should have come back hither ere
now, with a feeling that all was a dream and a mockery.’’ So strong, indeed, even in spite of Sophia, was
this sense of the unreality of the ‘‘grosser life’’, that he
professed a half-serious uncertainty whether he had
ever milked cows and hoed potatoes and raked hay at
West Roxbury at all. ‘‘And I take this to be one proof
that my life there was an unnatural and unsuitable,
and therefore an unreal, one. It already looks like a
dream behind me.’’ In such a dream, whenever his way
of life was official or specifically social, he was henceforth to walk.

When, therefore, late in September, Hawthorne
returned to the community, it was not as an even occasional laborer in the fields, but as an associate who had
invested his capital in the project, and hence had privileges as a boarder — the privileges which he hoped
would include the leisure and the solitude for writing.
If this hope should be fulfilled, and if the designs of
the brethren should prosper, there was still a possibility that he might settle at Brook Farm when he and
Sophia were man and wife. But as October wore on,
and the life of the community moved before him under
this new light, he saw with growing clarity that this
hope too must be abandoned. If his heart had been
in the community's experiment itself, Hawthorne could
only have been cheered by the animation that was now
more and more the spirit of the place. The half-dozen
of them who had been the advance-guard in April were
steadily being joined by new adventurers, attracted by
one aspect of the enterprise or another, so that the

miscellaneity which Ripley had aimed at was being rapidly achieved. Half-literate farmers from Vermont, printers, disillusioned clergymen, religious melancholiacs, rich young men from Providence, recent graduates of Harvard, seamstresses, idealistic widows, music teachers, and an increasing body of children — pupils in Marianne Ripley's school across the way — flocked through the rooms of the Hive, chatted and punned at the long dining tables like early Christians with a sense of humor, sang part songs as they washed dishes or pitched hay, and gathered in the evenings to discuss metaphysics or play charades or listen to readings from Shakespeare. But of all this hilarious group life Hawthorne could not make himself a part. He could look on, but he could not join in. "No one could have been more out of place than he in a mixed company," wrote Georgiana Kirby. "He was morbidly shy and reserved, needing to be shielded from his fellows, and obtaining the fruits of observation at second-hand." And a more tolerant chronicler, George Bradford, remembered that "he was shy and silent, and, though he mingled with the rest of the company in the evening gatherings in the hall and parlor of the Hive, he was apparently self-absorbed, but doubtless carefully observing and finding material for his writing."

That air of making mental notations which impressed both of these witnesses, he must undoubtedly have had. At no time in his life had he been in the thick of a concourse so rich as this was in material for scrutiny and analysis, and even in his prevailing mood Hawthorne was not too disaffected to remember his spectator's habit. But writing itself he could not find the detachment to resume.

I have not the sense of perfect seclusion — he wrote — which has always been essential to my power of producing anything. It is true, nobody intrudes into my room; but still I cannot be quiet. Nothing here is settled; everything is but beginning to arrange itself, and though thy husband would seem to have little to do with aught beside his own thoughts, still he cannot but partake of the ferment around him. My mind will not be abstracted. I must observe, and think, and feel, and content myself with catching glimpses of things which may be wrought out hereafter.

It is true that he finished at this time a little volume of "Biographical Stories for Children" — but it was writing that he could do with his left hand and less than half his mind. It is true, too, that he resumed the writing of a journal with more consistency than he had achieved since the summer in North Adams: but it is striking that there is much less than the usual proportion of personal descriptions and more than the usual proportion of nature notes in the entries for this period. However strong his interest in his associates may have been, it could apparently not overcome his present distaste for the social scene, or his irritable sense of being too closely affiliated with them; and he made — with the exception of a little seamstress from Boston — no studies of them. The crowds at Brighton Fair, to which he drove one day with William Allen, carrying a calf to be sold there, — the yeomen in their Sunday suits, the round-paunched country squires, the country loafers, the buckramed dandies from the city — these he could look at as from an advantageous distance, and he made notes on them in something of the old attentive manner. For the rest, Hawthorne found it more in consonance with his humor to take walks along the

Needham road, or to Newton and back by way of
Brighton and Jamaica Plain, or in the woods and
meadows along the Charles, laying himself under the
spell of the tonic October weather, remarking the pro-
cessional pomp of autumn gold and scarlet in the oaks
and maples and blueberry bushes, the solemnity of
crows cawing and flapping in the autumn woods, the
choleric conduct of a squirrel. Spectacles such as these
enhanced, instead of menacing, his privacy.

But it was not for the fostering of such methodical
unsociability that the communitarians of Brook Farm
had banded together, and Hawthorne, in spite of his
election to the chairmanship of the Committee on
Finance, lost little time in making other plans for the
winter and casting about for other arrangements for
Sophia and himself. His presence could have been but
little missed when he left West Roxbury in November.

At no time during these six or seven months, or the
ensuing period, could Hawthorne probably have given
any more abstract account of his dissatisfaction with
Brook Farm than his letters at the time expressed. Impatience, even disgust, with the unenlightened drudgery
of the fields; disappointment at his inability to settle
down, in the midst of so much bustle, to literary work;
restlessness induced by the delay of his marriage with
Sophia — were not these things reason enough for
abandoning an experiment in which he had never invested any impersonal hopes? Yet there were more
deep-seated reasons than these, sufficient as they were;
reasons which Hawthorne himself could never fully
have stated, but to which, in the record he made from
the vantage point of ten perspective years, he gave a sug-
gestive clue. Into the mouth of Coverdale, the narrator

of "The Blithedale Romance", he put these partial statements — statements which remind us that we are dealing with the author of "Wakefield" and "Peter Goldthwaite's Treasure."

I very soon became sensible — says Coverdale of his life at Blithedale — that, as regarded society at large, we stood in a position of new hostility, rather than new brotherhood . . . Constituting so pitiful a minority as now, we were inevitably estranged from the rest of mankind in pretty fair proportion with the strictness of our mutual bond among ourselves. . . . As matters now were — he observes later — I felt myself (and, having a decided tendency towards the actual, I never liked to feel it) getting quite out of my reckoning, with regard to the existing state of the world. I was beginning to lose the sense of what kind of a world it was, among innumerable schemes of what it might or ought to be. It was impossible, situated as we were, not to imbibe the idea that everything in nature and human existence was fluid, or fast becoming so . . . Our great globe floated in the atmosphere of infinite space like an unsubstantial bubble. No sagacious man will long retain his sagacity, if he live exclusively among reformers and progressive people, without returning periodically into the settled system of things, to correct himself by a new observation from that old standpoint.

Now manifestly this was not the whole truth: manifestly Hawthorne's "decided tendency towards the actual" — far as it was from being merely a fiction contrived for Coverdale — was constantly and sometimes hopelessly at war with the passion for isolation which really moved him in his desertion of Brook Farm. The life he was to lead for the ensuing three or four years was, to his great satisfaction, almost completely estranged from that of "the rest of mankind." Nevertheless, it is deeply true that he had longed, three years before, to find himself at the center, not on the lonely edge, of the real life of his time, of his America. What he now seemed to have learned was that, to all intents and purposes, that life had no center. No point, in any case, at which all the coöperating energies of a rich and integrated culture could be said to concentrate. No point on which the imagination could alight and from which it could contemplate all its proper objects. If Hawthorne's demand for unity and significance had been less exacting, he could no doubt have come to terms with both Boston and West Roxbury: as it was, what could he make of a world so imperfectly articulated, so motley, so cacophonous, as this world of venal bureaucrats, loutish farmers, poets of mystical experience, pig drovers, polished professors of literature, and reforming zealots? What common ground was there for one's feet to tread between Long Wharf and the Athenæum, between North Adams and West Roxbury? And if there was no common ground, if the Customhouse and Brook Farm could be brought into no fruitful contact, if both of them robbed him of his solitude and neither of them — Brook Farm less even than the other — enrolled him in an inclusive brotherhood with men, what motives could be valid enough to prevail against his deep desire for repose? The secret history of these last years had been a history of conflict between two necessities of his nature, or — in another phrasing — between the possibilities of American life and the values of isolation. The years had not been wasted, but decidedly they had ended in no triumph for the social party. And the issue was never to be defined in the same way again.

CHAPTER FOUR

MOSSES

"Men must know, that in this theatre of man's life it is reserved only for God and angels to be lookers on." — Bacon, "Advancement of Learning."

"THE solitude of a united two" — that was what, in Hawthorne's own language, he essentially desired, and what he was now to have with a virtual completeness that answered all his prayers. After three years' postponement, his marriage with Sophia, which he had long regarded as consummated in the ideal sense, became a civil fact in the summer after the departure from Brook Farm. A benignant fate, acting through the saintly person of Elizabeth Hoar, led the two of them to a spot where their dreams of a seclusion like that before the Fall could come as near realization as, at that historical date, was imaginable. During the preceding winter the Reverend Doctor Ezra Ripley of Concord had died at a patriarchal age, and since his son, Samuel Ripley, was at the time conducting a school in Waltham, the Old Manse, where Emersons and Ripleys had lived from pre-Revolutionary days, was temporarily without an occupant. Who could have occupied it more worthily or more happily than Nathaniel and Sophia Hawthorne? "As we could not live there yet," wrote Samuel Ripley to Emerson's Aunt Mary, after the Hawthornes moved in, "I am glad that it is inhabited by those who can value it for what it is, and for what it once contained of purity, piety, and worth."

How, indeed, could a man or woman of poetic sensibility fail to respond to the influential glamor of the place? Concord was the sleepiest and most peaceful of peaceful and sleepy villages, and the Old Manse was the most indolent domain in Concord. Set back a hundred paces from the road, approachable through an avenue of black-ash trees, weather-beaten, moss-grown, gambrel-roofed, it drowsed away its days in perfect indifference to the passage of worldly time, as if no conceivable emergency could threaten its vespertine quietude. The most deliberate of beans and squashes would always come to maturity in the vegetable garden that lay to one side; apples and pears and peaches would ripen through interminable summers, and drop of their own weight to the ground, in the little orchard that stretched downward behind the house; and the river at its foot would take its eternal way to the sea so sluggishly that one could scarcely guess at the direction of its current. All seasons would visit the place, of course, but it belonged with special justice to the late summer and fall, and even in the spring its air would be less vernal than autumnal. Inside, the chambers and hallways of the old house were filled, in their ancient austerity of line and finish, their want of the merely decorative, with clerkly and ancestral references that Sophia's prints and vases and astral lamps could brighten but could not profane. If men of God had dwelt here with singular fitness, it was clearly no less appropriate a residence for a poet, even a poet on a prolonged honeymoon.

The essential charm of the place was what Hawthorne called its "near retirement and accessible seclusion."

Without the bleakness of real isolation, it was sufficiently withdrawn, sufficiently shadowed and hedged
about, to make casual intrusion unlikely. In the quiet
ecstasy of their long-deferred union, Hawthorne and
Sophia took full advantage of this privacy, and recorded
with a kind of inverted avarice the rarity of their
visitations.

We were interrupted by no one — wrote Sophia after
a few months — except a short call now and then from
Elizabeth Hoar, who can hardly be called an earthly
inhabitant; and Mr. Emerson, whose face pictured the
promised land (which we were then enjoying), and in-
truded no more than a sunset, or a rich warble from a
bird.

Hawthorne himself was equally self-congratulatory.

Few, indeed — he wrote in his journal in August —
are the mortals who venture within our sacred precincts. George Prescott, who has not yet grown earthly
enough, I suppose, to be debarred from occasional visits
to Paradise, comes daily to bring three pints of milk
from some ambrosial cow; occasionally, also, he makes
an offering of mortal flowers, at the shrine of a certain
angelic personage. Mr. Emerson comes sometimes, and
has been so far favored as to be feasted on our nectar
and ambrosia. Mr. Thoreau has twice listened to the
music of the spheres, which, for our private conveni-
ence, we have packed into a musical box. Elizabeth
Hoar, who is much more at home among spirits than
among fleshly bodies, came hither a few times merely
to welcome us to the ethereal world; but latterly she
has vanished into some other region of infinite space.
One rash mortal, on the second Sunday after our arrival,
obtruded himself upon us in a gig. There have since

been three or four callers, who preposterously think that the courtesies of the lower world are to be responded to by people whose home is in Paradise.

There was no danger, now that Hawthorne had assumed the responsibilities of a family, that he would ever slip back into the eremitism of his youth; but his aversion to miscellaneous contacts had not been dispelled by his worldly experiences or his marriage, and for three years, while the Manse was their home, he indulged his unsociability without opposition, and even with Sophia's abetment. "During that time," wrote George William Curtis, "he was not seen, probably, by more than a dozen of the villagers" — and there were others than the inhabitants of Concord who suffered from his exaggerated shyness. On one occasion, the Manse was invaded by no less a person than Julia Ward Howe, with her husband, and what ill luck they had !

We presently entered the Manse — she later wrote — and were hospitably received by Mrs. Hawthorne in its modest parlor. While we talked with her, a step was heard descending the stair. Mrs. Hawthorne said, raising her voice, "My husband, I want you to come and see Dr. and Mrs. Howe." In obedience to this summons, Mr. Hawthorne showed himself at the door for a moment, and immediately disappeared. In this glimpse of him I had seen his handsome, fresh face and clear blue eyes. I recall even now the shape of the broad-brimmed straw hat that shaded his forehead. To my great disappointment, we saw nothing more of him. Mrs. Hawthorne consoled me as well as she could, and showed me, among other things, the bedroom furniture of which I had heard so much.

No, if any one had expected that love and marriage would prove to be channels through which Hawthorne would move toward other unconstrained and varied human relationships, he would have been grievously disenchanted by the outcome. It was far more as if that one profound intimacy were sufficient for the solidifying and vitalizing of his emotional life; as if that one cup were all he needed to slake the old thirst of the wilderness. It was as if, with his abandonment of utter solitude, the whole work of humanization were done, and he could now give over the tedious business of adapting himself to other men and women. "My wife is, in the strictest sense, my sole companion, and I need no other," he wrote in his journal; "there is no vacancy in my mind any more than in my heart. In truth, I have spent so many years in total seclusion from all human society, that it is no wonder if I now feel all my desires satisfied by this sole intercourse." And if the vibrancy of his tone here be set down to the credit of the first year after marriage, it is not merely on that ground that we can account for the misery of loneliness into which he allowed himself to fall whenever, during their Manse life, Sophia left him for short visits with her family in Boston. He seemed, on such occasions, to have lost all his old resources for the use of solitude without having acquired any new resources for companionship. As soon as Sophia had driven away down the avenue, desolation would settle upon his spirits; yet, with a kind of moody defiance, he would take a vow with himself to pass the whole period without speaking a word to any human being, and then be vexed if his Trappist intentions were thwarted by

Henry Thoreau unwittingly turning up at teatime for
a talk. It would not have occurred to him to seek out
Thoreau — or Emerson — or Ellery Channing — on his
own initiative; instead, he would attack the woodpile
in the hope that active exercise would still his inward
unquietness; he would make repeated, abortive attempts
to get through a tale of Tieck's on which he was exercising his small German; part of the morning he would
spend "scribbling", but without catching more than
"the glimmering of an idea" or finding that his mind
could be made to work "to any systematic purpose."
And if, as he sat reading at the western windows of his
study, there was a beautiful sunset to be seen, he found
that "I could not enjoy [it] sufficiently by myself to
induce me to lay aside the book." Such, no doubt, is
the penalty he pays whose personal relationships are
those of a fugitive, not a combatant.

The result, certainly, was that he formed no genuinely warm and unreserved friendships with even the
two or three people in Concord with whom he might
seem to have had a natural affiliation. Of Emerson he
could not share Sophia's worshipful opinion. It was a
pity, for Emerson was prepared to meet him at least
halfway with sympathy and respect: "Nature gives me
precious signs," he wrote in his journal the spring
after Hawthorne had moved to Concord, "in such persons as . . . Nathaniel Hawthorne, . . . that in democratic America she will not be democratized. How
cloistered and constitutionally sequestered from the
market and gossips!" Too cloistered, as it proved:
Emerson's own tentatives toward free intercourse came
to little or nothing, though there were repeated oppor-

tunities for the right spark to be struck. During the
first summer at the Manse, he was a not infrequent visitor, and at rare intervals managed to persuade Hawthorne to reciprocate his calls. Late in September of
the same year, the two of them went to the Shaker
Community at the village of Harvard on a walking trip
which occupied two days and was memorable to Hawthorne chiefly, it would appear, as the first occasion on
which he had spent the night away from home —
"for I never had a home before." After two weeks he
remembered nothing about the trip so well as the
fringed gentians which they saw growing by the road-
side. Once Emerson conducted Hawthorne and his
guest, George Hillard, on a walk to Walden Pond, and
took them a little out of their way to call on Edmund
Hosmer, the Concord farmer of whose innate sagacity
he had formed a high estimate. And after winter
descended upon them, he had the heroism to join
Hawthorne and Thoreau in skating upon the river —
an exercise for which he had no talent, and for which
he yielded the palm, with gracious allusiveness, to
Hawthorne.

Through all these passages, Hawthorne held himself
quietly aloof. The time had gone past, he managed to
convince himself, when Emerson's philosophy might
have helped him to solve the riddle of the universe:
"now, being happy, I felt as if there were no question
to be put", he confessed with ill-concealed relief. So long,
certainly, as he preserved this complacence, he could be
under no compulsion to pit his mind against Emerson's
in any equal combat, or to revise any of his own views
by getting at what was best in Emerson's central

thought. This would have meant a labor of penetration for which he now lacked the energy, and, remaining as he did on the surface, he was right enough about Emerson's infirmities and his own reasons for expecting no profit in that quarter. From Emerson the mere Transcendentalist, companion of the vaporous and oracular Alcott, Emerson "that everlasting rejecter of all that is and seeker for he knows not what" (as Hawthorne early described him), he undeniably had little to gain. With mere mystics, mere idealists, mere Platonic or Kantian visionaries he had already had traffic, and had learned that they could furnish none of the aliment that his imagination peculiarly demanded. In no light but this did he ever succeed in seeing Emerson — "Mr. Emerson, the mystic, stretching his hand out of cloudland in vain search for something real" — and since he had had his own not dissimilar difficulties, it is little wonder if he allowed their intercourse to remain perfunctory and dry.

Ellery Channing, in spite of his careless Transcendental poems, was a chip off another block. At first Hawthorne formed a none too favorable impression of him — disposing of him as "one of those queer and clever young men, whom Mr. Emerson . . . is continually picking up by way of a genius" — and he rejected in some alarm Margaret Fuller's suggestion that Ellery and her sister Mary, who had recently married, should add themselves as boarders to the household at the Manse. Later Ellery proved to be a more acceptable companion than Hawthorne had hoped: he was apparently genuinely eccentric without being by any means a fool, and he had a vein of poetry in his make-up that was none the less authentic for being overlaid with much that was crabbed, willful, and grotesque. A boat trip that the two of them made up the Assabet, the north branch of the Concord, rowing for a mile or more effortlessly upstream in the dense cool shadow of the overhanging maple and hemlock branches, cooking their supper in the open on its banks, and railing at society in a pleasantly Rousseauistic tone as they lay on the ground after eating, was one of the incidents that Hawthorne remembered with most satisfaction from his three years of life in Concord. Nevertheless, their companionship, if Ellery's own recollections are reliable, could never have emerged wholly from the shadow of Hawthorne's incurable diffidence. "I have walked much with him," Channing told Frank Sanborn; "but he was not fond of that exercise; he had the greatest aversion to company, — thought it a 'damnable bore', and would swear about it sometimes; he was a good swearer, you must know. He had the greatest difficulty in expressing himself in conversation. He would stammer and twist himself about."

Frequently, on their walks, he professed to remember, Hawthorne would become weary and give up the walk not from physical fatigue, but from sheer boredom. "Once in Concord I took him to Gowan's Swamp, a beautiful pool, not very large, between the old and the new Bedford Roads . . . It was a choice walk, to which Thoreau and I did not invite everybody. When we reached the place, Hawthorne said nothing, but just glanced about him and remarked: 'Let us get out of this dreadful hole!'" Something, clearly, was amiss in this partnership — something that is only hinted at in Hawthorne's remark, when Ellery was about to return to Concord after a long absence, that "I am rather glad than otherwise; but Ellery, so far as he has been developed to my observation, is but an imperfect substitute for Mr. Thoreau."

In Thoreau, certainly, Hawthorne had met his match for unsociability, and his interest was aroused as it never had been by the gregarious philosophers and reformers. Here was an individual who did not merely rail at ordinary social intercourse, but actually, after Hawthorne's own fashion, shunned it, and cultivated the arts of the solitary.

He is a singular character — Hawthorne recorded with evident if restrained enthusiasm — a young man with much of wild, original nature still remaining in him; and so far as he is sophisticated, it is in a way and method of his own. He is as ugly as sin, long-nosed, queer-mouthed, and with uncouth and rustic, although courteous manners, corresponding very well with such an exterior. But his ugliness is of an honest and agreeable fashion, and becomes him much better than beauty.

The heights of expansive mutuality were hardly to be scaled by two such devotees of the centrifugal, but there was a basis for real sympathy between them, and an odd sort of dry, laconic, austerely cordial friendship sprang up and grew sturdy during Hawthorne's first year in the Manse. Thoreau's passion for nature, though of a different quality from Hawthorne's, more direct, more studious, freer from subjective elements, had much of the same intense and perhaps misanthropic spirit; and Hawthorne delighted to learn from him about such matters as the variety among apparently similar blackbirds and the way the pond lily opens its blossom to the morning sunlight. From Thoreau he purchased the old boat — the *Musketaquid*, rechristened the *Pond-Lily* — in which he and his brother had made a famous trip down the Concord and the Merrimack, and from him acquired the art of navigating it, an art that proved more abstruse than Hawthorne had anticipated. It was with a regret he did not frequently feel that he heard from Thoreau, in the spring of 1843, the news of his imminent departure from Concord to take up his residence at Staten Island: "on my account, I should like to have him remain here," he wrote in his journal, "he being one of the few persons, I think, with whom to hold intercourse is like hearing the wind among the boughs of a forest-tree." But the regret, sincere as it was, was by no means violent; no more on Thoreau than on any third person was Hawthorne now dependent for companionship, and his departure made singularly little difference in the pattern of Hawthorne's days. Neither of them ever took energetic steps, in later years, to revive their friendship.

How self-contained, indeed, how independent of complex relations, how primitive (in that sense) were the occupations that made his three years' life at the Manse so happy and memorable a chapter in Hawthorne's experience! What a mellow and yet simplified pleasure it was, for example, to labor with spade and hoe in the earth, in the springtime, setting out a vegetable garden! And what a cheerful sense he had of being in conspiracy with nature, as he observed the

slow certain progress of his beans and peas and green
corn from day to day through the long sultry summer,
noting as time wore on the first occasions on which
these comfortable growths rewarded his care by appearing, after no transactions of the market place, on his
own dinner table! The very shapes of the ripening
squashes — like urns or vases with scalloped edges —
delighted him; and he rejoiced in the number of bees
that sucked honey from the blossoms, though (since
they came from heaven knew where) he himself would
never be the richer for it. The orchard was even less
care than the garden, needing only a little pruning
in the spring, the propping up of a too richly laden
bough in late August, and the labor of gathering up
the fruit that showered to the ground in embarrassing
quantities whenever a limb was shaken. To eke out
this so bountifully provided diet, and to give him
one more lazy employment, there were fish to be caught
in the river, uninviting as it looked in its muddy torpor — fish of which he could pull out a dozen or so
before breakfast on mornings when it was worth being
abroad for the mere sake of their bracing coolness.
Once, returning from a voyage he made alone in the
Pond-Lily up the north branch of the river, he caught
enough fish for the next day's breakfast: "but, partly
from a qualm of conscience, I finally put them all into
the water again, and saw them swim away as if nothing had happened." Why, in so liberal an atmosphere,
should one take thought even for one's breakfast on
the morrow?

A locality in which there was no spot for swimming
would have been only imperfectly a home for Haw-

thorne, and though he would have preferred the salt
waters of the sea, he was not disposed to complain
about the Concord, muddy as its waters were and likely
to be even warmer than the air. But how exhilarating,
in contrast with his morning dips in the river, was the
bath he once had, in George Hillard's company, in the
transparent waters of Walden Pond after Emerson had
left them! More than a year later, walking there
alone in early October, he was almost tempted to
bathe again: "though the water was thrillingly cold,
it was like the thrill of a happy death." But he contented himself with throwing sticks into it, and seeing
them "float suspended on an almost invisible medium."
The joys of outdoor bathing had to be confined to
warm weather, but only the extreme severity of winter
could keep him from taking the walks he had always
loved and now, alone or with Sophia, regarded as essential cadences in the rhythm of daily life. Something in
Ellery Channing's tastes as a walker must have clashed
with his own, for he himself never left record of a
wholly unsatisfactory excursion. Even the discordant
personality of Margaret Fuller repelled him far less
than usual when he came upon her, on his way home
from Emerson's, lying under the trees in Sleepy Hollow,
and he stopped and had talk with her about autumn
and the crows — and "the experiences of early childhood, whose influence remains upon the character after
the recollection of them has passed away." Ordinarily,
of course, he came upon no one; if he was with Sophia,
the two of them had enough to do to mark the wild
flowers that happened to be in bloom, and to gather as
many as they could carry home for their numerous

bowls and vases — laurel in its season, the blue-spired pickerel weed, the cardinal flower with its tragic portentous brilliance, and the flags and water lilies of the river and its banks. If he was alone, he could study from a hilltop, in the spring, the encroachments of the swollen river upon the contiguous fields, or, in the autumn, the gradual and gorgeous progress of decay in the Concord woods and meadows, and all summer long the murmurous many-colored life of animate and inanimate nature.

Protracted rainy spells in the summer and the rigors of endless winters kept them practically house-fast for long periods, but for neither Hawthorne nor his wife were there conceivable sources of ennui in each other's company, and the Manse itself was a house in which imprisonment by the rainiest or wintriest weather was rather a privilege than an affliction. Where could Hawthorne have felt more at home, on a wet dark day, than in the twilight of the arched and unfinished garret of the Manse: peering into the little whitewashed chamber where Emerson had written "Nature", turning up the odds and ends of "lumber" that generations had allowed to accumulate in the outer spaces, rummaging in the library of his predecessor — a dreary hoard of ancient theological works, printed sermons, controversies, and tracts, among which some old newspapers and almanacs seemed, by contrast, instinct with the authentic life of their era? And on long winter evenings, what could have been, for either of them, a more unalloyed luxury than for Hawthorne to read aloud from Shakespeare in the soft light of the astral lamp in his study while Sophia sat by and sewed, mar-

veling at the rich expressiveness of his voice? If there
was reason, at least to Sophia's mind, to believe that
the house was haunted — if a swishing sound as of
ministerial garments was sometimes heard in the parlor, and the noise of ghostly ministrations in the kitchen
at nights — so much the more perfect, in its own mode,
was the setting.

What wonder, then, if, in spite of their poverty,
pressing upon them increasingly as it did after the first
year, Hawthorne could feel that life in the Manse with
Sophia was a refuge from the ugliest of worlds, a refuge
he could scarcely be reproached for seeking, and attempting to preserve? "The fight with the world," he
recorded early in his journal, "the struggle of a man
among men, — the agony of the universal effort to
wrench the means of living from a host of greedy com-
petitors, — all this seems like a dream to me." And it
was only then, only when the ferment of "the grosser
world" had receded into remoteness and unreality, that
Hawthorne, shut up alone in his study on a winter
day, could take command again of his creative forces,
could muster his energies for the labor of invention,
could forget that he had been a measurer sufficiently to
remember that he had been even earlier a writer of
prose fiction. In that defended precinct, as in the solitary chamber of the Manning house, his imagination
could take wing and fly as it was impotent to do in any
less untenanted air. From this point of view, no revolution had been worked by the five years since "Twice-
Told Tales" had appeared.

Had no other change, however, in his status as a creative writer come about? Had not those five years

effected some deep shift in the very statement of his fundamental problems? If so, it was too early, during these Concord days, for the change to be appreciable. The problem of an audience and the problem of materials — these had been, from the beginning, inexorably with him, and it was singular how little either of them had yet taken on a new stress. Hawthorne, it is true, was now the author of a volume of collected tales as well as of two or three books for children, and his work did not have to go begging for acceptance among the magazine editors of the country. Yet the "Twice-Told Tales", as he observed some years later, had had but a limited and almost esoteric sale, and its distribution "was chiefly confined to New England"; in his late thirties, and after nearly twenty years of literary toil, he had no general or far-flung reputation, no basis on which he "could regard himself as addressing the American Public, or, indeed, any Public at all." "The reputation of the author of 'Twice-Told Tales'" declared Poe in 1846, "has been confined, until very lately, to literary society; and I have not been wrong, perhaps, in citing him as *the* example, *par excellence*, in this country, of the privately admired and publicly unappreciated man of genius . . . It was never the fashion (until lately) to speak of him in any summary of our best authors."

Two years before, in writing of himself under the veil of "M. de l'Aubepine", in a prefatory note to "Rappaccini's Daughter", Hawthorne himself had noted the same fact, and suggested an explanation that illuminates the whole terrain upon which he must be envisaged.

As a writer, he seems to occupy — he said — an unfortunate position between the Transcendentalists (who, under one name or another, have their share in all the current literature of the world) and the great body of pen-and-ink men who address the intellect and sympathies of the multitude. If not too refined, at all events too remote, too shadowy, and unsubstantial in his modes of development to suit the taste of the latter class, and yet too popular to satisfy the spiritual or metaphysical requisitions of the former, he must necessarily find himself without an audience, except here and there an individual or possibly an isolated clique.

A diagnosis, we must think, of quite unimpeachable soundness: Hawthorne had not shared the experience — he was incapable of sharing it — of either the Transcendentalists or the multitude; and how could he hope to address either party as from the vantage point of a common purpose, a common sense of the just and true? Such a reciprocity, in fact, he did not hope for; and that is partly the reason why he now failed to open up any really new territory of the imagination, to advance as far as he should have done beyond the ground covered by the "Twice-Told Tales."

For at the end of the creative period that coincided with his life in Concord, as Hawthorne collected his scattered tales and sketches for the volume of "Mosses from an Old Manse", it must have been clear that he had arrived at no fresh and permanent solution of the old problem of materials; that instead of having broken out a new pathway for himself, he had but followed to its impassable terminus an imaginative *cul de sac*. He felt this so strongly himself that he determined never to walk in that same way again, and promised his

readers, in the prefatory essay, that this would be his
last collection of such essays and tales: "unless I could
do better," he said, "I have done enough in this kind."
It was not that he had gained nothing from the long
holiday; not that he did not now write with a subtler
linguistic craft, a more practised chiaroscuro; not even
that he had not made one or two innovations in theme
and form. But the essential power had not been added
unto him, the power he himself must have had in
mind when he hinted that he had hoped to write a
novel in the Manse, and confessed his own opinion
that the "Mosses" had far too little of "external life"
about them to afford a "solid basis for a literary reputation." What could this have been but the power to
translate into fiction his patient observations of real
people on something like their own terms — with a
care, that is, for the roughness, the shifting contours,
the asymmetry of the human fact, and without the in-
tervention of a merely subjective speculation or an irresponsible allegory? Certainly Hawthorne had aimed at
attaining such a power; certainly that aim had been
present to him in his wanderings about the New England countryside, during the long days in Boston Harbor, and even in the restive weeks at Brook Farm: the
testimony of his studiously objective journals is too
plain for misunderstanding. Why did he not now
"make something more beautiful" of the sailor boy
from Malaga, or of the crippled soap-maker at North
Adams, or of the bewildered cuckold at Augusta?

It was not to these memories or these notes that he
turned for inspiration when he began to write again,
but to the abstract suggestions for sketches and tales

he had always entered in his journal. How remote are
these, in their inventive quality, from that other sort
of material! "To make a story of all strange and impossible things, — as the Salamander, the Phoenix."
And "A Virtuoso's Collection" is the outcome. "A
man to swallow a small snake, — and it to be a symbol
of a cherished sin" — a design that is followed out in
"Egotism; or, The Bosom Serpent." "To personify If
— But — And — Though, etc." — a suggestion that
proved, even for Hawthorne, too insubstantial to be
worked up into a tale, but one that is not unfairly
typical of a whole series of trifles which seem to have
amused him on his least imaginative side and which
he yet made use of, in the "Mosses", more than once.

In reading the least worthy of these pieces, one has
the painful impression of great capacities being wasted
on the production of the veriest bagatelles, the impression of a fine, high, uncommon energy being dissipated
in the service of cheap and silly ends. It is as if the fanciful exercises of a gifted boy were engrossing the
attention of a man in the full flood of his developed
powers. Consider such sketches as "A Select Party",
"The Hall of Fantasy", and "The Intelligence Office."
In the first of these, a Man of Fancy entertains in his
castle in the air a crowd of impossible guests, — the
Oldest Inhabitant, Monsieur On-Dit, Nobody, the
Clerk of the Weather, the Master Genius of American
Literature, Posterity — and these notables are described
with all the resources of a cold ingenuity. "The Hall
of Fantasy" is in a similar spiritual region: it is not
only the repository of the busts and statues of the great
imaginative writers of the past and the resort of living

ones, but also — and perhaps with a submerged significance — the resort of business men (whose characteristic schemes are thus satirized), of inventors, of cranks,
of reformers, and of the notorious Father Miller himself. In "The Intelligence Office" Hawthorne expands
the conception of a bureau whither all seekers for lost
objects flock, all persons with a quest or with something to exchange, and of a Man of Intelligence who,
like a Recording Angel, registers all these longings
and aspirations in a great folio, the Book of Wishes.
Like these three sketches, "A Virtuoso's Collection"
is a feat of enumeration, but it describes simply a mu-
seum of curiosities, and is the emptiest of the series.
No one of these, as we shall see, is merely empty: their
stiff texture is colored with dyes that have been fished
up from great depths; but how stiff and heavy in truth
that texture is, and how mechanical the work of weav-
ing it! Let them be read however unexactingly, yet the
faint artificial odor of triviality arises from them, so
tame and trashy are their organizing concepts. A literary artist who, at such a point in his development,
could give much of his time to the confection of these
gewgaws must be guilty of some radical mismanage-
ment in his creative economy; and these are four pieces
out of less than a score that Hawthorne wrote in the
Manse.

They were, moreover, in their weakly "symbolic",
their baldly schematic execution, symptoms of a growing devotion on Hawthorne's part to the allegorical
manner. At the outset, in the days of "Fanshawe", of
"The Gentle Boy", of "The Gray Champion", there
had been nothing to indicate that allegory was for him

an inevitable mode of literary utterance; there had been a good deal to indicate, in the first half-dozen years of his authorship, that his development might move in quite different and less Spenserian directions. It was only with such experiments as "The Great Carbuncle" and "Wakefield" in 1833 and the next year, that the manner began to impose itself upon him in a well-defined form, and only in the second series of the "Twice-Told Tales" that its presence, if not yet exclusive, was observably dominant. Now, with the exception of two or three familiar essays, he was to write nothing, during the productive period at the Manse, that did not bear the allegorical stamp. It had become his unique resource in narrative.

At its best, allegory had been, and was to be, the vehicle for Hawthorne of some of his most deeply creative designs. Such a form, it is true, would always have, in prose fiction, a secondary artistic value; would always betray some failure to find for the conception its perfect equivalent in terms of character and act. Nevertheless, in such tales as "Young Goodman Brown" and "Dr. Heidigger's Experiment" and "Lady Eleanore's Mantle", allegory had taken on a far from inconsiderable imaginative dignity; and this partly because it there had its roots far down in Hawthorne's emotional experience, partly because it was embodied in human figures not wholly unindividualized and thrown into a dramatic form not wholly arbitrary. He now attempted to extend the method to material of which neither of these things could be true, to material that was too much the product, on the one hand, of unripened observation, and, on the other, of cool reflection, to be capable of the same beauty and warmth. This material was, so to say, the general quality of American life as it had presented itself to Hawthorne during his years in "the world": that life had seemed to him overcast with unreality, — divided by unreal distinctions, driven by vain purposes, misled by false prophets, and cluttered with meaningless survivals from the past; but this was in itself an impalpable theme, and it is not surprising that, in seeking expression for it, he turned to the friendly form of allegory.

"The New Adam and Eve" was its first application. A newly created couple come into the world on the day following the fulfillment of Father Miller's prophecy — the sudden incidence of the Day of Doom — and find the world, though completely depopulated, still full of the untouched evidences of man's occupation. Much of what they observe, naturally, strikes their unperverted judgments as valueless and even revolting — the luxuries in a dry-goods store, the solemn atmosphere of a church, a courtroom, the rich interior of a Beacon Street mansion, the heaps of bills and specie in a bank, the cold gloom of a prison house, the halls of a university, and the white monuments in a great cemetery. A similar arraignment of an artificial society is contained in "The Procession of Life" — a sketch in which Hawthorne imagines that all the ordinary classifications of mankind are overthrown, and a great procession formed, under the leadership of the marshal Death, in which men and women take their places in new and more significant groupings: on the basis, not of their birth or fortune, but of their common wretchedness, their common guilt, their common intellectual power,

their common charity, and (most inclusive of all) their
common inability to find their proper places in the
world. "The Celestial Railroad" is a kind of parody
on Bunyan: it is a description of a new and easy way
to reach the Celestial City without the fatigues of a
pilgrimage — namely, by a railroad exploited by Mr.
Smooth-it-Away and engineered by Christian's old
enemy, Appolyon — but also, as it eventuates, without
a triumphant arrival. The central image in "Earth's
Holocaust" is a great bonfire on a western prairie to
which mankind brings all its worn-out trumpery for
destruction — all the paraphernalia of hereditary aris-
tocracy, the robes of royalty, the trappings of ecclesi-
asticism, the symbols of military power, the printed
literature of the world, and finally, as a symbol of pun-
itive justice, the gallows.

All these four allegories, as to a less degree the former
group, are colored, in spite of their frequently Rousseauistic language, by a strongly individual sense of the
vanity of much that passed for serious, the falseness of
much that passed for sound, in nineteenth-century
America. It was the reward — it was at least the consequence — of Hawthorne's detachment from the concerns of his contemporaries that he could see these
things so perspicaciously. Only because his own experience had been what it was could he envisage so
clearly the predicament of the unhappy man who comes
to the Intelligence Office in search of his true place in
the world — "my thing to do, which Nature intended
me to perform when she fashioned me thus awry, and
which I have vainly sought all my lifetime!" — and
of that multitude of the maladjusted who flock together

in the procession behind Death. Only because he was not himself involved could he thus satirize the acquisitive life so tellingly: could represent the citizens of the new Vanity Fair, bargaining away to one another their most precious possessions for empty honors and properties; could find solid business men in the Hall of Fancy concealing the extravagance of their dreams by the sobriety of their manner; could put rich men among the wretched and venal politicians among the guilty in the Procession of Life; could achieve the irony of that scene in a bank where Adam and Eve are confronted with the now visibly useless remains of a pursuit that had always been inherently futile. Who but a man whose inner life had been enriched and deepened by a proud pursuit of his own ends, a prolonged wrestling with subjective realities, could have conveyed so true an impression as Hawthorne did in all these sketches, of the pompous insignificance of what Emerson would call "things" and the solidity, in comparison, of human desires? How characteristic is his remark about the Book of Wishes — that it "is probably truer, as a representation of the human heart, than is the living drama of action as it evolves around us." And how penetrating is the upshot of "Earth's Holocaust" — the observation of a late comer (Satan himself) that the whole conflagration will have done away with as little evil as good since the true source of both is left intact: and "what" is that, as he says, "but the human heart itself?"

Why, then, with all this moral justness, do these allegories make, after all, so weak an appeal to the imagination? They have in them the substance of a

grand narrative satire on American society, but in fact
they are grandiose rather than grand; they have the
strength of plausibility, but not of the deepest persua-
siveness; their scenes and figures linger in the memory
in a pale, dusky, two-dimensional way, like line drawings seen through transparent paper; their outline is
noble, but their body is brittle and flimsy. Is it not
because something more than a perception of subjective
truth is required for a satire on mankind in its social
relations — because the power of such a satire, if it
were a great one, would derive partly too from its
fidelity to the large rhythms of human intercourse,
from its dramatic vigor and point? Allegory of a kind
might be its method, but its specific embodiment would
have to be embodiment in personality; and Hawthorne
had not yet shown the capacity for handling personality in fiction with a dramatic objectivity. His detachment, if it had its reward, had also this penalty; his
unwillingness to enter into spontaneous relations with
other men and women, his eagerness to escape from
social encounters, had come between him and a vivid
recreation of character. All the brilliance of his bonfire
and the wealth of its kindling, all the pomp of his well-
organized procession, all the ingenuity of his mechan-
ized pilgrimage, do not suffice to conceal from us the
bareness and abstractness of the devices themselves, or
the shadowiness of the human elements. The translation of the mere idea into artistic terms is but half
made, and we are distracted by the mingled sound of
two dialects. As satire, these four pieces are only ambiguous in their effect.

Hawthorne was on firmer ground in such a tale as

"The Artist of the Beautiful" in which much the same
criticism of the practical, worldly life is implicit. Here,
too, the design is allegorical, but it is allegory of the
earlier type: the abstractions — worldly sagacity, brute
strength, creative power — are embodied in the figures
of Peter Hovenden, the retired watchmaker; Robert
Danforth, the blacksmith who marries his daughter
Annie; and Owen Warland, the young watchmaker
who gives his life and strength to the incorporation of
ideal beauty. Character for its own sake, it is true,
can have no free play in types so simplified as these;
but into the drawing of Owen Warland, Hawthorne
could throw strong currents of self-knowledge and self-
analysis, and the sheer necessities of the tale's quasi-
dramatic movement give Peter Hovenden and Robert
Danforth and Annie a kind of provisional reality.
How much real experience lay behind the narration of
Owen Warland's long labors at his repeatedly frustrated
task of devising the perfect butterfly!—a task frustrated
by the cold inquiring skepticism of Peter Hovenden, by
the mere presence of the jovial but coarse-grained and
unimaginative blacksmith, by the failure of the well-
intentioned Annie to understand his aims. From all
these symbolic defeats Owen manages to recover, and
at length achieves the end of his creative travails — an
exquisite artificial butterfly, which he exhibits to Annie
and her husband and father, only to have it utterly
destroyed in the sturdy grasp of Robert and Annie's
very earthly child.

And as for Owen Warland, he looked placidly at
what seemed the ruin of his life's labor, and which
was yet no ruin. He had caught a far other butterfly

than this. When the artist rose high enough to achieve
the beautiful, the symbol by which he made it per-
ceptible to mortal senses became of little value in his
eyes while his spirit possessed itself in the enjoyment of
the reality.

Such had come to be Hawthorne's view of the creative life and its rewards in a society in which it had
to be led as an irrelevant activity on the margin. And
the whole parable was his criticism of a society in
which practical life was divorced from the creative
spirit and unilluminated by it.

Nothing, indeed, in the "Mosses from an Old Manse"
is more notable than the dark recurrence of the old
theme of isolation and its allied theme of guilt. With
Owen Warland there is no suggestion that his alienation from ordinary life was the cause of any criminality;
but it *is* suggested that, as with Peter Goldthwaite,
another consequence might have ensued. "The townspeople had one comprehensive explanation of all these
singularities. Owen Warland had gone mad! . . . Perhaps he was mad. The lack of sympathy — that contrast between himself and his neighbors which took
away the restraint of example — was enough to make
him so." It is for this kind of reason that the narrator
of "A Virtuoso's Collection" is horrified to discover
that his guide, the Virtuoso himself, is none other than
the Wandering Jew — whose voice has the bitter tone
"of one cut off from natural sympathies and blasted
with a doom that had been inflicted on no other human
being, and by the results of which he had ceased to be
human." Scarcely one of the enumerative and satirical
allegories is unmarked by the lurid streak of guilt: the

Virtuoso exhibits to his visitor a huge bundle which
proves to be Christian's burden of sin, and bids him
look into his own consciousness and memory for a list
of its contents; when Adam and Eve penetrate the
dreary shadows of a prison, the author observes that
"its patients bore the outward marks of that leprosy
with which all were more or less infected"; the regiment of guilt, in the Procession of Life, is filled up with
strange partnerships of the openly criminal and the
outwardly respectable; the human heart, in "Earth's
Holocaust", is described as a "foul cavern" from which
"will reissue all the shapes of wrong and misery — the
same old shapes or worse ones — which they have
taken such a vast deal of trouble to consume to ashes."
No more than this had Hawthorne's contacts with
real people ventilated or clarified his view of human
character.

Only in the work of this period, indeed — considering
how much had intervened between the "Twice-Told
Tales" and it — can we see with decisive vividness
how deep and indelible was the mark left on Hawthorne's imagination by those early unwholesome
experiences of estrangement, those early years of un-
checked, ingrowing fantasy. The best of the "Mosses
from an Old Manse" are but new handlings, new sym-
bolizations, of the themes of "The Minister's Black
Veil", "Young Goodman Brown", and "Lady Eleanore's Mantle." The ubiquity of secret guilt, the fatal
connection between isolation and evil, the flagrancy
therefore of spiritual pride — are not these, as we
have seen, at the heart of the old plots? And are they
not at the heart of "Egotism; or, The Bosom Serpent",

"The Christmas Banquet", "The Birthmark", and "Rappaccini's Daughter?"

Roderick Elliston, in "Egotism", is a brother to both Lady Eleanore Rochcliffe and Goodman Brown. His bosom the shuddering abode of a gnawing and hissing serpent, he nevertheless, in some of his moods, "prided and gloried himself on being marked out from the ordinary experience of mankind by the possession of a double nature, and a life within a life"; and yearning, in other moods, for fellowship, he finds that he can achieve only a horrid counterfeit of it — an insight into the festering places of other bosoms, where he detects the coiled monsters of hatred and lust or the diminutive, writhing snakes of spite and envy. "By Roderick's theory, every mortal bosom harbored either a brood of small serpents or one overgrown monster that had devoured all the rest." His liberation from his own unrelenting tormentor comes only when, on the reappearance of his wife, driven from him by his engrossing egotism, he has a single moment of self-forgetfulness in the idea of another. Is there not something inescapably impressive in Hawthorne's making Roderick Elliston the supposed author of one of his own tales, one of the "unpublished 'Allegories of the Heart'?"

This tale, at any rate, "The Christmas Banquet", would have been a natural one for Roderick Elliston, as well as for Hawthorne, to write. It is the story of an annual feast, instituted by an eccentric old gentleman's will, to which are bidden regularly, by the trustees, ten of the most miserable men or women they can discover. Year after year, among these misanthropes,

misfits, and hypochondriacs, appears a person who
gives no outward sign of having anything in common
with them, anything to justify his presence at their
dismal feast. Gervasye Hastings is a man blessed with
all the gifts of nature and fortune — high talent, great
wealth, an honorable rôle in public life, and, as the
years pass, a tender wife and promising daughters and
sons. Yet, in spite of the protests of his fellow guests,
Hastings' place in their midst is recurrently assured by
the steward of the feast, and at last, in his old age,
challenged to reveal the secret of his misfortune, he
replies feebly: "You will not understand it . . . None
have understood it, not even those who experience the
like. It is a chillness, a want of earnestness, a feeling
as if what should be my heart were a thing of vapor, a
haunting perception of unreality! Thus seeming to
possess all that other men have, all that men aim at,
I have really possessed nothing, neither joy nor griefs.
All things, all persons — as was truly said to me at
this table long and long ago — have been like shadows
flickering on the wall. It was so with my wife and children, with those who seemed my friends: it is so with
yourselves, whom I see now before me. Neither have
I myself any real existence, but am a shadow like the
rest." Thus, as the greatest of sinners is the man somehow cut off from normal sympathies, the most unhappy
wretch is the man who, whatever his intellectual gifts,
can neither share nor understand the ordinary emotions
of mankind.

Even the purest of intellectual aspirations, the aspiration toward perfection, Hawthorne seems to say, so far
as it tends to lead one away from imperfect humanity,

may have the deadliest consequences. This is the tragic discovery of Aylmer, the man of science in "The Birthmark", whose noble dissatisfaction with earthly imperfection is outraged by the tiny birthmark on the cheek of Georgiana, his otherwise perfectly beautiful wife, and whose attempt to eradicate it by his subtlest arts results successfully but at the terrible price of Georgiana's death. As the life fades out of her body, Aminadab, Aylmer's brutish servant, is heard to chuckle hoarsely.

Thus ever does the gross fatality of earth exult in its invariable triumph over the immortal essence which, in this dim sphere of half-development, demands the completeness of a higher state. Yet, had Aylmer reached a profounder wisdom, he need not thus have flung away the happiness which would have woven his mortal life of the self-same texture with the celestial. The momentary circumstance was too strong for him; he failed to look beyond the shadowy scope of time, and, living once for all in eternity, to find the perfect future in the present.

Aylmer's error, then, is his desire to attain concretely a purity above the human level — a desire in which, despite its consequences, there is no admixture of guilt. Perhaps it is the absence of this strain that keeps "The Birthmark" from having the somber force of Hawthorne's manner at its most characteristic.

Certainly none of these tales coerce the imagination with a brilliance at once so ardent and so sullen as that of "Rappaccini's Daughter." Yet its theme is close to the theme of "The Birthmark" — the evil wrought by the mere intellect working outside the boundaries of ordinary human concerns. Doctor Rappaccini, like Aylmer, cuts himself off from humanity by his pitiless passion for knowledge. "He cares infinitely more for science than for mankind," says Professor Baglioni, who represents the normal conscience, to young Giovanni Guasconti. "His patients are interesting to him only as subjects for some new experiment. He would sacrifice human life, his own among the rest, or whatever else was dearest to him, for the sake of adding so much as a grain of mustard seed to the great heap of his accumulated knowledge." When Rappaccini passes the professor and the young student on the street, and fixes his intent gaze upon Giovanni, there is "a peculiar quietness in the look, as if taking merely a speculative, not a human, interest in the young man." Unlike Aylmer, however, the sinister Rappaccini aims not at purity but at power, and at power achieved by no matter what gross and guilty means. To this end he sacrifices his beautiful daughter, Beatrice, by shutting her away from the world, immuring her in a garden where her only companions are the luxuriant noxious growths he has gathered there, so that, by imbibing only unwholesome airs, she will herself become a kind of poisonous human flower.

His purpose is accomplished, for Beatrice — estranged, as she says, from all society of her kind — is at last incapable of drawing vigor from "the common air", and her breath itself is deadly to ordinary plants and even insects. When Giovanni yields to the unhealthy spell and falls in love with her, it is to find himself, to his horror, losing his own sense of the normal and gradually acquiring the same envenomed nature.

It is with the responsibility for this fate that he taxes Beatrice in their last scene together in the garden: "Finding thy solitude wearisome, thou hast severed me likewise from all the warmth of life and enticed me into thy region of unspeakable horror!" In the meanwhile, however, Giovanni's friend the professor — in the hope, as he says, "of bringing back this miserable child within the limits of ordinary nature, from which her father's madness has estranged her" — has given him a vial containing a powerful antidote; and this Giovanni begs Beatrice to drink with him as a last resource in their hideous common plight. But the poison in Beatrice's make-up is too radical to be driven out with impunity, and, not unlike Georgiana, she dies at the feet of her father and Giovanni. "Rappaccini! Rappaccini!" cries Baglioni from a window above them, "and is *this* the upshot of your experiment?"

To the passionate energy of this tale Hawthorne had not before risen, save perhaps in "Young Goodman Brown"; and can we doubt that, like that earlier tale, its impetus came from far beneath the surface — lay, indeed, at the very center of his genius? It is true that in this disparagement of the intellect Hawthorne might simply have been following the example of his Transcendentalist acquaintances; might simply have been remembering some paragraph in "Nature", or some Kantian pronouncement of Alcott's, or one of Jones Very's sonnets; might, for that matter, have been paying tribute to the influence of any one of his romantic predecessors from Rousseau downwards. But in fact no such merely doctrinal incitement would have fertilized his imagination, or lent him the power to write

"Rappaccini's Daughter": for that he would have had
to pass through some strict personal experience of solitude and its unwholesomeness, and have had some
pressing personal sense of the evils of the speculative
intellect. The experience of solitude he had certainly
had to the full, and did he not have his private reasons
for dreading that his own interest in mankind might be
a coldly inquiring, a quasi-scientific interest? — he who
had said that "the most desirable mode of existence
might be that of a spiritualized Paul Pry hovering
invisible round man and woman, witnessing their
deeds, searching into their hearts, borrowing brightness from their felicity, and shade from their sorrow,
and retaining no emotion peculiar to himself." "To
have ice in one's blood" — that was the cryptic entry
Hawthorne had once made in his notebook, and had
he not had grounds for fearing that his own veins might
grow chill from observing the tragedies and comedies
of existence, and himself enacting none of them? At
Brook Farm, recording a masquerade in the woods, he
had described himself as one "whose nature it is to be
a mere spectator both of sport and serious business."
Was the distance between him and Doctor Rappaccini
an immeasurable one? Sophia had written to her
mother from Concord that "he is so seldom fully satisfied with weather, things, or people, that I am always
glad to find him pleased. Nothing short of perfection
can content him." Was this so far from Aylmer's
disastrous desire?

Surely it is the strain of subjective stresses they support, the burden they carry of interior conflicts, that
gives these tales what vibrancy and vividness they
have. And surely, too, they are themselves the best

illustration of the theme they all allegorize — the
menace offered by a cold or selfish or marginal way of
life to a healthy perception of human realities. For in
spite of their superiority to the satires in their dramatic
form, in their embodiment in personalities, the dramas
they represent are rather schemes than dramas, and the
personages that play them are rather masks than men.
Roderick Elliston, Gervayse Hastings, Aylmer and
Georgiana, even the four protagonists of "Rappaccini's Daughter" are, like the figures in "The Artist of
the Beautiful", the more or less transparently costumed symbols for the moral abstractions of the scheme.
Whatever reality they have they owe, not to their objective faithfulness, but to the draughts they make
upon their author's own vitality. Hawthorne had
already shown, in passage after passage in the note-
books, and indeed showed now in the essay (transferred
almost bodily from them) on the old apple dealer in
the Salem station, that he could write about real people
with truth and insight in the analytical form. He had not
yet shown that he could create real people in imaginary
confrontations and without the assistance of allegory.

Hawthorne himself had said, in the remarks on
M. de l'Aubépine, that his writings might have won
him greater reputation "but for an inveterate love of
allegory, which is apt to invest his plots and characters with the aspect of scenery and people in the clouds
and to steal away the human warmth out of his conceptions." In one of the tales of this period, "Drowne's
Wooden Image", he suggested, again in the language
of allegory, the same criticism of his art. Drowne is a
young wood-carver of Boston in the old days, whose
special practice is the carving of figureheads for vessels.

One day he is visited by the great painter Copley, who
praises his work for its extreme skill, though he detects
an inadequacy in it: "one other touch," he declares,
"might make this figure of General Wolfe, for instance,
a breathing and intelligent human creature." And
Drowne is aware of the implications of this: "I know,
he answers, "what you know as well, that the one
touch which you speak of as deficient is the only one
that would be truly valuable, and that without it these
works of mine are no better than worthless abortions.
There is the same difference between them and the
works of an inspired artist as between a sign-post daub
and one of your best pictures." Once in his life, however, Drowne transcends his limitations; executes a fig-
urehead, the image of a beautiful young woman, so
full of lifelike truth, so animated, so warmly colored
and delicately shaped, that the citizens of Boston mistake it, at first view, for an actual person. But Copley
guesses at the young carver's secret, guesses that for
once he has been inspired by a deep personal emotion,
for he has seen in Drowne's face "that expression of
human love which, in a spiritual sense, as the artist
could not help imagining, was the secret of the life
that had been breathed into this block of wood."
And indeed Drowne has had a model who has touched
his heart and not merely his workmanly mind.

"The one touch . . . that would be truly valuable!" Is it not that, precisely, that we miss in the
"Mosses from an Old Manse?" Yet from an artist
who can write with so cunning a hand and with a
craft so finished, how much have we not still the right
to anticipate!

CHAPTER FIVE

THE GOLDEN FLEECE

"True, the Golden Fleece may not be so valuable as you have thought it; but then there is nothing better in the world; and one must needs have an object, you know." — "Tanglewood Tales."

HAWTHORNE was a little more than forty that summer when, after three years in the Manse, the old house had to be surrendered to the Samuel Ripleys, returning now to Concord, and other considerations urged him to abandon the retired and idyllic life that he and Sophia had lived there. On the verge of middle age, he seemed to himself to have passed the point at which a man can look forward to any sweeping transformation in the aspect of his relations with the world; to have established himself, so far as society was concerned, in the rôle he would now play out to its quiet end. Not that he anticipated no changes in occupation or residence: such changes, indeed, he knew, might be recurrent and abrupt. But that he would ever move out of the moral circle, so to say, in which he now stood, he had no reason to hope or fear: he had made a graceful if decidedly minor reputation for himself as a writer of prose fiction; he had a small audience of appreciative readers and critics; his literary work would never fail of an outlet in the reviews of the period, and his books would be the source of a small but fairly dependable income; his civil experience and his access to the ears of politicians would put employment of that reasonably lucrative kind within his reach — and that was all. If he had ever dreamed of fame, of shining conspicuously and with an august brightness in the eyes of his countrymen, he had long since come to believe that dream a poetic delusion of youth, and he had yielded it up, at first reluctantly and regretfully, no doubt, but in the end with sufficient composure. Writing itself he had no intention of renouncing, but he was prepared to be rewarded for it mainly in its intrinsic satisfactions, and these, he had found, were not small.

Five years later, Hawthorne was one of the most illustrious of American authors. The literary glory that he had once envisaged as his special end, and had then been disciplined to forego, he had, suddenly and as it were inadvertently, achieved. He who had been content with the sale of a few hundred copies of the "Mosses", could speak of a first edition being exhausted in ten days. He who had enjoyed a kind of below-stairs fame as the author of "A Rill from the Town Pump", which had been much reprinted as a temperance tract, was now a widely read writer in Great Britain, admired by DeQuincey and Mary Russell Mitford and Robert Browning; and there was word of his being translated into German and French. "The obscurest man of letters in America" found that his house in the country was a Mecca for literary pilgrims; that he could scarcely answer the scores of letters that came to him from admirers, or the troubled queries from men and women in straits; that Oliver Wendell Holmes was proud to have had Hawthorne hold his horse for him, and that Washington Irving regarded his writings "as among the very best that have ever issued from the American press." Manifestly he had been wrong in thinking that "my writings do not, nor ever will, appeal to the broadest class of sympathies, and therefore will not obtain a very wide popularity." Manifestly there was more common ground than he had hoped or could believe, between himself and his compatriots and coevals. How strange that isolation should lead to this! — as if silence should become the means to communication. Had a miracle been wrought? Or was this the inevitable event? On the answer to these questions depends everything.

It was not only the return of its owners that made removal from the Manse imperative; the change would have been brought about by even more immediate necessities. These were, in short, economic: despite the bounty of the old clergyman's orchard and vegetable garden, Hawthorne and his wife had, certainly after the first year, found the problem of making both ends meet increasingly hard to solve, and it was only a matter of time before they would have to dismantle the little study, pack up Sophia's prints and vases, say farewell to "Paradise Regained", and pass forth between the two tall gateposts of rough-hewn stone at the end of their avenue. He had written industriously, especially during the winter months, and had disposed easily of his work to the *Democratic Review* and other magazines; but the income from this source was pitifully small and, worse yet, irregular; and the money he had invested in the Brook Farm project had never

come back to him. During their second spring in
Concord, a daughter had been born, and Hawthorne
might now call himself in the fullest sense a family
man: clearly the old economy of Eden would have to
be superseded by some more Jacksonian rule.

Fortunately a Democratic president was elected in
the fall of 1845, and Hawthorne, who had held office
under Van Buren, had a good claim on the new administration. Pierce, Bridge, and his other Democratic
friends lost no time in exerting their influence in party
councils, and even Charles Sumner, a Whig, early in
1846, wrote to Mrs. Bancroft, whose husband was to
be Secretary of the Navy, urging her to keep Hawthorne's name present to her husband's mind so that
"some post-office, some custom house, something, that
will yield daily bread, — anything in the gift of your
husband" might come to the relief of Hawthorne's
poverty. "As to Hawthorne," replied Bancroft, "I
have been most perseveringly his friend": and it is
true that he offered his former subordinate a position
in the Charlestown Navy Yard, but this Hawthorne
had declined. By that time he and his family were
settled in Salem; "here I am," he had written to Bridge,
"again established in the old chambers where I wasted
so many years of my life" — and something stronger
than a conscious purpose, something in the pull and
power of only half-forgotten habits, was impelling
him to remain there if he could. This was singular
enough, for Hawthorne had no reason, as he knew, to
love Salem or its people: he himself was inclined to
attribute "this strange, indolent, unjoyous attachment
for my native town" to the accumulated weight of

ancestral association with its soil. He might better have considered whether the twelve years of his youth were yet outlived. At all events, he was disappointed when the Salem postmastership was closed to him, and happy when he at last received, in the spring of 1846, an appointment as Surveyor in the Salem Customhouse.

For the next three years his life was divided between the Customhouse on Derby Street, where he spent his mornings, and the society of his family in each of the three houses they successively occupied. At no time were his spirits so oppressed by the mere routine of his work as they had repeatedly been at the Customhouse in Boston. For one thing, of course, he now had a home to return to, a refuge to which he could betake himself when the elements of business and politics became too murky for him. Impecunious as their way of living might be, — and for two years, until they moved to Mall Street, Hawthorne could have no study to himself, — how much better it was to rejoin Sophia and the children than to creep back to his bachelor quarters on Somerset Place after a day of salt-weighing, or to wander forlornly about the Boston Athenæum! In Salem, as in Concord, he and Sophia could have their evenings for each other's company, and as they never went out into society and were even less besieged than at the Manse, they could go on with their readings from the old authors and from such moderns as DeQuincey and Dickens. Further, Hawthorne now had a daughter, and, after a year and a half in Salem, a son; and as soon as they had passed the stage of babyhood, the activity and the childish prattle of Una and Julian offered themselves for observation of the curious

and conjectural kind he had hitherto expended on so
many grown-ups. What would come of it remained
to be seen; but Una particularly, with her strange
complexities of temper, her elvish inconstancies of
mood, her suggestion now of the angelic now of the
demonic in human nature, would clearly do well if
she kept out of her father's ink bottle in some future
inventive need.

At the Customhouse itself, Hawthorne was, if not
happier, certainly less low-spirited than at Long Wharf.
His hours there were shorter, and his duties as a surveyor, though humdrum enough, were less grimy and
less irksome than the measuring of coal and salt. The
business of the port was no longer what it had been in
the days "when India was a new region, and only
Salem knew the way thither": but shipments of pepper
still came in from Sumatra, hide ships docked there
occasionally from South America, and schooners with
wood from Nova Scotia were regular arrivals. A name
that Hawthorne protested he now neither sought nor
cared to have blazoned abroad on title pages was sten-
cilled with black ink on pepper bags, baskets of an-
natto, cigar boxes, "and bales of all kinds of dutiable
merchandise", to set the seal of legality upon them and
to carry them into mercantile quarters where it had
never been before and would never, so Hawthorne later
hoped, be seen again. The air he breathed was the
air of traffic and transport, but for all that it was an
air rather languid than heady. Save that he moved
from dock to office instead of from orchard to river,
and that he smelled salt water and tar instead of water
lilies and pine needles, there was not so vast a differ-

THE OLD CUSTOM HOUSE, BOSTON

THE CUSTOM HOUSE, SALEM

ence between this and his life in Concord as might appear. The Customhouse was more prosaic than the Manse, but it was scarcely less sleepy. It is true that Hawthorne congratulated himself on the ease with which, after long sojourn among philosophers and scholars and poets, he could adapt himself, without a murmur, to associates so secular, so little visited by fancies, as the soldierly old Collector, the gluttonous old Inspector, and the perfectly efficient Chief Clerk. Yet these men, and the Customhouse itself, were hardly closer to the center of practical life than the Old Manse and Henry Thoreau. They were either men who, like the Collector or the numerous aged sea captains who were now clerks, had retired from worldly activity, or men who, preferring the shelter of a berth in the spoils system, had never taken the plunge into it. It would not have been the most difficult thing in the world for Hawthorne to fall into the rhythm of their sluggish, frost-nipped, seldom-bestirred existence.

Indeed it was the dread of being conquered by the apathetic spirit of the office-holder, as much as any dissatisfaction with his duties themselves, that kept Hawthorne (on the conscious level) from accepting his present rôle as a permanent one.

Here was a fine prospect in the distance! — he was to write. — Not that the Surveyor brought the lesson home to himself, or admitted that he could be so utterly undone, either by continuance in office, or ejection. Yet my reflections were not the most comfortable. I began to grow melancholy and restless; continually prying into my mind, to discover which of its poor properties were gone, and what degree of detriment had already accrued to the remainder. I endeavoured to calculate how much longer I could stay in the Customhouse, and yet go forth a man. To confess the truth, it was my greatest apprehension, — as it would never be a measure of policy to turn out so quiet an individual as myself, and it being hardly in the nature of a public officer to resign, — it was my chief trouble, therefore, that I was likely to grow gray and decrepit in the Surveyorship, and become much such another animal as the old Inspector. Might it not, in the tedious lapse of official life that lay before me, finally be with me as it was with this venerable friend, — to make the dinner-hour the nucleus of the day, and to spend the rest of it, as an old dog spends it, asleep in the sunshine or in the shade? A dreary look-forward this, for a man who felt it to be the best definition of happiness to live throughout the whole range of his faculties and sensibilities!

Yet the danger in this direction was by no means so great as he doubtless feared. For one thing, the old habits of inertness and lethargy, though their roots were still in his make-up and might have been reawakened by the right conspiracy of circumstance, had slowly yielded ground — and were to yield it more and more rapidly — to what might seem to be a merely paradoxical desire for movement and change, a restless incapacity for continuing long in one place or at one employment. There had been other good reasons for escaping from the Boston Customhouse and Brook Farm, and for leaving Concord, as there were to be other good reasons for changes he was still to make; but behind all of these there was also something very like a fear of fixity, an undefined dread of the static.

He who had spent his youth in the immobility of a
monk was to spend his last years moving about with
the restlessness of a frontiersman or a gypsy, and death
was to come upon him, by no mere accident, away from
home. A paradox this might certainly seem, if it were
not also clear that the later impulse was at once a cor-
rection and a complement of the older: that, on the
one hand, restlessness was the only alternative to
apathy, and that, on the other, both were the expressions of an imperfect adjustment to his world. The
monk and the gypsy have congruities between them
that lie deeper than their divergences.

Other desires than the desire for change were to
threaten his present tenure. Hawthorne had not felt,
on leaving the Manse, the fatigued disgust with literary effort he had felt at the time of entering the
Boston Customhouse, and there were no signs that his
inspiration was running thin: "Rappaccini's Daughter"
was written late in the year before the move to Salem,
and the prefatory essay on "The Old Manse", in which
his manner was at its mellowest and most transparent,
was written six months or more after he had left Concord. Was it unreasonable for him to hope that, even
after he assumed his surveyorship, he might find the
impetus, on the long afternoons when he had leisure,
to keep his pen at work in the same way, and perhaps
to succeed with the novel he had failed to write in
the Manse? Certainly he did hope as much, and certainly he was chagrined to discover that his powers of
composition were benumbed as if by some abrupt paralysis. For nearly two years he wrote nothing. Then —

I am trying to resume my pen — he wrote to Long-fellow in November, 1847 — but the influence of my situation and customary associates are so anti-literary, that I know not whether I shall succeed. Whenever I sit alone or walk alone I find myself dreaming about stories, as of old; but these forenoons in the Custom-house undo all that the afternoons and evenings have done. I should be happier if I could write.

During the following year, though there can be no certainty about dates, he probably did write "The Great Stone Face" and the sketch, "Main Street." The first of these he need have been ashamed of at no period of his life; but he had said that he had done enough in this kind, and there was "an unquiet impulse" in him to go farther.

For some time, no one can now say how long, he was haunted by one of the physical symbols that so characteristically engaged him — by a symbol that had first entered his imagination ten years or more ago, when he had written "Endicott and the Red Cross." This was the embroidered letter "A" worn on the bosom of an adulteress who appears for a moment in that tale.

Sporting with her infamy — he had written — the lost and desperate creature had embroidered the fatal token in scarlet cloth, with golden thread and the nicest art of needlework; so that the capital A might have been thought to mean Admirable, or anything rather than Adulteress.

Now, the scarlet "A", if he had ever wholly forgotten it, rekindled itself in his imagination with a new and hotter radiance. For how deep a wrong might it not be the expiation, and of how terrible a loneliness the cause! And what if there might be a wrong greater than that which this woman had done, and a more awful punishment than hers? What if the scarlet letter might appear in other guises than this? Try as he would, he could not keep the lurid image out of his mind; and sooner or later, he knew, it would have to find its way out, like a splinter of steel from an old wound, in some new allegory.

But though he had at last found the energy to write three or four tales in the old vein, there was something in the atmosphere of the Customhouse, as there had been in Boston and at Brook Farm, that discomposed and enervated his faculties when he attempted to come to grips with this new preoccupation. As so often before, he could not be a bookkeeper and a poet at the same time!

My imagination — he was to confess — was a tarnished mirror. It would not reflect, or only with miserable dimness, the figures with which I did my best to people it. The characters of the narrative would not be warmed and rendered malleable by any heat that I could kindle at my intellectual forge. . . . The same torpor, as regarded the capacity for intellectual effort, accompanied me home, and weighed upon me in the chamber which I most absurdly termed my study.

And how could it have been otherwise, at so advanced an hour, with a writer whose periods of productivity had always been periods of undistracted leisure? He need not, as he did, have regarded the impotence from which he now suffered as perhaps incorrigible. But he was tormented by it with growing intensity. "An entire class of susceptibilities" — that was how he was later to put it — "and a gift connected with them — of no great richness or value, but the best I had — was gone from me." He could make nothing, for the moment, of the dark and distant realities that wavered in the gleam of the scarlet letter.

Why, however, could he not in these straits put to some creative use the near and not unfruitful realities of the Customhouse? If his imagination would not operate freely on remote materials, what was to keep it from playing to good effect over the scene and the characters about him? He realized that they were by no means empty of import. The Collector had been one of the celebrated generals of the War of 1812, and most of the ancient inmates of the Customhouse had led tumultuous and highly colored lives on the quarter-deck or in the forecastle. Much of the farce and melo-drama of commerce enacted itself daily before his eyes. Why, with all this about him, should he try to fling himself back into another age, and insist on creating an imaginary world?

The wiser effort would have been, to diffuse thought and imagination through the opaque substance of today, and thus to make it a bright transparency; to spiritual-ize the burden that began to weigh so heavily; to seek, resolutely, the true and indestructible value that lay hidden in the petty and wearisome incidents, and ordi-nary characters, with which I was now conversant. The fault was mine. The page of life that was spread out before me seemed dull and commonplace, only be-cause I had not fathomed its deeper import. A better book than I shall ever write was there; leaf after leaf presenting itself to me, just as it was written out by the reality of the flitting hour, and vanishing as fast as written, only because my brain wanted the insight and my hand the cunning to transcribe it. At some future day, it may be, I shall remember a few scattered fragments and broken paragraphs, and write them down, and find the letters turn to gold upon the page.

Apparently the old clerks were to go the way of the sailor boy from Malaga and the soap-maker at North Adams.

With these contesting necessities, Hawthorne's present situation could not have been a very stable one, and, despite the distastefulness of the circumstances, he was not inconsolably afflicted by the series of political misadventures which, in the summer of 1849, deprived him of his surveyorship. His earlier intentions of resigning had no doubt been vague enough, but they had existed, and he later compared himself to a man who should lay plans for committing suicide, and should then, "although beyond his hopes, meet with the good hap to be murdered." It is true that his sensibilities were deeply offended, and his spirits depressed, by the unseemly spectacle of low chicanery and falsehood that was now offered to him; and that for the moment his nerves were sufficiently exasperated for him to express himself with unwonted violence and even bitterness. "I must confess," he wrote to Longfellow, "it stirs up a little of the devil within me, to find myself hunted by these political bloodhounds. If they succeed in getting me out of office, I will surely immolate one or two of them." It is true, also, that his economic prospects were none too bright, and that the strain of this anxiety, added to the other stresses under which he had labored, led him to take temporarily a very somber view of his position in the world. "It is something else besides pride," he wrote gloomily to his Cambridge friend, George Hillard, "that teaches me that ill-success in life is really and justly a matter of shame. I am ashamed of it, and I ought to be. The fault of a failure is attributable — in a great degree at least — to the man who fails." And within a few weeks he was to pass through what he called "the darkest hour I ever lived", in the bedchamber of his mother who lay dying, with all the inarticulateness between them, while Una and Julian shouted and laughed at play in the yard below: "and then I looked at my poor dying mother, and seemed to see the whole of human existence at once, standing in the dusty midst of it."

Not all these accumulating reverses, however, could keep Hawthorne, so deep was the "unquiet impulse" within him, from seizing the opportunity he at last had to work out the creative possibilities of the scarlet letter. "Oh, then," Sophia had exclaimed, when he brought her the news of his discharge, "you can write your book!" And as she proceeded to exhibit to him a little hoard of dollars that she had husbanded out of their weekly income, and as George Hillard, on behalf of a group of friends, came forward with a generous advance of the same sort, the most urgent problem was, for a few months, satisfactorily solved. At the end of that time, as on a similar occasion before, he could say:

The life of the Custom-House lies like a dream behind me. The old Inspector . . . and all those other venerable personages . . . are but shadows in my view. . . . The merchants, — Pingree, Phillips, Shepard, Upton,

Kimball, Bertram, Hunt, — . . . how little time has
it required to disconnect me from them all, not merely
in act, but recollection! It is with an effort that I recall
the figures and appellations of these few.

For meanwhile he had been living in a world as unlike theirs as a world could be, the world of early Puritan Massachusetts, or rather — since even that was
not quite antipodal — of Hester Prynne and little Pearl,
of Arthur Dimmesdale, of Roger Chillingworth, and
the sinister symbol in which their lives are focussed.
Never before, in his career as a writer, had Hawthorne
been visited by a creative mood so intense or so prolonged; never before had he striven so severely with
the difficulties of the creative process; never before had
he been so irresistibly dominated by the creatures of
his imagination. The constrained energies of several
years had been liberated, and in spite of the storm and
stress he had just passed through, he could say that
"he was happier, while straying through the gloom of
these sunless fantasies, than at any time since he had
quitted the Old Manse."

The product of these strenuous months, and of the
long brooding that had preceded them, was a work
on a different scale from anything Hawthorne had
attempted since "Fanshawe": the conception of the
tale that foliated from the scarlet letter would not
confine itself within the limits of "Rappaccini's Daughter", but grew and expanded in his mind with every
renewal of his attention to it. In a sense, at least, he
had at last written his novel. But he had been too
vehemently wrought upon by the sustained effort to be
able to form a cool judgment of what he had done.

Commonly he was able to detach himself almost too easily and coolly from what he had written, but in this instance what he called "my own adamant" was quite overcome when he. read the last scene of the book to Sophia immediately after writing it: "tried to read it, rather, for my voice swelled and heaved, as if I were tossed up and down on an ocean as it subsides after a storm." He could explain this away, in retrospect, by saying that "I was in a very nervous state then, having gone through a great diversity and severity of emotion, while writing it, for many months past": but how can we doubt that "The Scarlet Letter" itself had drawn heavily upon that emotion and heightened it with its own imaginative vitality? "To tell you the truth," he wrote to Bridge, "it is — (I hope Mrs. Bridge is not present) — it is positively a hell-fired story, into which I found it almost impossible to throw any cheering light." This he regarded as, from one point of view, a disadvantage; but his prevailing sense was of his own inability to steer the tale in any other direction than the one it had itself taken.

At all events, Hawthorne was convinced that what he had written, deeply as he himself had been affected by it, could have no claim on the popularity his other writings had so signally missed. "Who would risk publishing a book for *me*, the most unpopular writer in America?" he had asked, despondently and challengingly, his friend, J. T. Fields, the publisher, while he was still at work on the first chapters of the story; and even after Fields, in his enthusiasm for these, had insisted on his finishing the book, and had promised to start it off with a large edition, Hawthorne could not

believe that this argued anything but friendship and
generosity. How could so dolorous a narrative of
guilt and retribution, relieved so little by the strong
sunlight of humor and easy hopefulness, be expected
to invoke the regard of the Dickens-loving, Longfellow-
loving American public? How could "The Scarlet Letter" triumph where the "Twice-Told Tales" and the
"Mosses", with so much more as even they had of the
genial and the Goldsmithian, had failed? No, the only
thing that could save it from disaster, he at first thought,
would be to make it merely one of a series of short
tales to be included together in a volume; and when
Fields had dissuaded him from this, and induced him to
extend the story of the scarlet letter to the length of a
book, Hawthorne could not bring himself to publish it
on its own merits. To offset its cheerlessness, he wrote
a prefatory essay on the Customhouse, in the "familiar"
vein of the essay on the Old Manse, and insisted on its
appearing in the opening pages of the new book. "It
would be funny," he wrote to Fields, "if, seeing the
further passages so dark and dismal, [my guests] should
all choose to stop there!" And a year later, when his
outlook should have changed radically, he could say
that "the preliminary chapter was what gave 'The
Scarlet Letter' its vogue."

All this did but demonstrate how completely Hawthorne was out of touch with his potential audience,
for the new book was an immediate and decisive success. This was the book of which a first edition of two
thousand copies was exhausted in ten days, and which
gave Hawthorne, almost over night, an international
reputation. Suddenly, at what seemed the lowest ebb

of his literary fortunes, he stepped out of the shadow and the stillness and found himself standing in the intense light of the fame he had quite given over expecting. The name that Poe had declared was seldom mentioned in any list of the best writers, was from now on to be habitually included at or near the top; a book on the homes of American authors, for example, to be published in a year or two, was to contain as a matter of course a chapter on the Old Manse. Wherever Hawthorne went from now on it was to be not as the obscurest literary man in America, but as the author of "The Scarlet Letter." He had won, for what it might be worth, the Golden Fleece!

The effect upon his own mind of this abrupt access of glory was at once striking and ambiguous. No longer could he complain of having to write for an irresponsive world, of a "total lack of sympathy" with his purposes. No longer need he say, as he had said to Fields, "I have no money to indemnify a publisher's losses on my account." A publisher was not likely to lose money henceforth on any book of his. On the contrary, his successive volumes were to be awaited with much the same expectancy that preceded the appearance of a book of Longfellow's, and Hawthorne could be aware of this with every page he wrote. The numbness, naturally, was thus taken out of his fingers, and the chillness out of his heart: from now on he could write in a moral atmosphere that was warm if it was not remarkably light. "As long as people will buy," he declared a year later to Bridge, "I shall keep at work, and I find that my facility for labor increases with the demand for it." Within a period of less than four years, indeed, he

wrote almost as much as he had written and published
in all the earlier part of his life — three novels or
"romances" (with a fourth taking shape in his mind),
two books for children, two or three tales, and a biography. It is true that the income from his books was
just insufficient for the needs of a growing family;
but if it had not been for this, Hawthorne might well
have gone on indefinitely writing for his incredible new
public. As it was, he continued to write with a kind
of unworried fluency whenever he had leisure and
health, and to lay plans for new books even when he
was unable to work at them.

Yet with all the refreshment and reassurance of this
new popular status went a curious incomprehension of
the real grounds for it, whatever they were; a curious
unwillingness to accept it on its face value. We have
seen how confident Hawthorne had been that no work
which embodied so much of his own imaginative life
as "The Scarlet Letter" could possibly have an intrinsic
validity for many readers, and how stubbornly he had
insisted that its success was owing to the essay on the
Customhouse. Now he persevered in believing that
there was some chasm between himself and his audience
which either could not be bridged at all or could be
bridged only by some feat of wary foresight. When he
had written "The House of the Seven Gables" he confessed to Bridge that he thought it "a work more characteristic of my mind, and more proper and natural for
me to write, than 'The Scarlet Letter'; but for that
very reason, less likely to interest the public." When
he began to consider his next book, "I mean," he said,
"to put an extra touch of the devil into it, for I doubt

whether the public will stand for two quiet books in succession without my losing ground." And, with "The Blithedale Romance" behind him, he wrote of a book which he was about to begin, and "which, if possible, I mean to make more genial than the last." What readers he had, he seemed to say, could not be counted upon; they could only be circumvented! And at the best it was a matter of luck. "My own opinion," he wrote to Fields in 1860, "is, that I am not really a popular writer, and that what popularity I have gained is chiefly accidental, and owing to other causes than my own kind or degree of merit." It had not been too late for his fingers to be thawed by popular approval; but, with all that lay behind him, it had been too late for his mind to be disarmed and reconciled by it. In this sense, he continued to write as if in the old solitude.

Fame of some sort, nevertheless, as he could not deny, had come to him; and was it not, despite its long postponement, a pure and lively satisfaction? If so, Hawthorne could have felt it only intermittently: he never confessed to the feeling in so many words. Some notion of the factitiousness of all glory, or perhaps merely of this particular kind, kept him from anything like complacency.

How slowly I have made my way in life! — he exclaimed in a letter to Bridge early in 1851. — How much is still to be done! How little worth — outwardly speaking — is all that I have achieved! The bubble reputation is as much a bubble in literature as in war, and I should not be one whit the happier if mine were world-wide and time-long than I was when nobody but yourself had faith in me.

This has the ring of exaggeration, but he was prepared to go still further in stating his indifference.
"The only sensible ends of literature," he added, "are,
first, the pleasurable toil of writing; second, the grati-
fication of one's family and friends; and, lastly, the
solid cash." So thoroughly as this had he learned the
lesson that in the America of his time literary distinction, no matter how great or how deservedly won, was
in itself a thing of minor consequence. The solid cash
he was never ashamed to mention, and the proceeds
from his books were always to be for him a legitimate
topic for reference. His disenchantment as regarded
fame was to persist to the end. "You can tell, far better than I," he wrote to Longfellow during the last
months of his life, "whether there is ever anything
worth having in literary reputation, and whether the
best achievements seem to have any substance after
they grow cold."

By the time "The Scarlet Letter" was going through
the press, Hawthorne was again weary of Salem, weary
of the place where so much that had been grievous and
disconsolate in his life was present to him — of "the
old wooden houses, the mud and dust, the dead level of
site and sentiment, the chill east wind, and the chillest
of social atmospheres" — and restively eager to find
some new abode for himself and his family where all
these associations could be put behind. The most likely
spot seemed, after some casting about, to be the neighborhood of Lenox in the western part of the State; and
thither, in the late spring, he and Sophia, with the two
children, betook themselves. He turned his face from

Salem — for the last time, so far as residence was concerned — without regret.

Henceforth, it ceases to be a reality of my life. I am a citizen of somewhere else. My good townspeople will not much regret me; for — though it has been as dear an object as any, in my literary efforts, to be of some importance in their eyes, and to win myself a pleasant memory in this abode and burial-place of so many of my forefathers — *there* has never been, for me, the genial atmosphere which a literary man requires, in order to ripen the best harvest of his mind.

Lenox itself proved to be acceptable as a dwelling place only for a period of less than two years, but its setting was as different from Salem's as Hawthorne could have desired, and his life there, with all the exceptions that have to be made, was a kind of return to the regimen of the days in the Manse. In Concord they had been practically in the country, and here they literally were. A little frame house painted red — Hawthorne called it, dutifully, "the Scarlet Letter" — with its southern windows looking out over the waters of Stockbridge Bowl and at the smooth and placid slopes of Monument Mountain beyond, was their new Castle of Indolence. During his customhouse life Hawthorne had suffered from finding that the befogged mental state into which he had fallen went with him on his seashore walks and rambles in the country, refusing even to yield to the charm of nature that had formerly invigorated and renewed him; and he now rejoiced to discover that among the Berkshire hills — where he looked, as some one said, "like a banished lord" — this charm was as fresh and vivid as ever.

14 MALL STREET, SALEM

HAWTHORNE'S BIRTHPLACE

Una and Julian were now old enough to be his companions abroad, and hour after hour he spent with them —
swimming in the lake or rowing about on it in the
summer, and fishing not very earnestly in what was to
be known in literature as Shadow Brook; going nutting
in the autumn among the intricate gold-flecked shadows
of what was to be known as Tanglewood; and in the
winter building snow houses, or taking adventurous
walks across the ice-sheeted lake. There are more
than traces of the old flame in the notations, which
begin to reappear in his notebooks, on the delicate
splendor of winter sunsets, the manifold effects of color
and shadow on the mountain sides, and the appearance
of trailing arbutus and columbines in the spring woods.

In Lenox too, as in Concord, they found themselves
in an atmosphere of letters and art — though again
with differences perhaps more striking than the parallel. Fanny Kemble, the actress, who lived near by,
proved as good a friend as Elizabeth Hoar; but she
could scarcely have reminded them of that other-
worldly presence when she came pounding up to the
gate on her great black horse, summoned Julian for a
gallop astride the pommel of her saddle, and then, returning with him, drew rein, held the boy out at arm's
length, and shouted, "Take your boy! — Julian the
Apostate!" In Stockbridge, a few miles away, lived
the Cockney Dumas, G. P. R. James, author of "Darn-
ley", "Richelieu", and uncounted other romances in
the Flamboyant Style, who was even now dictating to
three or four secretaries simultaneously at the rate of
two volumes a year, and who yet found time to live an
arduous social life. It was for Hawthorne one of the

disasters of their Lenox period when on a day of violent thunder showers, with Sophia and Una away in
Boston, the whole James family, overtaken on a pleasure-
excursion by the elements, descended upon him and
Julian, beseeching shelter, and were, for humanity's
sake, afforded it, at the cost of considerable perturba-
tion to their shy and unresourceful host. Fortunately,
the excellent James himself was in a loquacious mood;
so that, with an exchange of views on English and
American periodicals, and on the Puritans — "about
whom we agreed pretty well" — and with some remi-
niscences of James' childhood for Julian's benefit, the
ordeal was finally passed. In Pittsfield, to the north,
lived Doctor O. W. Holmes, in the summer time; the
occasion has already been alluded to when he drove over
with a friend to see the view from the windows of the
little house, and being unwilling to leave his horse alone,
received what he regarded as the signal honor of having
his horse held by the author of "The Scarlet Letter."

A molluscan habit, however, that had not yielded
notably to the advances of Emerson and Thoreau, was
not likely to be seriously threatened by the near presence of the bluff James and the breezy Holmes. If these
had been his only literary neighbors, Hawthorne would
have remained as uncommunicative in Lenox as he had
been for five years in Salem. As it happened, a far more
closely related spirit was just now a dweller in these
parts, and was to conquer, so far as we can gather, more
territory in Hawthorne's confidence than any of these
others. This was Herman Melville, the man who had
lived among the cannibals in the valley of Typee, and
who was now living at Arrowhead, his farm on the

hither side of Pittsfield, "shaping out", as Eustace
Bright tells his young listeners in "A Wonder Book",
"the gigantic conception of his 'White Whale'." During the first summer in Lenox a friendship sprang up
between the two with a suddenness and warmth unique
in Hawthorne's record. On the fifth of August they
were both in a party which made the ascent of Monument Mountain and dined afterwards with a Mr. Field
of Stockbridge; on the seventh, Hawthorne wrote to
Bridge: "I met Melville the other day, and liked him
so much that I have asked him to spend a few days with
me before leaving these parts." Thereafter, since the
cordiality was returned and multiplied, Melville became a frequent visitor at the little red house, riding
over from Pittsfield on horseback with his great New-
foundland dog, reciting his South Sea adventures to the
whole family with an actor's representational vigor,
and sitting up until all hours with Hawthorne talking "about time and eternity, things of this world and of
the next, and all possible and impossible matters."

It was, on the surface, a singular alliance, and could
hardly have promised well in an observer's eyes. How
could a life have been less like Hawthorne's than the
life that Melville, his junior by fifteen years, had led? —
Melville who had shipped before the mast in an English
vessel at the age of seventeen, had later been a sailor
on a whaling ship in the South Seas, had deserted it
with one companion in the Marquesas and spent four
months among the too hospitable natives of Typee, had
made his way into the penetralia of the palace of Queen
Pomaree of Tahiti, and had just missed flogging by
order of the captain on an American man-of-war;

Melville whose companions had been ne'er-do-well ship surgeons and outlandish harpooneers and Polynesian chiefs; Melville who had tramped the water-side streets of Liverpool, and basked on the beach sands at Honolulu, and watched from the masthead of a whaler the sunrise on the becalmed Pacific. How could a man who had seen so much of the world as this be drawn to a recluse like Hawthorne, or how could Hawthorne get into communication with him? Even as authors, had they shown any common inspiration in such dissimilar books as "Typee" and "Mosses from an Old Manse", or as "White Jacket" and "The Scarlet Letter?" Why, of all the men of letters in the world — or in western Massachusetts — did Melville seize upon Nathaniel Hawthorne as the one human being to whom he could utter his deepest intentions and betray his secretest fears?

The truth is, it was only externally that their experiences had been so incongruous. Through all the press and bustle of his adventurous life, Melville had gone about locked up in a solitariness no whit less bleak and overcast than Hawthorne's own; had suffered from as acute a sense of incurable isolation from his kind. "Call me Ishmael," he enjoins the reader, at the opening of "Moby-Dick": and he had felt more than once, in his moods of saturnine self-torment, that his hand was against every man's and every man's hand against him. Like Hawthorne, he had come early to the discovery that he could make no agreeable terms with the world about him; like Hawthorne, he had met disaster in every attempt to live its life and accept its current goods. His "dismal chamber" had been the stinking, crowded murk of the forecastle on an unseaworthy whaler; but it had been, for a born poet and philosopher, no less a wilderness. His Customhouse had been the New York State Bank at Albany and his brother Gansevoort's fur store, and he had fled from them as Hawthorne had fled from Long Wharf and Derby Street. Loneliness and pride — had not these two ruled Melville's life between them?

Oh, man! — he cries in his greatest book — admire and model thyself after the whale! Do thou, too, remain warm among ice. Do thou, too, live in this world without being of it. Be cool at the equator; keep thy blood fluid at the Pole. Like the great dome of St. Peter's, and like the great whale, retain, O man! in all seasons, a temperature of thine own.

In this book, which he was now laboring over at Pittsfield, he created a symbol of the lonely intellect as monumental as any of Hawthorne's; for what else than this is Captain Ahab, bent inflexibly on his cruel purpose, sharing his meaning with no man, pursuing his single prey through the calms and storms of the greatest seas, and going down at last in wild defeat under the lashings of its mighty tail? We have reason to believe that in the figure of Ethan Brand, Hawthorne made a kind of portrait of his new friend: certainly the tradition that he did so is by no means hard to accept.

Until he met Hawthorne, Melville had known no man whom he could admit as a spiritual equal, no man of such a stature as to achieve his own tragic vision of human life. But he had already read the "Mosses from an Old Manse", and praised the book for its dark and serious truth, and was ready to grasp Hawthorne's hand

as one giant among the pigmies would grasp another's.
"The divine magnet is on you," he wrote, "and my
magnet responds. Which is the biggest? A foolish
question, — they are *One*." They were one, he felt,
in their power to deny what all the rest of their contemporaries were asserting. "There is the grand truth
about Nathaniel Hawthorne," he declared in a letter
to its author praising "The House of the Seven Gables."

He says NO! in thunder; but the Devil himself cannot
make him say *yes*. For all men who say *yes*, lie; and all
men who say *no*, — why, they are in the happy condition of judicious, unincumbered travellers in Europe;
they cross the frontiers into Eternity with nothing but
a carpet-bag, — that is to say, the Ego. Whereas those
yes-gentry, they travel with heaps of baggage, and,
damn them! they will never get through the Customhouse.

Hawthorne and he were one, he felt, in their capacity
for holding themselves aloof:

In reading some of Goethe's sayings, so worshipped
by his votaries, I came across this, "*Live in the all*."
That is to say, your separate identity is but a wretched
one, — good; but get out of yourself, spread and expand
yourself, and bring to yourself the tinglings of life that
are felt in the flowers and the woods, that are felt in
the planets Saturn and Venus, and the Fixed Stars.
What nonsense! Here is a fellow with a raging tooth-
ache. "My dear boy," Goethe says to him, "you are
sorely afflicted with that tooth; but you must *live in the
all*, and then you will be happy!" As with all great
genius, there is an immense deal of flummery in Goethe,
and in proportion to my own contact with him, a monstrous deal of it in me. . . . P. S. "Amen!" saith
Hawthorne.

What wonder if, feeling this parity and sympathy between them as he did, Melville expanded in the warmth, however moderate, of Hawthorne's friendship, and poured out his doubts and anxieties and mutinous impulses to him as he would have scorned to do to any other man? What wonder if he allowed Hawthorne more than a glance into "the tornadoed Atlantic of my being!" "Knowing you," he wrote, "persuades me more than the Bible of our immortality": and certainly, for a man whose life had been divided between the respectable mercantile families of New York and Albany and the populations of the seven seas, the author of "The Scarlet Letter" was, as an intimate, a godsend for which he could not be too grateful. Whatever Hawthorne's friendship may have been intrinsically worth — and Melville no doubt exaggerated somewhat their congruities — it was probably the awareness of his understanding presence in the neighborhood that helped Melville more than anything else through the oceanic struggles of composing "Moby-Dick." His dedicating the book to Hawthorne is a witness to this, and his deep satisfaction in Hawthorne's praise of it is another:

Your joy-giving and exultation-breeding letter is not my reward for my ditcher's work with that book, but is the good goddess's bonus over and above what was stipulated for — for not one man in five cycles, who is wise, will expect appreciative recognition from his fellows, or any one of them. . . . In my proud, humble way, — a shepherd-king, — I was lord of a little vale in the solitary Crimea; but you have now given me the crown of India. . . . A sense of unspeakable security is in me this moment, on account of your having understood the book.

Unhappily there were miseries and confusions in Melville's spirit that not even Hawthorne's sympathy could appease; after "Moby-Dick", his lips were never again to be touched with the true flame, and before many years he was to sink into a "long quietus" of solitude and silence for which even Hawthorne's experience had no parallel.

As for the older man, what rôle did this quick-flowering friendship play in his spiritual affairs? Did Melville throw for Hawthorne any new light on the darkness of human destiny, or distress him with any new enigmas to be solved? No full answer to these questions can be given, since Hawthorne's letters to Melville have been destroyed, but it is hardly likely that at this stage Hawthorne's spiritual course could be altered by any such deflecting pressure. If he had not long since put off his particular Sphinx with some acceptable answer, it would have been too late for Melville to add to either his enlightenment or his perplexity; and indeed Hawthorne, partly because in his domestic life he had attained repose, partly because he had never suspected the universe of the blackest treacheries, could feel neither the need nor the desire for reassurance. Melville he must have valued, not as a philosopher, but as a man who was as little committed as he to the prevailing affirmations, and who spoke to him out of an isolation as immitigable as his own. Their imaginations were sufficiently akin so that Hawthorne could seriously consider making a book out of materials that Melville had given him. But no more than Emerson or Thoreau could Melville exercise a lasting sway over his mind; and when they met, after five years, in England, Hawthorne was able to write of him with warmth and admiration but with character-istic detachment:

It is strange how he persists — and has persisted, ever since I knew him, and probably long before — in wandering to and fro over these deserts, as dismal and monotonous as the sandhills amid which we were sit-ting. He can neither believe nor be comfortable in his unbelief; and he is too honest and courageous not to try to do one or the other. If he were a religious man, he would be one of the most truly religious and rever-ential; he has a very high and noble nature, and is better worth immortality than most of us.

For several months after their arrival in Lenox, Haw-thorne had been too exhausted from the travail of writing "The Scarlet Letter", and too eager for an out-of-doors existence, to be capable of falling to work at once on a new book. With the restorative lapse of the summer weeks, however, and with the accumulating assurances of his new fame, his energies had revived, and early in September he had begun a new romance — a romance in which the Salem that he had now left be-hind him for good appeared as almost a protagonist in the action. As winter closed in upon them his seasonal habits of composition asserted themselves, and he wrote with so steady an application and so untroubled a flu-ency that by the early days of January he had finished "The House of the Seven Gables."

Sometimes, when tired of it — he had written to Fields in November — it strikes me that the whole is an absurdity, from beginning to end; but the fact is, in writing a romance, a man is always, or always ought

to be, careering on the utmost verge of a precipi-
tous absurdity, and the skill lies in coming as close as
possible, without actually tumbling over.

He felt, as we have seen, that the book was a more
natural one for him to write than "The Scarlet Letter";
but he did not expect it to be so well received, and was
not surprised when it actually proved to be less dramatically popular. His fingers were now warmed to the
task of writing: early in the following summer, unwilling to let them remain idle, and not yet ready to begin
a new romance, he spent four or five weeks composing
the group of mythical tales for children that made up
"The Wonder Book." For some time the purpose of
using his Brook Farm experience for a novel had been
in his mind, and in the fall he began "The Blithedale Romance", which was to be finished the following spring.

Meanwhile, dissatisfaction with Lenox as a place of
residence had been growing upon him.

Please God — he wrote to Fields toward the end of
the summer — I mean to look you in the face towards
the end of next week; at all events, within ten days. I
have stayed here too long and too constantly. To tell
you a secret, I am sick to death of Berkshire, and hate
to think of spending another winter here. . . . The
air and climate do not agree with my health at all;
and, for the first time since I was a boy, I have felt
languid and dispirited during almost my whole residence here.

This was a moody exaggeration, but it was clear
that Lenox had had its day; after some hesitation
over the possibility of moving into Fanny Kemble's
house, which she had offered them for the winter, the

Hawthornes dismantled the little red cottage and, on a dreary November day, took their way eastward again — this time to West Newton, a suburb of Boston, where they were to spend the winter in the house of their relatives, the Horace Manns. Here, within walking distance of its setting, "The Blithedale Romance" was written; but West Newton could not be a permanent abode, and during most of the winter Hawthorne was occupied with the problem of finding a new home. Nowhere had they yet been better content with their immediate world than in Concord, and now that more than six years lay between them and their tranquil life in the Manse, their thoughts turned in that direction as toward their inevitable home.

There was no question of their going back to the Manse itself, but when it became known in Concord — chiefly through Ellery Channing, of whom Hawthorne had made inquiries — that they were looking for a house, Bronson Alcott came forward with a proposal to sell them the Hillside, where after returning to Concord from Boston he had been living for a year or two past. This was a pre-Revolutionary house on the old Boston Road, not far beyond Emerson's, upon which Alcott had exercised without let his euphuistic fancies, but which did not repel the Hawthornes on that account, and attracted them because of its pleasant situation at the foot of a hillside covered with locust trees and young oaks and elms. Indeed, Hawthorne was so much pleased by the prospect it offered of a quiet countrified existence that he bought it with little hesitation, and, rechristening it the Wayside, moved over from West Newton and took possession of it late in the spring of 1852. By the time Sophia had hung the Endymion in Hawthorne's study, and set up the cast of Apollo in one corner, and found space for Correggio's Madonna in the drawing-room; and by the time Mr. Emerson and Henry Thoreau and Ellery Channing had severally dropped in to welcome them back to Concord, they could feel that they were resuming their old way of life with only such changes as they rejoiced to have made in the meanwhile.

Here it might well have seemed that Hawthorne would now remain forever, calmly composing one romance after another, each of which he would hope to make "more genial" than its predecessor; receiving without too much distress the visitors who, drawn by the magnetism of his name, had more and more to be predicted; and retreating now and then to the wooded ridge of the hillside behind the house where he could pace back and forth alone and "think of nothing at all", which, as he said, would be "equivalent to thinking of all manner of things." In fact, they had, for the present, hardly more than a year to live in the Wayside. While they were in the process of getting settled, the Democratic national convention met in Baltimore, and after failing to select any of its salient men, nominated as a dark horse, on the thirty-fifth ballot, General Franklin Pierce of New Hampshire. This was a turn of affairs in the political world that could scarcely fail to have its repercussion in Hawthorne's life, and the form that this was likely to take became evident when, a few days later, the new candidate requested him, as his oldest friend and chief literary acquaintance, to write the campaign biography.

It was well for Pierce that he could appeal in this
need to Hawthorne, for no other man of letters in the
north, of equal distinction, would have met the request
with anything but contempt; and it is eloquent of
Hawthorne's insulation from the strongest spiritual
currents of his time that, in spite of other reluctances,
he at last undertook the task with a good conscience.
At a moment when men like Emerson, Thoreau, Lowell,
Whittier, G. W. Curtis, and even Holmes and Longfellow had made up their minds that slavery was a
tragic evil and would sooner or later have to go, Hawthorne found nothing distasteful in the idea of thus
allying himself with a steadfast political friend of the
slaveholder. Of the man whom Emerson called "that
paltry Franklin Pierce", and whom Lowell described
derisively by comparing him with Elijah Pogram,
Hawthorne could say privately that "I have come
seriously to the conclusion that he has in him many of
the chief elements of a great ruler." Much of this, to
be sure, may be set down to political hostility on the
one side, and to personal friendship on the other; but
not so easily can we explain away Hawthorne's devotion not only to the man but to the partisan. For this
there can be no accounting, unless we remember the
dismal chamber, and the flight from the Boston Customhouse, and the more than physical seclusion of the
Manse, and all the blindness and deafness to the central
issues of American life that these things imply. Only
a man partially blind and deaf could have moved,
without gross incongruity, among the spirits of Brook
Farm and Concord, and have remained a Democrat.

Within a few months after "Uncle Tom's Cabin"

had appeared, and less than a decade before Fort Sumter, Hawthorne could write this paragraph in his life of Pierce:

He comes before the people of the United States at a remarkable era in the history of this country and of the world. The two great parties of the nation appear — at least to an observer somewhat removed from both — to have nearly merged into one another; for they preserve the attitude of political antagonism rather through the effect of their old organizations than because any great and radical principles are at present in dispute between them. The measures advocated by the one party, and resisted by the other, through a long series of years, have now ceased to be the pivots on which the election turns. . . . Both parties, it may likewise be said, are united in one common purpose, — that of preserving our sacred Union, as the immovable basis from which the destinies, not of America alone, but of mankind at large, may be carried upward and consummated. And thus men stand together, in unwonted quiet and harmony, awaiting the new movement in advance which all these tokens indicate.

"In unwonted quiet and harmony!" What, then, might be regarded as dissonance and turmoil?

It was, at any rate, no uncertainty about his Democratic loyalties that made Hawthorne hesitate for a moment to concede to Pierce's request, and even to make one effort to be exempted. This he did because he disliked to have the appearance of selling his services for political reward: so strong was this feeling that he spoke of Pierce, with humorous overemphasis, in a letter to Fields, as having "reached that altitude when a man, careful of his personal dignity, will begin to think of cutting his acquaintance." Pierce, however,

proved adamant, and Hawthorne, unwilling to seem
deficient in friendship, promised himself that he would
accept no favors from the Democrats if they triumphed;
and wrote the book. For the purposes of American
politics it was a mild and weakly colored little volume,
and it could not have won many votes for its subject.
Happily for Pierce, he did not need them; he was elected
in November by an enormous electoral plurality over
his opponent. Even before the election, Hawthorne
had begun to reconsider the promise he had made
himself:

Before undertaking the book — he wrote to Bridge in
October — I made an inward resolution that I would
accept no office from him; but, to say the truth, I doubt
whether it would not be rather folly than heroism to
adhere to this purpose in case he should offer me anything particularly good. We shall see. A foreign
mission I could not afford to take. The consulship at
Liverpool I might.

And the consulship at Liverpool he did accept. His
appointment to the post was one of the first acts of the
new administration; and, as it was one of the most
lucrative offices in the president's gift, Hawthorne was
too conscious of his economic duty to his family to
reject it.

In April, shortly after Pierce's inauguration, Hawthorne, in company with Ticknor, Fields' partner, took
a trip to Washington to make one or two requests of
the new president in person. Donald Grant Mitchell,
a younger man of letters, was staying at Willard's
Hotel at the same time, and preserved for us an impression of Hawthorne as he now appeared.

Mr. Hawthorne was then nearing fifty — strong, erect, broad-shouldered, alert — his abundant hair touched with gray, his features all cast in Greek mould and his fine eyes full of searchingness, and yet of kindliness; his voice deep, with a weighty, resounding quality, as if hearing echoes of things unspoken; no arrogance, no assurance even, but rather there hung about his manner and his speech a cloud of self-distrust, of *mal-aise*, as if he were on the defensive, and determined to rest there. Withal it was a winning shyness; and when — somewhat later — his jolly friend Ticknor tapped him on the shoulder, and told him how some lad wanted to be presented, there was something almost painful in the abashed manner with which the famous author awaited a school-boy's homage — cringing under such contact with conventional usage, as a schoolgirl might.

On a fine cloudless day early in the following July, the Cunard steamship *Niagara* sailed out of Boston Harbor bearing the new American consul at Liverpool and his family, and was saluted for his sake by the guns on Castle Island and by the flags of incoming vessels. The consul himself stood at the rail of the afterdeck with two children, watching the hills and headlands of Boston recede and grow dim in the afternoon light. "Go away, tiresome old land!" sang out the two children with the easy infidelity of their years, and were rebuked by a word and a serious look from their father.

CHAPTER SIX

THE HOUSE OF PRIDE

"It was a goodly heape for to behould,
And spake the praises of the workmans witt."
— "The Faerie Queene", Book I

WHEN Hawthorne sailed for England to take up his official duties at Liverpool, he had behind him, with the
exception of one book, all the finished and momentous
work he was to do in imaginative literature. If he had
never afterwards resumed his pen, his station as a creative writer would not have been essentially different
from what it is; and we may pause at this point to
inquire, in the light of all that has since fallen out,
what that station is. In the concerns of the age in
which he lived our emotions are no longer engaged;
whatever local and immediate motives his writings may
have served and satisfied have long ago ceased to animate us. Any sway those writings may now exercise
over our imaginations must rest on the basis of some
persistent and general consent, not on such suffrages of
neighbors and contemporaries as have largely hitherto
defined its limits. It is a question we should now ask
whether Hawthorne's work has in it the qualities of
major imaginative literature, whether we can continue
to read it with the kind of pleasure we take in the
poems and plays and novels that have created a desirable and permanent home for the imagination. Is
Hawthorne, for American literature, the kind of writer

whose work, focussing so much of the common experience, takes on the character we call epic? Is it, in any
sense, Homeric, Dantesque, Shakespearean? Have any
of his books the validity of "Don Quixote", or the
"Comédie Humaine", or "Tom Jones", or "War and
Peace?" Or have they some minor but authentic virtue that must be expressed in other terms?

Every one knows what it is that makes major literature of such books as these. The creative achievement they represent is the product of two forces. In
the first place, the writer of such a book must have
shared fully and directly some central spiritual experience of his people and his time, must have been moved
by desires not merely personal or fugitive, and have
won some typical triumph or gone down in some typical defeat. Through all the books of this kind blow
the winds, if not of doctrine, at least of a general spiritual necessity; upon them all is stamped the seal of a
catholic adventure. "Paradise Lost" is not merely
Milton, but the Protestant spirit in seventeenth-century
England; "Père Goriot" and "Cousin Pons" and
"Eugénie Grandet" are not merely Balzac, but the lust
for power and place in the France of the July Monarchy. Milton and Balzac and all writers of the first
order, whatever their idiosyncrasies, have played out
in their own fortunes some representative drama of
which their work is at once the outcome and the ultimate record. In the second place, this experience is
embodied, artistically, in the idiom of personality; is
translated from its native formlessness, abstractness,
subjectivity, into concrete and dramatic terms. On
the fullness and truth with which they reproduce the

facts of human character, as much as on their catholic-
ity, the imaginative acceptableness of such books
depends. Their pages swarm with "representative
men" and representative women, and it is these that
prolong and reënforce their ascendancy over the mind.
Paolo and Francesca, the Wife of Bath, Sancho Panza,
Falstaff, Tom Jones, César Birotteau, Bazároff, — characters such as these seem to exist in three dimensions, to
speak and act with the uncontrollable and unpredict-
able variety of actual speech and conduct; and, as a
result, they are the perpetual and heroic emblems of
certain prime experiences that men have. In the fulfillment of these two demands consists the authority of
the greatest literature. These are commonplaces, but
they must be restated here if the question about Hawthorne is to be clarified.

How completely does the work of Hawthorne fulfill
these demands? Is it the literary memorial of a focal
chapter in our spiritual history? Does it bear witness
to its author's participation in some generic destiny?
Has it, in short, a broadly representative value? And
how great is its dramatic truth? Has it added to our
literary heritage any Wife of Bath, any Tom Jones,
any Bazároff? Only when we have answered these
questions shall we have approached a conclusive
estimate.

At this point, with the work of his great period
before us, and with what we have already seen of all
that preceded it, we can at least say what were the central motives in Hawthorne's own experience, and detect their overtones sounding through his literary
utterance. Whether that experience was typical or not

is another question, and must wait for another answer. He had, at any rate, begun life by repudiating any allegiance to the prevailing purposes of his countrymen, by setting before himself a lonely and unfashionable goal, and by divorcing himself, physically and ideally, from the great middle current of American enterprise. He sat down by the wayside, as he himself said, and for years he had remained sitting there, growing more and more apart from ordinary humanity, losing gradually his capacity for warm and open relations with men and women, allowing a cold, inquiring, analytic interest in them to take more and more entire possession of his mind. All this kept Hawthorne from orienting himself humanly and, so to say, socially; from expanding on all sides as a personality, and multiplying his points of fruitful contact with reality; from achieving roundness and relief as a man. Gradually the conviction had grown in his mind that he was committing the unpardonable sin in thus arrogating to himself a right and rank above or aside from those of other men. A sense of guilt began to molest him in his solitude, and a dread lest he should now be unable to regain his footing in the general and morally significant march. This he at length made an effort to do; but his essay was an experiment not so much in participation on a vital level, as in mere association on a mechanical one; his real gifts were not called into play, and his real usefulness to society was not exploited; the experiment was a failure, and he had never repeated it with the same hopes. It is unlikely, indeed, that Hawthorne perceived the true grounds for his defeat; he doubtless

THE HOUSE OF PRIDE 185

abandoned the hope of participating fully and tellingly in the life about him, and contented himself with making the most of his rôle as a husband and father. This, at any rate, was a positive relationship, however marginal, and it saved him from the charge of entire heartlessness he might otherwise have brought against himself. Such was the experience on which his imagination was nourished, and of which his work is the expression.

In this light, it should be obvious why Hawthorne's tales and novels can be called an elaborate study of the centrifugal. They are a dramatization of all those social and psychological forces that lead to disunion, fragmentation, dispersion, incoherence. "The wages of estrangement is death" — that might be printed as a legend on the threshold of all of them; the causes and consequences of estrangement is their consistent theme. And numerous as are the forms which estrangement takes in this drama, it is clear that they all have their roots in an error for which there is no better single word than pride. It may be the pride of family and position that cuts men off, in their own esteem, from ordinary necessities and the vulgar fate; it may be the cold pride of speculative curiosity, preying irresponsibly upon the privacies of other hearts; it may be the noble pride that shrinks from revealing guilt when secrecy may seem to accomplish a greater good, or the intellectual arrogance of a man dedicated to a limited ideal; it may be spiritual pride in its subtlest and most metaphysical form. In any case, it is irreconcilable with a truly human solidarity; it sets men at odds with one another, instead of at peace; and its

unavoidable consequences are frustration and despair, —
the maiming, the debasing, or the impoverishment of
the healthy personality. "All that seems most real
about us," Hawthorne had once written to Sophia,
"is but the thinnest substance of a dream, — till the
heart is touched"; and to this emptiness, this fraudu-
lence, this spectral unreality in all conduct that springs
merely from the intellect or the will, he continually
recurred. Not in that direction, he seemed to say, lie
union and abundant life.

Consider the complex thematic coherence of the tales
and novels of Hawthorne's great productive period.
Fanciful satire in "Feathertop", idyllic allegory in
"The Great Stone Face", lurid "terror" in "Ethan
Brand" — all draw their vitality from one pregnant
center. What is the fate of the poor scarecrow in the
first of these but a parable on the vanity of all character,
all distinction, that is the product of mere ingenuity
and designing craft, unwarmed by any deep feeling or
desire? "Many a fine gentleman," observes Mother
Rigby pithily, "has a pumpkin-head, as well as my
scarecrow": and Feathertop is unique, we gather, only
because he catches sight in a mirror of his true and
trashy self, and thereupon gives over the sorry pre-
tence of grandeur. The three distinguished visitors in
"The Great Stone Face" are in the same factitious class.
How could Ernest pretend that any one of them resem-
bled the great countenance of the crag in its massive
and benign humanity, when a genuinely humane expression was lacking in all of them — in the shrewd, selfish
features of Mr. Gathergold; in the war-worn visage of
Old Blood-and-Thunder, "full of energy, and expres-

sive of an iron will" but without "gentle wisdom"
or "deep, broad, tender sympathies"; in the grand
heroic face of Old Stony Phiz, the orator, with its
gloomy revelation of a life that, "with all its high
performances, was vague and empty, because no high
purpose had endowed it with reality." And why does
Ethan Brand fling himself to death in the lime-kiln
except because he has discovered, in his search for
the Unpardonable Sin, that he alone has been guilty
of it? — "the sin of an intellect that triumphed over
the sense of brotherhood with man and reverence for
God, and sacrificed everything to its own mighty
claims! The only sin that deserves a recompense of immortal agony!" His mental powers had been developed
so highly that he at last stood quite alone in his emi-
nence: "but where was the heart? That, indeed, had
withered, — had contracted, — had hardened, — had
perished! It had ceased to partake of the universal
throb. He had lost his hold of the magnetic chain of
humanity."

Like Ethan Brand, in this tragic respect, are the
protagonists of Hawthorne's three middle romances.
They have all, in their several ways, lost their hold
of the magnetic chain of humanity. Separation, division, and the starvation of their spiritual lives is the
fate that overtakes them all. And a destruction like
Ethan Brand's, even when it is not consummated, is
implicit in their miserable destinies.

In nothing that Hawthorne wrote are the tragic possibilities of the theme more richly and intensely realized
than in "The Scarlet Letter." What makes the outcome of its events so pitiful and terrible is not simply

that a great sin has had its retribution, but that the harmony of several related lives has been fatally jangled, that they have all been set at odds with the general purposes of the life about them, that all the fair potentialities of personal development have miscarried grievously and come to nothing. When we first hear of the embroidered letter shining on Hester Prynne's bosom, as she stands at the prison door with her child in her arms, it is to be told that the letter "had the effect of a spell, taking her out of the ordinary relations with humanity, and enclosing her in a sphere by herself." It is not for the intrinsic flagrance of the sin she has committed, but for the waywardness and irregularity of all wrongdoing, that she is punished; and the penalty is made to suit the offense, since Hester Prynne can never regain her innocent and normal status among men. In expiation of what she has done, she may adopt the rôle of a sister of charity, and thus come to have a certain part to perform in the world: "in all her intercourse with society, however, there was nothing that made her feel as if she belonged to it. Every gesture, every word, and even the silence of those with whom she came in contact, implied, and often expressed, that she was banished, and as much alone as if she inhabited another sphere, or communicated with the common nature by other organs and senses than the rest of human kind." In consequence of this alienation, the luxuriance and warmth of her personality undergo a kind of blight, and become austerity, coldness, and a rigid strength. Passion and feeling give way, in the movement of her life, to thought; and her thinking itself becomes bolder and more speculative, expressive not

so much of her whole being as of a specialized and
"unwomanly" function. At length she loses her clear
sense of human realities — loses it so far as to suppose
that she and Dimmesdale can achieve happiness by
mere escape from the dangers and difficulties that beset
them separately. No wonder Roger Chillingworth, in
their interview on the edge of the forest, is moved to
cry out, "Woman, I could wellnigh pity thee! . . .
Thou hadst great elements. Peradventure, hadst thou
met earlier with a better love than mine, this evil had
not been. *I pity thee, for the good that has been wasted in
thy nature!*"

Frustration like that which falls to the lot of Hester
Prynne is the punishment of the man who has shared
her guilt; and Dimmesdale is made to suffer even more
atrociously than she because he has deepened his original wrongdoing by the secrecy with which he has
invested it. This cuts him off still more effectually
from the redemptive force of normal human relations.
"There was an air about this young minister," we are
told when he first appears, "as of a being who felt
himself quite astray and at a loss in the pathway of
human existence, and could only be at ease in some
seclusion of his own." His noblest faculties and highest purposes seem engaged in the concealment of what
he has done; the reverence in which he is held by his
parishioners, and the pure spiritual influence he exercises upon them, are specious voices pleading against
confession. But in all this there is too large an element
of the unpardonable sin, too abject a surrender to spiritual pride; and the minister gradually discovers how
deadly is its effect upon his moral world.

It is the unspeakable misery of a life so false as his, that it steals the pith and substance out of whatever realities there are around us, and which were meant by Heaven to be the spirit's joy and nutriment. To the untrue man, the whole universe is false, — it is impalpable, — it shrinks to nothing within his grasp.

In such a world, the fruits of personal character cannot ripen; and Dimmesdale's nature, like Hester's, is finally perverted and vitiated by the central falsity of his life. His refined spirituality becomes the instrument for a diseased self-persecution; his spiritual insight turns into a loathsome apprehension of the evil in other men's breasts. As he returns through the town after his interview with Hester in the forest, Dimmesdale is tempted at every step to perpetrate some monstrous impropriety of speech or act — the symbol of a moral sense gone hopelessly awry. Of this disastrous process there can be but one fit culmination, and that is reached and realized by the minister's public self-exposure and death. His own breast has been seared by the scarlet letter!

Neither Hester Prynne nor Dimmesdale, however, is represented as the greatest sinner of the drama, and their punishments are less terrible than that of the third chief personage. The pride of the detached intellect is Roger Chillingworth's error, and it is this, not the wayward passion of the other two, that lies at the very root of the whole tragedy. The initial wrong was committed by the aging man of science who tried to bring warmth into his own benumbed existence by attaching to himself the radiance and vigor of Hester's youth. Her weakness was but the less culpable product of his folly. "I have greatly wronged thee," murmurs

Hester in her first interview with her husband. "We have wronged each other," he has the justice to answer. When Hester Prynne tries later to overcome her hatred for the old man by recalling their early life together, she cannot find it in her heart to forgive him: "it seemed a fouler offence committed by Roger Chillingworth, than any which had since been done him, that, in the time when her heart knew no better, he had persuaded her to fancy herself happy by his side." And Chillingworth does not rest content with having brought so much wrong to pass; he applies his great intellectual powers and his vast learning to the task of discovering Hester's partner in guilt, and of then wreaking a subtle revenge upon him. As he does so he ceases to be a man and becomes a moral monster.

In a word, old Roger Chillingworth was a striking evidence of man's faculty of transforming himself into a devil, if he will only, for a reasonable space of time, undertake a devil's office. This unhappy person had effected such a transformation, by devoting himself, for seven years, to the constant analysis of a heart full of torture, and deriving his enjoyment thence, and adding fuel to those fiery tortures which he analyzed and gloated over.

No trespass committed in passion can vie with this icy and ingenious iniquity. "That old man's revenge," says Dimmesdale to Hester, "has been blacker than my sin. He has violated, in cold blood, the sanctity of a human heart. Thou and I, Hester, never did so!" Of all the spiritual ruin symbolized by the scarlet letter, no part is more awful than the destruction of Roger Chillingworth.

What gives this first of his four chief romances its unique position of greatness in Hawthorne's work is the intense integrity of its tragic effect, the strictness with which the painful implications of the theme are allowed to work themselves out to the last bitter stroke. So much cannot be said of the others, and certainly not of "The House of the Seven Gables", into which Hawthorne rejoiced to have let more "sunshine." Nevertheless the materials here are only less somber in themselves than the materials of "The Scarlet Letter", and here too the forces of disintegration are represented as in full play — so truly in full play that the happy outcome must be felt to be far too little organic. How many of the motives that operate most powerfully in this story are motives that spring from some other sources than the heart! How many of them are motives that spring from loneliness or lead inevitably to it! The evil machinery of the drama is first set in motion by the heartless greed and unscrupling pride of the earliest Pyncheon, who sticks at no cruelty or fraud in his design of founding a great family, and who, on the very threshold of achieving it, is visited by so ironic a fate. Upon one generation after another of his descendants falls the curse of the man he has injured, falls really in the form of Colonel Pyncheon's worst qualities, and more than once with the same retribution. Even the beautiful Alice Pyncheon, who has no other fault than "a certain gentle and cold stateliness" that sets her apart from the world's vulgar mass, is made to suffer deep humiliation for this one taint of pride.

In the generation which enacts the drama proper,

this dark ancestral heritage bears its final fruit of division, coldness, and falsity. Of the three Pyncheons in the direct line — the Judge, Hepzibah, and Clifford — no one is a normally developed human being, living in the right and genial relations with his fellow men or with the others. They are all of them partial and imperfect characters, and they are all punished dreadfully on that account. Judge Pyncheon, whose nemesis is the most unsparing, is the coldest and falsest of the three. He is, indeed, Hawthorne's only elaborate study of the hypocrite, and it is instructive to see how the light and shade are disposed. Dominated by a narrow, self-seeking purpose, devoted to his own aggrandizement through wealth and worldly power, the Judge allows this to triumph over every humane consideration, and even over the limited loyalty of blood relationship; and he does not scruple to take upon his conscience an inactive falsehood that brings about the ruin of his cousin's life. The human beings closest to him, his wife and his son, go down before the hardness and harshness of his will, the one to an early death, the other to disinheritance and exile. In the end, as if he had not already done Hepzibah and Clifford enough injury, the Judge is willing to destroy what little peace is left to them in order to satisfy a grotesque and abstract greed. Yet all the while, so false is the very principle of his existence, the Judge is an honored and distinguished citizen, marked out by the warm benevolence of his manner, and the munificence of his public charities. At the moment when he is making his cruellest attack upon his cousins, he is about to be nominated by his party for the highest office in the commonwealth. It is at this point, when the unreality of his whole life is most atrociously exaggerated, that the Judge is stricken by the ancestral death blow, sitting alone in the parlor of the house of the seven gables.

Hepzibah and Clifford Pyncheon are pathetic figures where the Judge is an object of satire, but their pathos lies similarly in their radical limitations of spirit. In Hepzibah the old empty pride of family has run into the sands of a dry and sterile gentility, and through long years of seclusion she falls quite out of pace with the ordinary march of existence, losing all the vitality and suppleness that may have been latent in her, until at last she forgets the secret of easy personal intercourse. Her punishment is that when a great human need is forced upon her she has no longer the power to deal with it: all the rigor and angularity of her character come between her and the services she yearns to render to Clifford. "In her grief and wounded pride, Hepzibah had spent her life in divesting herself of friends; she had wilfully cast off the support which God has ordained his creatures to need from one another; and it was now her punishment, that Clifford and herself would fall the easier victims to their kindred enemy." If her life ends in a kind of victory, it is because she has, after all, been moved most strongly by human love, no matter how restricted in its scope. The wreck of a personality that is Clifford Pyncheon is the product of not quite the same forces: it consists partly in the original defectiveness of his character, and partly in the effects of his long and hideous isolation from humanity within the walls of a prison. From the beginning a man of the type that "can always be pricked

more acutely through his sense of the beautiful and har-
monious than through his heart", Clifford loses, in
his prison years, all other capacities, and retains only
the tremulous vestige of this. On no such basis could
his normal status as a man be reëstablished. He continues to the end to be the shadow or the fragment of a
character.

Still another sort of incompleteness is illustrated in
the person of young Holgrave, the daguerreotypist and
the descendant of that Matthew Maule whom Colonel
Pyncheon had so fatefully wronged. In him the stub-
born independence of his line culminates, and takes the
form both of a footloose personal existence, and of a
speculative detachment from the beliefs and purposes
of his countrymen. On the better side, this detachment gives to his thinking an uncommon boldness and
sweep; on the darker side, it threatens whatever warmth
and passion there may be in his make-up.

He was — as Phoebe Pyncheon decides early in their
acquaintance — too calm and cool an observer. Phoebe
felt his eye, often; his heart, seldom or never. He took
a certain kind of interest in Hepzibah and her brother,
and Phoebe herself. He studied them attentively, and
allowed no slightest circumstance of their individualities to escape him. He was ready to do them whatever
good he might; but, after all, he never exactly made
common cause with them, nor gave any reliable evidence that he loved them better, in proportion as he
knew them more. In his relations with them, he
seemed to be in quest of mental food, not heart-suste-
nance. Phoebe could not conceive what interested him
so much in her friends and herself, intellectually, since
he cared nothing for them, or, comparatively, so little,
as objects of human affection.

Here are all the elements of the major Hawthornesque tragedy, but for once Hawthorne does not let them move to their due catastrophe, and Holgrave comes to no such end as Chillingworth or Ethan Brand or Hollingsworth. If there is any parable suggested in his fate, it is contained in his final surrender to the forces of normal humanity represented by the healthy and commonplace little Phoebe; his love for her, however factitious dramatically, is at least an evidence that his intellect has not been in complete control. Perhaps, indeed, it is Phoebe who saves the whole group of them from the dismal destinies that their own characters seem to foreshadow.

Elements of the same sort are at work in "The Blithedale Romance", but here they are redeemed by no such sanative influence. Love, as in the other novels, is present as a force; but it is crossed and complicated by too many destructive forces to have free play, and the drama ends in a catastrophe only less consummate than that of "The Scarlet Letter." Both the foreground and the background are occupied by men and women who have lost their hold on the principle of human integration. So far as the book is a record of the Brook Farm chapter, it is, as we have seen, a criticism of the experiment on just these grounds: Coverdale discovers at Blithedale, as Hawthorne had done at Brook Farm, that a new hostility rather than a new brotherhood was the note of the relation between the communists and society at large, and Zenobia expresses the feeling they both have when she exclaims: "Of all the varieties of mock-life, we have surely blundered into the very emptiest mockery in our effort to establish the one true system." How fit a setting is this community of come-outers for a drama of selfishness and pride!

For it is pride and selfishness, in their obvious and in their obscurer forms, that play such tragic havoc with the lives of Zenobia and Hollingsworth, and make a victim of Priscilla, and render Coverdale's own life so hollow and unprofitable. It is not easy to say which of the first two is, in this respect, the more culpable; but it is upon Hollingsworth that the weight of analytical emphasis falls. With all his innate capacity for tenderness and affection, Hollingsworth's actual relations with humanity are as narrow and hard as if he were a simple egoist; and this because he has allowed himself to be dominated by a fixed and special philanthropic purpose to which he is willing to sacrifice every other duty and every other human demand. The result is that he is more terribly egoistic than sheer selfishness could make him. His very membership in the socialist community is but a perfunctory one, and a means to his own, not the collective, end. "I began to discern," says Coverdale, early in the book, "that he had come among us actuated by no real sympathy with our feelings and hopes, but chiefly because we were estranging ourselves from the world, with which his lonely and exclusive object in life had already put him at odds." Astigmatism of the moral vision is the inevitable penalty for all this; and Coverdale discovers early, what Zenobia discovers in the end, that Hollingsworth must be dealt with rather as a maniac than as a man.

This was a result exceedingly sad to contemplate.
. . . Sad, indeed, but by no means unusual. He had
taught his benevolence to pour its warm tide exclusively through one channel; so that there was nothing
to spare for other great manifestations of love to man,
nor scarcely for the nutriment of individual attach-
ments, unless they could minister, in some way, to the
terrible egotism which he mistook for an angel of God.
. . . He knew absolutely nothing, except in a single
direction, where he had thought so energetically, and
felt to such a depth, that, no doubt, the entire reason
and justice of the universe appeared to be concentrated
thitherward.

Of such selfishness as Hollingsworth's there can be,
in Hawthorne's dramatic scheme, but one result; yet
Hollingsworth is not solely responsible for the series
of defeats with which this story ends. His particular
species of egotism is met and matched by the richer and
warmer but no less fatal pride of which Zenobia is the
prey. Like Hester Prynne, Zenobia is represented as a
woman singularly endowed with personal and intellectual brightnesses: a bold and independent thinker, a
writer, an actress of genuine power, and, in her somewhat operatic way, a great beauty. More even than
Hester Prynne, she should, with such gifts, have accomplished some large purpose, achieved some fine
triumph of human capacity. With Zenobia, again, it
is pride that substitutes defeat for victory. Early in
his acquaintance with her, Coverdale discovers this
radical defect in her personality — a defect of which
he chooses to see a symbol in the exotic flower which
Zenobia habitually wears in her hair. "So brilliant, so
rare, so costly, as it must have been, and yet enduring

only for a day, it was more indicative of the pride and pomp which had a luxuriant growth in Zenobia's character than if a great diamond had sparkled among her hair." For Hawthorne, further, there is a special sense in which Zenobia's pride is an aberration from the human norm: it is the pride of a woman who takes satisfaction not in her peculiar powers as a woman, but in powers with which she makes herself a competitor with men. If a man can err as Ethan Brand did, he seems to say, so much the more terrible is it when a woman, whose intellect is not her finest faculty, lays claim to superiority on intellectual grounds. Once more, then, in Zenobia's tragedy we have the old story of estrangement and its penalty. On the verge of suicide, she herself perceives this, and says as much to Coverdale in that mocking, unhappy colloquy which they hold together in the wood: if he seeks a moral in her story, she says, he can find it in this:

. . . that the whole universe, her own sex and yours, and Providence, or Destiny, to boot, make common cause against the woman who swerves one hair's-breadth out of the beaten track. Yes; and add (for I may as well own it, now) that, with that one hair's-breadth, she goes all astray and never sees the world in its true aspect afterwards.

In the confrontation of Hollingsworth and Zenobia, two various embodiments of selfishness are pitted against each other; and between them they destroy not only their own power and happiness, but the power and happiness of the one other person, Priscilla, who is made to depend wholly on their love. Hollingsworth seeks to exploit Zenobia's passion for him in the interests of his own selfish purpose, and of any such self-surrender Zenobia is incapable. She, on her part, is willing to interpose herself between Hollingsworth and Priscilla, in the full knowledge that their happiness can be insured by their being brought together, and in spite of the obligations of an older sister to Priscilla. In the sequel, Zenobia is completely frustrated; and, as if to make the perfect happiness of the other two impossible, she punishes them, as well as herself, by committing suicide. What little happiness remains to Hollingsworth and Priscilla is the fruit of Hollingsworth's having acted, at last, on a sudden impulse of unselfishness.

Not content with enforcing his theme so irresistibly in the drama limited to these three, Hawthorne fills in the background with other incorporations of the great sin. The peculiarly chill and ungenial light in which the whole narrative unrolls itself may be laid to the account of Miles Coverdale, who observes and records it all, with (for the most part) unsympathetic detachment — "making my prey of people's individualities, as my custom was." For this vice Coverdale too, as he realizes midway through the story, pays a penalty: "that cold tendency, between instinct and intellect, which made me pry with a speculative interest into people's passions and impulses, appeared to have gone far towards unhumanizing my heart." It is for this reason that he feels so sharp a distaste for the presence and the memory of Zenobia's former lover, Westervelt, the man with the glistening false teeth, who can see no good reason for her suicide: "Yet the Professor's tone represented that of worldly society at large, where

a cold skepticism smothers what it can of our spiritual
aspirations, and makes the rest ridiculous. I detested
this kind of man; and all the more because a part of
my own nature showed itself responsive to him."
Westervelt, unlike the others, is redeemed by no single
trait of compassion or warm-heartedness; and Coverdale
suggests that, if Heaven were to deal justly with such
a man, it would annihilate him. Observe, finally,
that, speaking merely in terms of narrative, the whole
story has its roots in a defective personality — in the
personality of Zenobia's and Priscilla's father, "Fauntleroy", whose whole being, in his princely youth,
"seemed to have crystallized itself into an external
splendor, wherewith he glittered in the eyes of the
world, and had no other life than upon this gaudy
surface." His love for his wife, "though it showed
largely, was superficial, like all his other manifestations
and developments." And, after escaping from the consequences of the crime he has committed, after losing
all that has given his life any show of substance, he
virtually loses his identity. "Nor could it have been
otherwise. The man had laid no real touch on any mortal's heart. . . . He seemed to leave no vacancy; a
phenomenon which, like many others that attended his
brief career, went far to prove the illusiveness of his
existence." So we know him in the main action of the
story as Old Moodie, the most insubstantial character
in fiction.

So complete as this, then, is the thematic unity of
Hawthorne's imaginative treatment of human life.
So consistent as this is his reading of human personality. So constantly did he return to the question,

What are the forces that abet, what are the forces that impede, a rich personal development? If Hawthorne had no claim to greatness as an imaginative writer, he could lay claim to high distinction on the sole ground of his absorption in this one essential problem. And how can we deny that his answer is the answer that, in language perhaps not quite the same as Hawthorne's, must finally be given? To some men of our own time it has become clear that the personal life is not to be enriched or amplified by mere self-assertion; that devotion to impersonal or, better, supra-personal ends is the true method of personal development; that romantic individualism is at war with the ideals of individuality. The intellect, it is true, is not being discredited as Hawthorne may seem to have discredited it; but indeed his anti-intellectualism was not of the school against which our generation has reacted. Between Hawthorne and the Transcendentalists there was no real affiliation. Enough should have been said to demonstrate that he distrusted the regnant intellect not because it inhibits, but because (in a sense) it encourages, the free expansion of temperament; because, at any rate, the domination of a man by his intellect, uncorrected by any appeal to the full normal life of humanity, leads him away from the center toward some waste and dismal region such as that to which Ethan Brand is exiled. Since Hawthorne's time the case for ethical and cultural centralization has been fully and variously stated. In an era given over to the centrifugal, he may be said to have anticipated the argument.

"An era given over to the centrifugal!" Is it not with some such phrase that we must finish our answer to the first of the two questions with which this chapter began — the question, namely, whether Hawthorne's work is the literary memorial of a focal chapter in our spiritual history? At this point the question virtually answers itself. What human theme could have been closer than Hawthorne's to the drift of American life in his day — and indeed of American life from the beginning? A movement from the center outwards: that, if a single phrase will do it, sums up what now appears to be the major aspect of our history. Dispersion, not convergence, has been the American process; and this on every level, from the most mechanical to the most vital. What have been our grand national types of personality? The explorer, with his face turned toward the unknown; the adventurous colonist; the Protestant sectarian, determined to worship his own God even in the wilderness; the Baptist, the Quaker, the Methodist; the freebooter and the smuggler; the colonial revolutionary; the pioneer, with his chronic defections; the sectional patriot and the secessionist; the come-outer, the claim-jumper, the Mormon, the founder of communities; the Transcendentalist, preaching the gospel of self-reliance; the philosophic anarchist in his hut in the woods; the economic individualist and the captain of industry; the go-getter, the tax-dodger, the bootlegger. The best and the worst of humanity, not to be confounded in one gesture of repudiation, but united after all in their common distrust of centrality, their noble or their ignoble lawlessness, their domination by spiritual pride. United in their refusal to work together on any but a false basis. United, finally, in paying the penalty for disunion —

in becoming partial and lopsided personalities, men and women of one dimension, august or vulgar cranks. How can we forget the Dimmesdales and Hollingsworths and Pyncheons who have divided our life among them?

We come back to Hawthorne himself. Against this larger background it is plain that his experience was only apparently unique. He failed to participate, we have said; but it would be truer to say that he participated by failing to participate. This is the paradox of his career, and the secret of his otherwise unaccountable significance as a writer. He was at odds with the society about him; but the elements of that society were, in a special sense, at odds with one another. He divorced himself from the great middle current of American enterprise; but that current itself was a current away from the equator. His very estrangement from his fellows was but emblematic of their own estrangement from one another or their collective estrangement from the main body of human experience. In this light, the chamber under the eaves is symbolic not only of the isolation of Thoreau in his hut at Walden, of Melville on the high seas and among the Polynesians, of Poe at Fordham, of Emily Dickinson in her solitary room, of Henry James and Whistler aloof in England; but of the spiritual isolation in which Americans on many levels have preferred to live rather than lend themselves to a general and articulated purpose. In this light, Hawthorne's feeling that he could become "a man among men" merely by measuring coal in Boston Harbor or digging potatoes at Brook Farm is emblematic of the illusion most Americans have suffered from, that they could achieve social integrity by learning to "coöperate", and attain harmony by striving for standardization. He failed in this, as we have seen, but at least his failure was not merely private; at least it had the stateliness of the typical. And in general it is manifest that if, on the surface, Hawthorne shared little in what was important to his countrymen, beneath the surface he shared fully in what was the most important of all.

It is on this ground that his greatness as an imaginative writer most solidly rests. Unwilling at first to accept any easy adjustment to the world about him and dissatisfied later with the unreal adjustment he did make, Hawthorne was forced in his own life to taste the harshest fruits of disunion and isolation; and, unlike many lesser men, he faced, without blinking, the terrible and tragic light that he saw gleaming at the end of that road. He laid no flattering unctions to his soul. He refused to mitigate the tragedy. He did not turn his tales and novels into defenses of his own mistakes. If his imagination had been impoverished on one side, it had been deepened and disciplined on another; and he allowed Ethan Brand and Dimmesdale and Judge Pyncheon and Zenobia to pass to their miserable deaths without one sentimental gesture to save them. They become, in consequence, whatever else they are, the authentic fictional representatives of a vast chapter in cultural history. Their tragedies embody the darker side of American personal life. Sooner or later, if the imagination was to function here at all, that chapter was to be put on record; sooner or later that darker side was to be exposed and dramatized.

"Ethan Brand" and "The Scarlet Letter" are that
exposure, that record; as such, they are permanently
valid as literature.

A further question, however, remains. Valid as
Hawthorne's tales and novels are as the records of a
spiritual era, do they have the highest validity of imaginative fiction? Do they do, for the life they represent,
what the epic, the drama, the novel, at their best, have
always done? At this point, the implied comparison
forces itself upon us. We know what we have a right
to expect of a writer who aims at the fullest truth. We
know that human life can be represented in literature
with the utmost breadth and reach, with infinite animation, color, and clarity, with unlimited fineness and
precision. Men and women in action can be shown, by
an illusion, as they exist in actuality. Not only our
sense of the marvelous, of the picturesque, of the exceptional, but our sense of the generally true, of the commonplace, of the racily normal, can be appealed to with
success. In the greatest dramas, the greatest novels,
the action advances freely and energetically from one
credible incident to another, against a large background of social or national life, in a setting flooded
with hard, clear, natural sunlight, among human
beings who belong in the center of their own worlds.
Human beings, moreover, who exist, so to say, in
their own right; who prove nothing beyond their own
independent vitality; who are remembered not as abstractions or as agitated shadows but as personalities
in high relief. Falling short of this standard, fiction
can hardly be first-rate.

As a writer of fiction, Hawthorne is plainly not of

the first order. His very fidelity to his own experience, his fidelity to the tragic side of American life, kept him from becoming — shall we say it arbitrarily? — a Fielding, a Balzac, a Tolstoi. Nourished by isolation, disciplined by estrangement, his imagination could and did develop, in high degree, a kind of power; it could not and did not develop the true dramatic robustness, the true realistic energy, of the great writer. His stories do not enact themselves in the open, in the midst of things, in the sunlight; his men and women do not achieve the kind of illusory life that would give them, for their own sakes, a permanent sway over the memory. He failed to do what it was always his moral, if never his artistic, intention to do. For there can be little doubt that he wrote, not as he would, but as he found he could. In this connection, nothing could be more revelatory than his own remark, in a letter to Fields about the work of Anthony Trollope:

It is odd enough that my own individual taste is for quite another class of novels than those which I myself am able to write. If I were to meet with such books as mine by another writer, I don't believe I should be able to get through them. Have you ever read the novels of Anthony Trollope? They precisely suit my taste; solid and substantial, written on the strength of beef and through the inspiration of ale, and just as real as if some giant had hewn a great lump out of the earth, and put it under a glass case, with all its inhabitants going about their daily business, and not suspecting that they were made a show of.

It would be peculiarly fatuous to compare Hawthorne with Trollope to Hawthorne's discredit; yet he himself suggested the comparison between his taste and his performance, and this suggests a comparison between his performance and his purpose. Together they are the measure of his relative failure as a writer.

The test of observable reality, as he himself saw, is the important one; but it was a test he was unwilling to invite. He knew, all in all, a great deal, by observation, about the American scene in his day; he could conceivably have made it the setting for his tales; but he preferred to evade the responsibilities this would have laid upon him. In the choice of a landscape for his action, Hawthorne confessed that he aimed at the irresponsible. "His present concern with the socialist community," he declared in the preface to "Blithedale", "is merely to establish a theatre, a little removed from the highway of ordinary travel, where the creatures of his brain may play their phantasmagorical antics, *without exposing them to too close a comparison with the actual events of real lives.* [The italics are not his.]" He was even prepared to defend this with a bad argument.

In the old countries, with which fiction has long been conversant, a certain conventional privilege seems to be awarded to the romancer; his work is not put exactly side by side with nature; and he is allowed a license with regard to every-day probability, in view of the improved effects which he is bound to produce thereby. Among ourselves, on the contrary, there is as yet no such Faery Land, so like the real world, that, in a suitable remoteness, one cannot well tell the difference, but with an atmosphere of strange enchantment, beheld through which the inhabitants have a propriety of their own. This atmosphere is what the American romancer needs. In its absence, the beings of imagination are compelled to show themselves in the same category as actually living mortals; a necessity that generally renders the paint and pasteboard of their composition but too painfully discernible. With the idea of partially obviating this difficulty (*the sense of which has always pressed very heavily upon him*), the author has ventured to make free with his old and affectionately remembered home at Brook Farm, as being certainly the most romantic episode of his own life, — essentially a day-dream, and yet a fact, — and thus offering an available foothold between fiction and reality

A confession so ingenuous is of course disarming: but we need not accept it as the last word. We may reserve our own judgment of a theater "a little removed from the highway of ordinary travel." It will have its advantages, no doubt; but its disadvantages will be radical, and of these we are conscious on the very threshold of "The Blithedale Romance", of "The House of the Seven Gables", — yes, even of "The Scarlet Letter." Recall how the curtain rises in each of them. A kind of prologue, in the first, in which Old Moodie shuffles across the stage; and then the main action begins — a ride from Boston in a snowstorm over whitening country roads to Blithedale, the refuge, the isolated farm. In the second, an ancient, moldering house, with seven fantastic gables, on a little-used side street of a sleepy New England town, where a spinster is just opening a cent-shop. And in the third, the space before the prison door in seventeenth-century Boston, where a crowd of Puritan citizens and magistrates has gathered. How could we be bidden more frankly to a kind of imaginative truancy? How could we be more carefully warned to expect no natural sunlight?

We get, in fact, even less than we might foresee. For

even Blithedale is not the scene of "The Blithedale Romance"; we escape as promptly as possible from the great kitchen and living room of the farmhouse, where the life of the colonists goes forward; we escape from the bean field and the potato patch where the men labor together; we retreat with singular dispatch to Coverdale's sick chamber, and then to the shadowy recesses of the woods lying about the farm; and at length we abandon the farm altogether, and pursue Zenobia, by way of the alleys of the city, to her heavily curtained apartments and the hocus-pocus of the Veiled Lady. Not even the sleepy New England town is the scene of "The Seven Gables." The author "would be glad", said Hawthorne in the preface, "if . . . the book may be read strictly as a Romance, having a great deal more to do with the clouds overhead than with any portion of the actual soil of the County of Essex." And indeed we leave the real Salem behind us effectually when we open the half-door of the cent-shop and find ourselves peering about in the twilight of those low-ceilinged rooms. The rumble of the outside world, it is true, does not wholly die away; occasional visitors from without intrude upon this privacy; but how much of the darkling charm of the book depends precisely on this carefully managed contrast! It enhances, instead of compromising, our sense of delightful remoteness. There is no danger of our taking too seriously the background of Essex County. Or, in "The Scarlet Letter", the background of Puritan Boston. It would be easy, if it were necessary, to argue that no such Boston ever existed in reality. Of course it is not necessary. Even as a setting, the Boston of "The Scarlet

THE WAYSIDE

Courtesy of J. W. Ames

THE OLD MANSE FROM THE WEST

Letter" was not chosen for its own sake, or because the homely facts of its real life were important to the romancer; it was chosen because it was remote in time, and because all that was picturesque and peculiar in its outward aspect could be exploited to aggravate the contrast with nineteenth-century America. Boston is not so much a background as a back-drop; and even as such it recedes into the distance, at many of the crises of the tale, to give way to the lonely marshes along the Charles or the depths of the primeval forest. In all three books the theater is considerably more than "a little" removed from the highway of ordinary travel.

To say all this is only to formulate the obvious, and in saying it we appear to be reproaching the author, egregiously, for executing his conscious purpose. Of the consequences, however, we have a right to judge; and it is one of the unhappy consequences of focalizing a dramatic scene thus distantly that the whole action of the drama becomes a little dreamlike, inelastic, un-gainly, and ill-spaced, like the action of men moving to an unaccustomed music. Hawthorne himself defined the difference involved when he noted, in his English journal, that several scenes of an opera based on "The Scarlet Letter" had recently been performed with success in New York. "I should think," he added searchingly, "it might possibly succeed as an opera, though it would certainly fail as a play." It would not be easy to make operas out of "The Blithedale Romance" and "The House of the Seven Gables": it would be impossible to turn them into plays. How much of what we miss in them is suggested by the word "operatic!" How stiff is the movement of incident and episode; how self-conscious, frequently, are the groupings; how studied are the pantomime and gesture! In "Blithedale", indeed, it is almost as if we were sitting too far from the stage, observing the whole action through glasses, but overhearing only a little of what is said, so seldom are Hollingsworth and Zenobia and Priscilla allowed to confront one another naturally and easily, so constantly is our attention distracted by scenes that serve no good narrative purpose. Zenobia must be brought to the front of the stage in tableau costume to tell the tiresome legend of "The Silvery Veil"; Coverdale's flight to Boston is the clumsiest device for shifting the scene of Zenobia's relations to Priscilla; the masquerade of the colonists in the woods serves no organic function in the drama, and retards its movement at the wrong point; the fate of Hollingsworth and Priscilla is conveyed to us in a final scene as mechanical as a last bow of marionettes. Only the fine narration of Zenobia's suicide saves the book from falling to pieces through its own craziness of structure.

All this is less true of "The Seven Gables" and far less true of "The Scarlet Letter", but these books too suffer in different degrees from a sort of woodenness in their narrative movement. The scene is set elaborately in the former; the lines are drawn and the colors disposed with the last subtlety; all the properties are in exquisite keeping, and the lights are adjusted and readjusted with marvelous atmospheric skill; but the action, in the midst of this impeccable "atmosphere", is halting, torpid, and badly emphasized. Not that there are not wonderful feats of narration; no one can forget the relation of Clifford Pyncheon's uncanny homecoming, or the Judge's nightlong vigil in the parlor of the deserted mansion. But what happens momentously is painfully out of proportion to what is so copiously told. The sudden death of an avaricious hypocrite, the return from prison of a wronged man, a happy love affair between the last of the Pyncheons and the last of the Maules — these are the substance of the drama, but they are too small a portion of the substance of the book. There are plenty of "scenes", to be sure: but the curtain rises and falls upon them too abruptly, and the principle of coherence among them is less dramatic than pictorial. The story of the cent-shop takes up three deliberate chapters; a Sunday afternoon in the Pyncheon garden is described in leisurely detail; young Holgrave, like Zenobia, holds up the course of the narrative with a tale of his own, which just falls short of the jejune; the Italian boy with the barrel organ is an agent of tedium, not of speed; and, at a luckless moment for the narrator, Hepzibah and Clifford escape from the old mansion to set off on a railway journey that comes close to undoing the book. All this is delightful in its way — it is even beguiling — but it is not dramatically arresting; and "The Seven Gables" is more impressive than "Blithedale" only because the setting itself is more artfully managed, and because the story, such as it is, is better adjusted to it.

Compared with either of these, "The Scarlet Letter" is a triumph of swiftness, simplification, and emphasis; unlike either of them, in short, it is a great book. Here there is none of that apparent uncertainty of purpose that debilitates "Blithedale", or that sluggishness of movement that makes "The Seven Gables" a sustained anticlimax. Nothing could be clearer than the dramatic purpose of "The Scarlet Letter", or better regulated than its progress. Almost literally, nothing is told that does not need to be told; nothing essential, as in "Blithedale", is left out. In its singleness of direction, in its integrity of effect, "The Scarlet Letter" has the perfection of the best of Hawthorne's short tales. But we have spoken of the woodenness of its narrative movement; and, with all possible qualifications of that term, we must recur to it. The parallel with the short tales illuminates the point: "The Scarlet Letter" is an expansion, an apotheosis, of "The Gray Champion", of "Young Goodman Brown", of "Rappaccini's Daughter", of "Ethan Brand"; and, as in all these, its action is seen at a certain distance, or through some insubstantial veil, enlarged, simplified, ennobled, and ever so slightly stiffened, so that we miss the easy gestures, the impulsive motions, of real life. Stateliness is distinctly the effect of those groupings about the pillory, of that conference in the Governor's Hall, and even of those intimate scenes between husband and wife, or between lover and mistress, or between mother and child. The book gains, in just this way, its special character of elevation without coldness; but elevation is not the prime virtue of great fiction, and "The Scarlet Letter" has too much the quality of a pageant — or of an opera ! — to be a novel of the very first order.

This retardation — or, if you will, this ennobling — of the action is, we have said, one of the consequences of establishing a theater a little removed from the highway of ordinary travel. As Hawthorne himself pointed out, there is another and more important consequence, which is that in this way the beings of the romancer's imagination are not compelled "to show themselves in the same category as actually living mortals." In his own view, or at least in his own words, this is a clear advantage. From a more critical angle, it is an advantage only to an author who, wishing to deal somehow with the materials of experience, to make some appeal to our interest in character and in human conflicts, is unwilling to expose himself to the tests imposed by our awakened sense of human truth. Such a writer would have his cake and eat it too. He would manipulate moral problems, but not in the setting in which alone they are momentous. He would represent character in action, but character constructed irresponsibly and developed in the most arbitrary way. He would combine the materials of tragedy or comedy with the methods of the masque. As readers, therefore, we are encouraged to anticipate something we do not receive. We ask for the illusion of personality, and are given a synthetic substitute for it, or, at the best, a provisional illusion that does not survive reflection. The chief source of power in fiction is, as a result, dried up; and we must look elsewhere for the memorable. This is the final count in the indictment of Hawthorne as a prose romancer.

It will not do, of course, to brush aside with a single gesture all the men and women in his tales and novels as puppets equally mechanical. A few of them are the products of his most authentic creativity, and approximate the living truth of all but the greatest characters in fiction. Hester Prynne, by a miracle of sympathy, triumphs over her merely representative rôle, her function as a moral symbol, and emerges into relief as a woman who can be conceived, not only as an Adulteress, but as a mother, or even as a friend. We can believe in Arthur Dimmesdale, because we do actually see him from several sides, and can identify ourselves with him at more than one moment. With a stroke or two more at one point, a stroke or two less at another, Clifford Pyncheon, tenuous as his very existence is, would come to life with the subtlest animation. But the truth of even these personages is imperfect, and if we go beyond them, what do we encounter? A series of Feathertops, more or less cunningly disguised, who do not have Feathertop's excuse for their basic flimsiness. It would be too much to expect that Ernest or Ethan Brand, figures in brief allegories, should be recognizable as human beings; and in fact they are the merest ciphers; but surely we might expect that Chillingworth or Zenobia, Judge Pyncheon or Hollingsworth, Priscilla or Holgrave, with the scope of a novel to move in, would survive in our memories as credible men and women. Instead, they survive as monsters or as shadows, as optical illusions, as flutterings of misty light or foci of sultry heat. We remember the themes they illustrate; it would be an exaggeration to say that we remember them.

What is amazing, perhaps, is that they have as much illusiveness as they do; for they are the agents of a fictional intention that it would be hard to reconcile with real objectivity. There is no reason, of course, why a plot should not exemplify a general human truth; but to begin with that truth too sharply defined is not to encourage spontaneity in the actors. Hawthorne trusted in his observation of life itself too little: he leaned upon his deductions from it too much. He may have been right in supposing that the inheritance of guilty pride is a force for destruction and death; but in "The Seven Gables" this theme is not enacted by the characters, it is imposed upon them. No wonder their action is constrained, and their language stilted. No wonder that the Judge reminds us of some Avarice in an old morality, or that Phoebe, called in as the first Pyncheon to learn humility, is so effectively self-effacing — and so banal. It is the same in "The Blithedale Romance": Hollingsworth and Zenobia are not a selfish man and a selfish woman, but embodied Selfishness in two forms; they are, in the strictest sense, opposing forces, not opponents; and their real life as characters is extraordinarily abstract. Priscilla's rôle requires her to be crushed between them, and the feat is not a difficult one; there is, as the author says, "a lack of human substance in her", and we believe him when he adds: "it seemed as if, were she to stand up in a sunbeam, it would pass right through her figure, and trace out the cracked and dusty window-panes upon the naked floor." In "The Scarlet Letter" the theme is still more implacable, and its effect on Chillingworth and little Pearl is to transform them, the one into a hideous, the other into an exquisite, symbol. Hester and Dimmesdale, as we have said, escape with their lives — doubtless because, in Hawthorne's imagination, the theme was narrowly identified with them from the beginning; but even these two have elements of formalism in their make-up that deprive them of the utmost vitality. Even in what they do we feel that there is more coercion than volition.

Coercion, in fact, in more senses than one, is at work throughout these books to inhibit the free play of individual will. It is not only that the themes of Hawthorne's romances are too plainly envisaged at the outset to allow scope for character to develop: it is also that those schemes are defined too closely in terms of a repressive fatalism. We have seen how true they are when applied with a certain freedom to the facts of American experience, but the force of that application does not depend on our premising a dark and melodramatic determinism. The thoughtful determinist knows at what point the will becomes virtually free, and he is not tempted to explain all conduct by reference to Destiny or Fate. It is eloquent of Hawthorne's own surrender to the movement outward that he preferred to think of personal tragedy as the product of mysterious agencies outside the personality. Hence we hear far too much in these stories of inescapable influences and irreversible destinies. The characters assume far too complacently that they are the prey of forces against which it is useless for them to struggle, and this is the chief secret of their inanity. Zenobia is typical of them when — in answer to Coverdale's question, "Did you come away of your own free will?" — she replies: "I am blown about like a leaf. . . . I never have any free will." Hollingsworth is typical of them when, admitting that his most marked trait is an inflexible severity of purpose, he declares, as with a helpless detachment: "Mortal man has no right to be so inflexible as it is *my nature and necessity* to be." Hepzibah is typical in regarding as "an hereditary trait" her inapplicability to any useful purpose. Against such a background, we may be surprised, again, that these men and women have so much reality as they do.

True as Hawthorne's "thesis" is, when stated carefully in abstract terms, it is consistent, as he applies it, with a conception of character that is singularly false. According to this conception, freedom of choice exists, but on so narrow a basis that, once exercised in the wrong direction, it is forever resigned. We have seen how Zenobia attributes her downfall to her having swerved a hair's-breadth out of the beaten track; and, even more notably, we might recall Hawthorne's own statement of the "moral" of "The Seven Gables": "the truth, namely, that the wrongdoing of one generation lives into the successive ones, and, divesting itself of every temporary advantage, becomes a pure and uncontrollable mischief." Here the wrong choice is made, not only once by an individual, but once by a long-lived family. And on this preter-Calvinist theory the whole of "The Scarlet Letter" is based. Roger Chillingworth phrases it most fully in that interview with Hester when the woman begs him to undo the worst of the ill that has been done by exercising his privilege of pardoning them.

"Peace, Hester, peace!" replied the old man, with gloomy sternness. "It is not granted me to pardon. I have no such power as thou tellest me of. My old faith, long forgotten, comes back to me, and explains all that we do, and all we suffer. By thy first step awry thou didst plant the germ of evil; but since that moment, it has all been a dark necessity. Ye that have wronged me are not sinful, save in a kind of typical illusion; neither am I fiend-like, who have snatched a fiend's office from his hands. It is our fate. Let the black flower blossom as it may! Now go thy ways, and deal as thou wilt with yonder man."

In such a speech, this fatalism takes on a solemn grandeur; and, in "The Scarlet Letter" at least, it is exemplified so austerely and with a poetic energy so unmistakable that we can scarcely lament its abstract falsity. But false, on reflection, we know it to be; and we are prepared to find it elsewhere devitalizing character and drama. So blossoms the black flower of the imagination.

More might be said, much more, about Hawthorne's achievement as a writer; a dozen other aspects of his fiction are worth attention: but enough should have been said to define his unique status in our literature. We must not overrate, we are not likely to underrate, what he did. He is one of those writers who have said too much, who have had too serious an insight into human experience, ever to be ignored or forgotten. In the nineteenth century he was one of the half-dozen American writers to come to grips with the essential difficulties of the good life; and, his native endowment being that of a genius, he reported upon his adventures in a series of tales and novels that are stamped all over with imaginative significance. To compare him with Poe, for example, is to compare a typical major writer with a typical minor one, to compare high seriousness with intrinsic frivolity. Poe's work, for all its tortured and distressing beauty, remains the natural expression of a merely abnormal temperament, a merely abnormal experience; Hawthorne's, with all its limitations, is plainly the product of a normal or super-normal temperament, and of a generally relevant experience. "The Scarlet Letter" is one of those books which, like "The Pilgrim's Progress" — to take a convenient parallel —

lays claim to our attention on philosophic and impersonal grounds. It allegorizes a conflict and a tragic triumph which are continually fought and won.

In saying so much, however, we have hinted at the limits we must set to Hawthorne's greatness. Serious as "The Pilgrim's Progress" is, it is less serious than "Hamlet" or "Tom Jones"; and this because it simplifies the drama of human struggle at the expense of dramatic truth, and is essentially false to the facts of personality. In other words, it is an allegory, and an allegory at its best, and truest, makes to the imagination only a secondary appeal. It would be idle to push this analogy very far; but, rather for illustration than for argument, and with a dozen reservations, we may say that the world into which Hawthorne's fiction takes us is like the world of "The Faerie Queene", or of "The Pilgrim's Progress", or of "Rasselas", not like the world of the great dramatists and novelists. We move in it among embodiments of our most momentous passions, our most urgent desires, our most vital conflicts; and these we cannot fail to recognize for what they are. But we miss "the one touch that would be truly valuable" — the touch of illusive personality — and, missing it, we must qualify our assent.

CHAPTER SEVEN

"Two Hundred and Eighteen Years"

"My ancestor left England in 1635. I return in 1853. I sometimes feel as if I myself had been absent these two hundred and eighteen years — leaving England just emerging from the feudal system, and finding it on the verge of republicanism. It brings the two far-separated points of time very closely together, to view the matter thus." — "English Note-books", October 9, 1854.

ALL but a few biographies, like all but a few lives, decline at the end to an anticlimax; and we have reached the point in our own narrative beyond which the sense of accumulating significance relaxes. It is not only that Hawthorne as a man, at the date of his departure for England, was to pass through no more experiences of a deeply modifying power; it is also that Hawthorne as a writer had already his important work behind him. What might have to be said on this score if "Blithedale" had been followed at a short interval by that next projected romance, it is vain to speculate: we know only that Hawthorne was conscious, at that point, of no impediment to his productiveness, and that, when he did return to imaginative writing, it was after five or six years of official service and foreign life had aged him in proportion, and weakened (as we shall see) his hold on immediate reality. As a developing writer Hawthorne's career virtually came to an end at West Newton; as a person, during the last decade of his life, he was rather to show the effects of all that had gone before, than to grow in response to new influences. Yet without those last ten years we should not perceive the whole relevance of Hawthorne's career, and it is lucky for his biographers, if it was not entirely for him, that President Pierce, with other considerations in mind, appointed him to the consulship at Liverpool.

It was a beautifully symbolic voyage on which the steamship *Niagara* carried the new consul across the untroubled Atlantic in July, 1853. On a different level, those earlier excursions into the midst of things — at Long Wharf in Boston, at Brook Farm, at the Salem Customhouse — were now to be, for the last time, repeated. In Boston, at West Roxbury, at Salem, it was Hawthorne the recluse, Hawthorne the self-alienated, plunging, or at least wading, into the central stream of normal American enterprise to test his powers of participation; in England and Italy, it was Hawthorne the American — Hawthorne whom we may, if we choose, regard simply as such — returning to the historical center with reference to which, even at that time, America was on the circumference. The new excursion was of course unique; there was now no question of a real return, a real participation. It is only by an easy metaphor that we may draw the parallel, but on those grounds it is real enough. In England and Italy, Hawthorne was brought face to face with the main body of European experience: at this late date, what was he to make of it? Well, as before, he was to vacillate between two attitudes, between readiness and reluctance, between imaginative participation and imaginative withdrawal, between denial and assent.

From the hour when the *Niagara* steamed up the channel of the Mersey to the hour when its sister ship
(whose name is not preserved) steamed out of the same
waters, this subtle conflict went on in Hawthorne's
breast. On the one hand, his delightful sense — in
England and, for other reasons, in Italy — of being at
length "at home", of having retraced the ancestral
footsteps, of returning somewhere after a long absence;
on the other hand, his distressing awareness of having
ceased to "belong", of having lost irretrievably his
hold on the principle of solidarity, of being at the best
a welcome alien. To the chronic contradictions of his
whole foreign residence, this paradox is the sufficient
key. It explains his love of England and his scorn or
his distrust of Englishmen, his nostalgia for Rome
and his sense of relief on leaving it. And it explains
— this slight, incessant contest — his periods of dull
fatigue and depression, and, at the end, his growing
melancholia. Not with impunity was such a warfare
to be carried on for seven years.

So far as his consulship itself was concerned, there
was no implicit conflict. Hawthorne, as we know,
had long since abandoned the illusion that in official
service he could find a significant employment for his
powers. From the beginning he found his consular
routine irksome, his duties onerous; but this he had
expected, and, though he was rebellious, he was hardly
disappointed. Indeed, the dingy little room in Washington Chambers, not more than five paces from end to end
— with the engraving of the Tennessee State House on
the wall, and the bust of General Jackson on the bookcase, and the octavo volumes of American Statutes *in*

the bookcase — could scarcely have seemed anything
but a prison to a man so restless as Hawthorne had
come to be. With the gray Liverpool fog curtaining
the two windowpanes, and the lamplight flickering
drearily inside, what a dismal cell it must have been!
And how tediously its dismalness must have been
enhanced, for Hawthorne, by the round of petty or vex-
atious duties that filled his day! Deputations of his
fellow citizens coming needlessly to pay their respects
to a terribly bored representative; harmless lunatics
waiting upon him for sympathy or assistance; penniless
vagabonds — genuine or counterfeit fellow countrymen
— besieging him for financial aid; sailors with battered
visages or their arms in slings, complaining of mistreatment by their officers, or ship captains making repre-
sentations against their men — these, with occasional
exceptions, were his regular visitors. No wonder
Hawthorne, never too resilient at the best, groaned
inwardly as he walked up the two flights of steps to
his office.

For the last week or two — he wrote in his journal,
in the summer of 1855 — I have passed my time between
the hotel and the Consulate, and a weary life it is, and
one that leaves little of profit behind it. I am sick to
death of my office, — brutal captains and brutal sailors;
continual complaints of mutual wrong, which I have
no power to set right, and which, indeed, seem to have
no right on either side; calls of idleness or ceremony
from my travelling countrymen, who seldom know
what they are in search of at the commencement of
their tour, and never have attained any desirable end
at the close of it; beggars, cheats, simpletons, unfor-
tunates, so mixed up that it is impossible to distinguish

one from another, and so, in self-defense, the Consul distrusts them all. I see many specimens of mankind, but come to the conclusion that there is but little variety among them, after all.

It had taken him but a few weeks to grow weary of his duties at Long Wharf and to lose patience with the facts of life at Brook Farm; and he was not long in giving vent to his distaste for an office to which he had bound himself for four years.

I suppose — he wrote to Ticknor early in his first December in Liverpool — I suppose Baring Brothers have already advised you of my depositing £300 to your credit. If it had been £3000, I would kick the office to the devil, and come home again. I am sick of it, and long for my hillside; and — what I thought I should never long for — my pen!

From the beginning of his ventures into officialdom, Hawthorne had been singularly frank and realistic in his attitude toward the money involved; but he had never been more simply and eagerly mercenary than in Liverpool. "Invest — invest — invest!" he exhorted Ticknor early in 1854. "I am in a hurry to be rich enough to get away from this dismal and forlorn hole."

During the following spring, a bill for the remodelling of the diplomatic and consular service was introduced into Congress; and Hawthorne, foreseeing the drastic curtailment of his income, berated, in his letters to Ticknor and Bridge, the authors of the offensive bill — "those jackasses in Washington" — and even the American system itself. "Our Government grows more intolerable every day," he complained. "I wish it might be changed to a monarchy." Every letter to

Ticknor — not unnaturally, since he was Hawthorne's financial agent — was filled with the nicest financial calculations; and all the while Hawthorne was crying out against the tediousness of his position itself. "I could not possibly live in this infernal hole," he protested, "if it were not for the pleasure of sending you a thousand or two of dollars"; and, in the fall of 1856, referring to his chances under Buchanan, "nothing earthly," he wrote, "would induce me to stay in office another winter after the coming one." When, finally, in the summer of 1857, he was able to send in his resignation to the new president, it was with a sense of release that he had never felt so joyfully before, even at the end of his Boston service. "Thank Heaven, I am a sovereign again, and no longer a servant," he wrote in his journal, apropos of a visit to the American Minister in London; and to Ticknor, a little earlier, he wrote, with mingled weariness and anticipation:

In good earnest the cares and toils of office have given me a long shove onward towards old age during these past four years. Italy may perhaps revive me a little. . . . I wish I were a little richer; and I doubt whether you would ever advertise another book by the "author of the Scarlet Letter." Still, I thank God for bringing me through this consular business so well.

Not that the four years in England, or even those parts of his term when he was acting purely as a consul, were a dead loss to Hawthorne the observer of men. At Long Wharf and on Derby Street in Salem, he had never wholly ceased to take an interest in the life about him; and in Liverpool his tiresome responsibilities were occasionally relieved by incidents that smacked too richly

of human frailty or human suffering not to engage his
interest. So deeply ironic had his view of human character become that he could scarcely conceal the satisfaction he took in the spectacle of a highly reputable
American clergyman turning up at the consulate, in a
damaged condition, after a spree in the brothels of
Liverpool; or in that of an American woman protesting
that her son, committed to an English asylum, was
"the best, purest, most innocent child that ever was",
when Hawthorne knew "that the young gentleman
had been in company with a lady, two nights, at a
hotel here, and, from the items of his bill, had had a
particularly jolly time." Now and then his duties
brought him closer to the brutality and dull grime of
existence than he had ever been before. His journal
takes on a new note of the Dickensian: "In the afternoon, at three o'clock, I attended the funeral of Captain
Auld"; "I was sent for to the police court the other
morning, in the case of an American sailor accused of
robbing a shipmate at sea"; "at the police court on
Saturday, I attended the case of the second mate and
four seamen of the John and Albert, for assaulting,
beating, and stabbing the chief mate"; "I went yesterday to a hospital to take the oath of a mate to a protest." Dingy law courts, asylums, hospitals, the
coroner's office, cheap undertaking parlors, became
familiar places to him; and manifestly he preferred them
to the little room in Washington Chambers: interviews
with dying sailors might be trying, but they were interludes of tough reality in what seemed to him the
phantasmal march of meaningless functions at the
consulate.

Meanwhile, however, the four and a half years in England were not being wholly absorbed in those functions. Of mere official service Hawthorne had seen enough already, and, except for the incidental adventures we have spoken of, he was to learn nothing essentially novel from his work as a consul. What was now really unique in his situation was of course, as we have said, that he found himself for the first time on foreign soil, physically as well as psychically remote from his countrymen, dropped down in the midst of another way of life to which, as an individual, he was not born, and to which he could never properly belong. Was he to find it more, or less, congenial than his own country? On one side, certainly, more. To the end of the seven years, he was to look back at America with the feelings of a man who has escaped at last from something he has always been wearied by. "It sickens me to look back to America," he confessed to Bridge early in 1854. "I am sick to death of the continual fuss and tumult and excitement and bad blood which we keep up about political topics. If it were not for my children I should probably never return, but — after quitting office — should go to Italy, and live and die there." Two more years in England served only to confirm this mood: "I must confess," he said in a letter to Ticknor, "I am in no hurry to return to America. To say the truth, it looks like an infernally disagreeable country, from this side of the water." And from Italy, after the same lapse of time, he could write: "I wish I were a little more patriotic; but, to confess the truth, I had rather be a sojourner in any other country than return to my own. The United States are fit for many excellent purposes, but they are certainly not fit to live in." So easy as this might it appear to be for a man to tear up his roots from his native soil.

Nor was it merely a negative aversion to America that kept Hawthorne, on the whole, so contented in Europe for seven years. Positively, too, he persuaded himself that England or even Italy could be a home for him in his old age.

If I were in your position — he wrote to Longfellow — I think I should make my home on this side of the water — though always with an indefinite and never-to-be-executed intention to go back and die in my native land. America is a good land for young people, but not for those who are past their prime. It is impossible to grow old comfortably there, for nothing keeps you in countenance. . . . Everything is so delightfully sluggish here! . . . A man of individuality and refinement can certainly live far more comfortably here — provided he has the means to live at all — than in New England.

In the same mood he declared to Ticknor: "I wish we could annex this island to the Union, and that I could have an estate here in Warwickshire"; and from London he wrote: "I think I never should be weary of London, and it will cost me many pangs to quit it finally, without a prospect of returning. It is singular, that I feel more at home and familiar there than even in Boston, or in old Salem itself." Again, toward the end of his consular term: "I shall leave the consulate joyfully, but England with some regret; for it is a good country to live in, and if I were rich enough, I doubt whether I should ever leave it for a permanent residence elsewhere."

"Our old home!" — that was the light in which, to the descendant of William Hathorne, the England even of the nineteenth century, in its physical aspects, presented itself. Whatever he might think or say of Englishmen as individuals, of the active life of contemporary England — of its institutions, its manners, its interests — England itself, England the island, so to say, England the garden, drew him to itself gently, magnetically, irresistibly. It was not as a stranger in an unfriendly country, but as an exile who had returned home, that Hawthorne, in the early weeks of his Liverpool life, set forth on walks into the rural vicinity of the city, to Bebbington, to Eastham, to Tranmere. Different as every object of sight might be from anything in New England — softer as the English oaks might be than the elms of Salem, greener as the hedges might be than the stone walls of Massachusetts — all were as familiar to his eyes as if he were looking upon them, not for the first, but for the thousandth time. The sense of being on his own ground, among these lawns and parks, these crowded churchyards, these thatched and stone-built farmhouses, was with him from the beginning, and never left him. Eastham, for example, "is the finest old English village I have seen, with many antique houses, and with altogether a rural and picturesque aspect, unlike anything in America, and yet possessing a familiar look as if it were something I had dreamed of." At Newby Bridge, in the Lake Country, after a visit to Furness Abbey, it was the same: "We reached home somewhere about eight o'clock, — home I see I have called it; and it seems as homelike a spot as any we have found in England, —

the old inn, close by the bridge, beside the clear river, pleasantly overshadowed by trees. It is entirely English, and like nothing that one sees in America; and yet I feel as if I might have lived here a long while ago, and had now come back because I retained pleasant recollections of it."

In "Our Old Home", at the end of a chapter on Leamington and Warwickshire, there is a passage that memorializes this whole aspect of Hawthorne's English experience.

Almost always — he says — in visiting such scenes as I have been attempting to describe, I had a singular sense of having been there before. The ivy-grown English churches (even that of Bebbington, the first that I beheld) were quite as familiar to me, when fresh from home, as the old wooden meeting-house in Salem, which used, on wintry Sabbaths, to be the frozen purgatory of my childhood. This was a bewildering, yet very delightful emotion fluttering about me like a faint summer wind, and filling my imagination with a thousand half-remembrances, which looked as vivid as sunshine, at a side-glance, but faded quite away whenever I attempted to grasp and define them. Of course, the explanation of the mystery was, that history, poetry, and fiction, books of travel, and the talk of tourists, had given me pretty accurate preconceptions of the common objects of English scenery, and these, being long ago vivified by a youthful fancy, had insensibly taken their places among the images of things actually seen. Yet the illusion was often so powerful, that I almost doubted whether such airy remembrances might not be a sort of innate idea, the print of a recollection in some ancestral mind, transmitted, with fainter and fainter impress through several descents, to my own. I felt, indeed, like the stalwart progenitor in person, returning to the hereditary haunts after more than two hundred years, and finding the church, the hall, the farm-house, the cottage, hardly changed during his long absence, — the same shady by-paths and hedge-lanes, the same veiled sky, and green lustre of the lawns and fields, — while his own affinities for these things, a little obscured by disuse, were reviving at every step.

Only some home-coming emotion such as this, only some more than literary piety, could have fortified Hawthorne through four years spent (in the literal sense) so homelessly, so restlessly, and — in some aspects — so disconsolately; could have given him the strength for those incessant and heroic tours into every corner of the island, burdened with the responsibility of small children, and repeatedly fatigued almost to the breaking point with the labors of mere sight-seeing. Sustained at the beginning by curiosity, he continued to the end to be rewarded by something more substantial. "I must go again and again and again to Chester," he resolved in October, 1853, "for I suppose there is not a more curious place in the world." Three years later, making a trip thither with Herman Melville, he could still say: "I love to take every opportunity of going to Chester" — and he added, significantly — "it being the one only place, within easy reach of Liverpool, which possesses any old English interest." For it was, as we should expect, the England of which the musty Chester rows were emblematic, that really called to him with this powerful authority. Not the collieries of Nottingham, not the factories of Manchester, not even the parliamentary benches of Westminster; but Furness

Abbey, Hampton Court, Leicester's Hospital in War-
wick, Smithell's Hall, the Close at Peterborough, the
gardens of New College, and the cathedrals of England,
from Durham to Saint Paul's — these were the things
he sought out eagerly, and lingered over as if he would
never willingly leave them. Wherever the past had
laid its hand most unmistakably, and loitered on with
quiet insistence into the present, Hawthorne was most
delighted, and from such places he was most reluctant
to go away.

In the Close at Salisbury, surrounded by ancient epis-
copal residences, he felt that he had never been on any
spot more fit for a permanent home. At Gloucester, he
was fascinated by the cloisters: "even at this day, if
I were a canon of Gloucester, I would put that dim
ambulatory to a good use." "I should like well," he
elsewhere confessed, recording his impressions of the
ancient garden of Leicester's Hospital — where he
found the twelve aged beneficiaries of the Earl of
Leicester hobbling about in their stately, old-world
seclusion — "I should like well to sit down among
them there, and find out what is really the bitter and
the sweet of such a sort of life." And at Peterborough,
more than anywhere else, he felt that life could here
be led, from one point of view, almost ideally.

Of all the lovely churchyards that I ever beheld,
that of Peterborough Cathedral seems to me the most
delightful; so quiet it is, so solemnly and nobly cheerful, so verdant, so sweetly shadowed, and so presided
over by the noble minster, and surrounded by quiet,
ancient, and comely habitations of Christian men. The
most delightful place, the most enviable as a residence,
in all this world, seemed to me that of the Bishop's

secretary, standing in the rear of the cathedral, and bordering on the churchyard; so that you seem to pass through hallowed precincts in order to come at it, and find it a sort of Paradise, the holier and sweeter for the dead men that sleep so near. We looked through the gateway into the lawn, which really looked as if it hardly belonged to this world, so bright and soft the sunshine was, so fresh the grass, so lovely the trees, so trimmed and refined, and softened down, was the whole nature of the spot; and so shut in and guarded from all intrusion. It is in vain to write about; nowhere but in England can there be such a spot, nor anywhere but in the close of Peterborough Cathedral.

Such were Hawthorne's emotions on the historic ground from which, in a sense, he had all his life been an exile. These colleges, these cloisters, these abbeys, were not mere spectacles for the sight-seer; not, to an American, mere curiosities, in the same order as Buddhist temples or Chinese palaces; they were the visible dwelling places of a continuous human experience with which he himself had deep affiliations, and from which he could not really regard himself as an alien. If he had not made these pilgrimages, we should never have known quite how acute, there in Concord and Salem, was his nostalgia for the old home. As it is, to give our view of him the true pictorial depth, we must envisage Hawthorne, not only on the rocky stretches of the North Shore, nor along the reaches of the Concord River, nor in the alleys and byways of Boston, but among the ragged arches of Melrose Abbey, or before the monuments in Saint Paul's, or on the banks of the "stripling Thames" near Nuneham Courtney. "What a wonderful land!" he exclaimed, with a gush of strong feeling, on returning from one of these expeditions. "It is our forefathers' land; our land, for I will not give up such a precious inheritance."

So much for that side of the picture. There was, as there was bound to be, another and a more unpleasant side. For, however emphatically he might claim England as "our land", however boldly he might refuse to give it up, neither Hawthorne nor any American could have forgotten for a single moment, or on a single spot of British ground, that he was here incorrigibly a foreigner. That sense of being somehow at home was indeed what he called it, — an illusion; what was real, if far less striking, was the sense of being away from home, and this, in his soberer moods, was vividly present to him. "As I sat in this English house," he recorded, when early in their first fall they had found temporary quarters, "with the chill, rainy English twilight brooding over the lawn, and a coal-fire to keep me comfortable on the first evening of September, . . . I felt that I should never be quite at home here." No, for all his hereditary yearnings, Hawthorne was not and could not be an Englishman; among the material symbols of English life, among the movements of English society, he was flatly and finally an outsider. But an outsider, of course, with a difference; and the result of that unhappy paradox was that he went about, from the beginning, with the most conspicuous of chips set defiantly upon his shoulder, to be jostled or shaken off at the slightest contact. To speak without metaphor, Hawthorne indemnified himself for his exclusion from the real life of England by adopting an exaggerated and truculent nationalism, — a nationalism

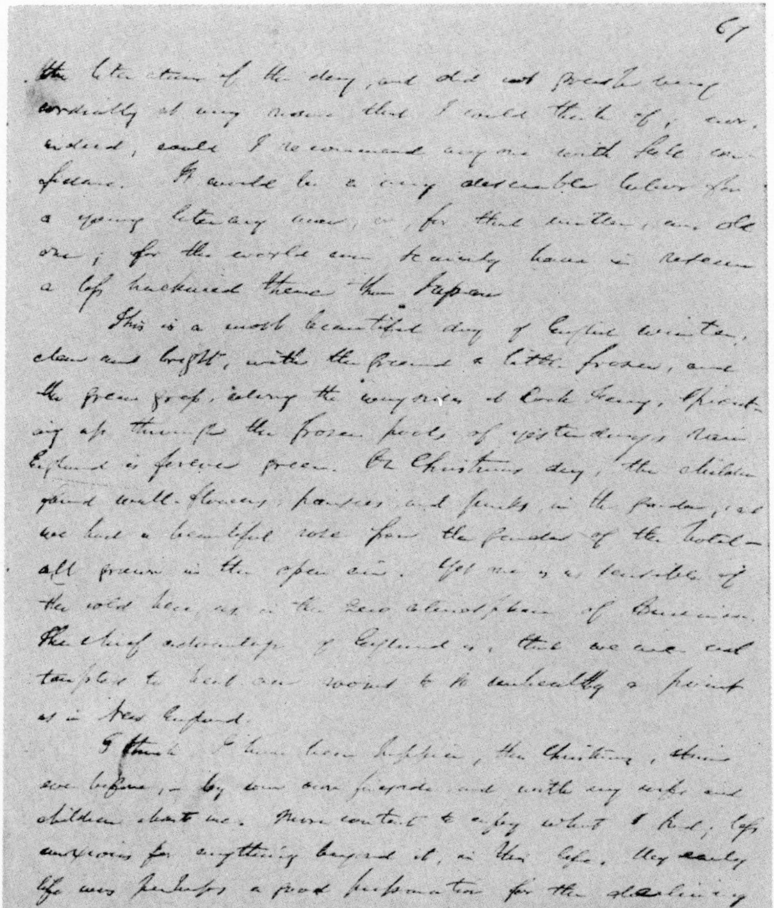
67

the literature of the day, and did not speak very cordially of any name that I could think of; nor, indeed, could I recommend anyone with full confidence. It would be a very desirable labor for a young literary man, or, for that matter, an old one; for the world can scarcely have a less hackneyed theme than Japan.

This is a most beautiful day of English winter, clear and bright, with the ground a little frozen, and the green grass, along the wayside at Rock Ferry, sprouting up through the frozen pools of yesterday's rain. England is forever green. On Christmas day, the children found wall-flowers, pansies and pinks in the garden; and we had a beautiful rose from the garden of the hotel — all grown in the open air. Yet one is sensible of the cold here, as in the zero atmosphere of America. The chief advantage of England is, that we are not tempted to heat our rooms to so unhealthy a point as in New England.

I think I have been happier, this Christmas, than ever before, — by our own fireside and with my wife and children about me. More content to enjoy what I had; less anxious for anything beyond it, in this life. My early life was perhaps a good preparation for the declining

Courtesy of the Pierpont Morgan Library

A PAGE FROM HAWTHORNE'S ENGLISH JOURNAL
DECEMBER 28, 1854

most incongruous with his other expressions about America, but quite congruous with the habitual asperity of his tone in speaking of English institutions and Englishmen.

On what other ground, if we remember the aversion with which he looked back to America, can we explain those outbursts of almost passionate patriotism that alternated with it? For that sentiment in its simpler forms Hawthorne had, by temperament, but the slightest capacity; for patriotism as a compensation, his capacities were evidently great. "After all the slanders against Americans," he wrote to Ticknor, "there is no people worthy even to take the second place behind us, for liberality of idea and practice. The more I see of the rest of the world, the better I think of my own country (not that I like it very enthusiastically, either)." In August, 1855, he was expressing a hope that "two years on the Continent will perhaps revive my patriotism." Yet learning, a year later, of Ticknor's distress over the Kansas troubles, he was reassuring him like the veriest jingo: "We shall grow and flourish in spite of the devil. Affairs do not look so very bad, at this distance, whatever they may seem to you who are in the midst of the confusion. For my part, I keep a steadfast faith in the destinies of my own country, and will not be staggered, whatever happens." Beyond a doubt, we may regard as Hawthorne's own the feelings that, in "Dr. Grimshawe's Secret", he ascribed to his hero, Redcliffe: "I am not fit to be here, — I, so strongly susceptible of a newer, more stirring life than these men lead; I, who feel that, whatever the thought and cultivation of England may be, my own countrymen have

gone forward a long, long march beyond them, not intellectually, but in a way that gives them a further
start."

At Mrs. Blodgett's boarding house, where he lodged
during his wife's absence in London, and where all the
other boarders, mostly shipmasters, were Americans,
Hawthorne managed to be confirmed in this feeling.
"Really, I do not know any other place in England,"
he protested, "where a man can be made so sensible
that he lives in a progressive world, as here in Mrs.
Blodgett's boarding house."   On returning to London:
"My mind had been considerably enlivened, and my
sense of American superiority renewed, by intercourse
with these people."   As he observed Englishmen, in the
mass or as individuals, the challenging contrast was
never far from his thoughts.   During his first year at
the consulate, he was sought out by the old poet,
Barry Cornwall — of whom, on the whole, his impressions were agreeable; but he could not refrain from
observing that "an American of the same intellectual
calibre would have more token of it in his manner and
personal appearance, and would have a more refined
aspect; his head, however, has a good outline, and
would look well in marble; but the English complexion
takes greatly from its chasteness and dignity."   "Every
Englishman," he concluded, "has an outward case of
such undeniable flesh and blood that I doubt whether
it is best to see the poets of this country.   Our pale,
thin, Yankee aspect is the fitter garniture for poets."
Monckton Milnes, who called on him a little later, he
found "pleasant and sensible"; but "an intellectual
and refined American," he insisted, "is a higher man

than he — a higher and a finer one." Inevitably, now and then, he was thrown with Englishmen such as Leigh Hunt, to whom these invidious generalizations could not well be applied; sensitive and high-mettled men whom he could not fail to recognize for what they were. But he had his solution for that problem!

There is not an English trait in him, from head to foot, neither intellectually nor physically; no beef, no ale or stout; and this is the reason that the English have appreciated him no better and that they leave this sweet and delicate poet poor, and with scanty laurels, in his old age. It is his American blood (his mother was a Pennsylvanian) that gives him whatever excellence he has — the fineness, subtlety, and grace that characterize him — and his person, too, is thoroughly American.

Of William Allingham he could not say the same, but he could record that "his face was intelligent, dark, pleasing, and not at all John Bullish."

So alert, indeed, was Hawthorne to these national disharmonies, so exposed were his sensibilities to every lurking antagonism, that it was easy for him to convince himself of a settled, if somewhat abstract, grudge against Americans on the part of all Englishmen. He himself was the object of much kindness and hospitality in England, but this he was prepared to discount. "If an Englishman," he recorded, "were individually acquainted with all our twenty-five millions of Americans, and liked every one of them, and believed that each man of those millions was a Christian, honest, upright, and kind, he would doubt, despise, and hate them in the aggregate, however he might love and

honor the individuals." Persuaded as he was of this
inclusive and immedicable rancor, nothing could have
pleased him more than to have it confirmed, on one
occasion, by a certain Mr. Watson, a merchant of
Manchester.

He is the only Englishman, I think, whom I have
met, who fairly acknowledges that the English do cherish doubt, jealousy, suspicion, in short, an unfriendly
feeling towards the Americans. It is wonderful how
every American, whatever class of the English he min-
gles with, is conscious of this feeling, and how no
Englishman, except this sole Mr. Watson, will confess it.

It pleased him even — pleased him who, all the
while, felt himself on so strangely homelike a soil —
to contemplate what seemed to him the inevitable
clash of interests between England and America as
nations, and the unhappy consequences, for England, it
was bound to have. "There is an account to settle
between us and them for the contemptuous jealousy
with which (since it has ceased to be unmitigated contempt) they regard us; and if they do not make us
amends by coming humbly to ask our assistance, they
must do it by fairly acknowledging us as their masters."
And elsewhere: "The truth is, there is a spirit lacking
in England, which *we* do not lack, and for the want of
which she will have to resign a foremost position
among the nations, even if there were not enough other
circumstances to compel her to do so."

The middle years of Hawthorne's stay in England
were years that saw considerable diplomatic tension
between the two countries, and always Hawthorne
rejoiced at the display of American aggressiveness.

You will see by the newspapers — he wrote to Bridge, in the summer of 1856 — that John Bull is in a pretty high state of excitement in relation to American affairs; but, in my opinion, Frank Pierce has taken the right course to bring matters to an amicable settlement. The recognition of Walker was a prudent measure as well as a decided one. It has angered the British, and has mortified them to the heart's core; but it has satisfied them that we are in earnest, and that their further action will be in peril of a war, which they would be very loath to encounter.

During a similar crisis, the fall before, he had written to Mrs. Hawthorne, who was spending the winter months in Lisbon for her health: "We hold the fate of England in our hands, and it is time we crushed her — blind, ridiculous, old lump of beef, sodden in strong beer, that she is; not but what she has still vitality enough to do us a good deal of mischief, before we quite annihilate her."

It was a favorite notion of his, as these passages suggest, that England as a nation had had its hour and was now on the downward slope. "Thank God," he exclaimed in a letter to Ticknor, "England's day is past forever. I have such a conviction of the decline and fall of England, that I am about as well satisfied as if it had already taken place. And yet," he added — for the dilemma was always with him — "and yet I like John Bull, too." Indeed, it would have been strange if Hawthorne, turning always as he did to the ruinous or at least weathered monuments of England's past, and insulating himself from all the elements of vitality in her present, had not had this settled belief in England's doom. Certainly one had one's choice in the fifties:

one could linger romantically over every stone surviving
from the England of Grosseteste or Wycliffe or Gaunt,
over every alleyway haunted by the shades of Addison
or Swift or Goldsmith; or on the other hand one could
keep one's eyes and ears open to miss nothing said or
done in the England that was just then preparing for
"The Origin of Species", that was listening however
reluctantly to the sermons of Kingsley and Maurice,
that was hovering on the verge of the Second Reform
Bill, and giving refuge to Mazzini and Marx. To this
latter England Hawthorne was steadily indifferent:
probably, in fact, he scarcely knew of its existence, and
would quite have failed to understand it in any case.
"On the whole," he wrote, with a droll touch of
provincialism, "I think the English Conservatives are
the men best worth knowing. The Liberals, with all
their zeal for novelty, originate nothing; and one feels
a little disgusted to find them setting forth their poor
little views of progress, — especially if one happens to
have been a Brook Farmer!" Decidedly, the English
Liberals of the fifties had their limitations; but could
infelicity go farther than in this parallel between the
world of Bright and Spencer and the world of the West
Roxbury communists? It was born, of course, of perfect
incomprehension; and we are not surprised to find
Hawthorne reflecting, as he strolled about in the shadows of Westminster Abbey, that the glory of the old
church "is the glory of a declining empire. . . . It
sums up all. Its beauty and magnificence are made
out of ideas that are gone by."

Out of such intangible materials was compounded
that odd malevolence with which, for four years,

Hawthorne scrutinized the play of British personality, the attitudes of British life; and which deprives his observations, sound as they sometimes are, of the validity that springs from a friendly detachment. We would credit him more willingly if he tried to persuade us of less. He goes too far, he denounces too peevishly, for us to follow him. We may rather rejoice not to have been present at that tea in St. John's Wood where, with a couple of American women, Hawthorne sat talking about the Americans and the English, "especially dwelling on the defects of the latter, — among which we reckoned a wretched meanness in money transactions, a lack of any embroidery of honor and liberality in their dealings, so that they require close watching, or they will be sure to take you at advantage." We are sometimes diverted, but we are more frequently mortified, by the waspishness and — not to put too fine a point upon it — the tastelessness of his notes on the manners, the appearance, the habits of his metaphorical hosts. When he observes that "the English do not know how to rejoice", or that "they feel nothing, and bring themselves no nearer to God when they pray than when they play at cards", or that the English idea of good conversation is probably "something like plum-pudding, — as heavy, but seldom so rich", we are not struck, as we should be, by the possible truth of the criticism, but by the unwholesome petulance of its tone. Something other, and something less respectable, than accomplished observation lay behind those gross descriptions of English personal grossness, or behind such an ill-advised passage as this: "The English probably eat with more simple enjoyment than any other people; not ravenously, as we often do, and not exquisitely and artificially, like the French, but deliberately and vigorously, and with due absorption in the business, so that nothing good is lost upon them. They are a wise breed of animals." The outsider, in such passages, is avenging himself too palpably.

Such was the opposition of sentiments that waged itself in Hawthorne's spirit to the last months of his stay in England. What wonder if, during all that time, he was never wholly at peace — if, for example, he was still, in the midst of his family happiness, visited by the old dream he wrote of, the dream that he was still in college, with a sense of having been there unconscionably long, and having quite failed to make the same progress as his contemporaries, "and I seem to meet some of them with a feeling of shame and depression that broods over me when I think of it, even now." "How strange," he added, "that it should come now, when I may call myself famous and prosperous! — when I am happy, too! — still that same dream of life hopelessly a failure." What wonder if, even on his vacations from the consulate, on visits to the spots he most longed to see, he was repeatedly afflicted with a sudden boredom, a sudden emotional fatigue, and cried out bitterly against the duties of sight-seeing. What wonder if, during Mrs. Hawthorne's absence on the continent, he suffered "woefully" and protractedly from low spirits.

Really, I have no pleasure in anything — he wrote at the time — and I feel my tread to be heavier, and my physical movement more sluggish than in happier times; a weight is always upon me. . . . Nothing gives me any joy. I have learned what the bitterness of exile is, in these days; and I never should have known it but for the absence of my wife. "Remote, unfriended, melancholy, slow," — I can perfectly appreciate that line of Goldsmith; for it well expresses my own torpid, unenterprising, joyless state of mind and heart. I am like an uprooted plant, wilted and drooping. Life seems so purposeless as not to be worth the trouble of carrying it on any further.

Early in 1858, a free man once more, Hawthorne left England with his family for the continent; after ten days in France, spent mostly in Paris, they moved on at once to Rome, where the spring months were passed; the summer of 1858 was spent in Florence, where the Hawthornes occupied successively the Casa del Bello and the Villa Montauto; and in the fall, returning as they had come by *vettura*, and stopping off for a few days in Siena with the Storys, they were again in Rome until the late spring of 1859. Leaving Rome for the second and last time, they spent two or three more weeks on the continent, chiefly in France and Switzerland; and at length returned to England, where Hawthorne, who had already made great headway with a new romance, remained for another year — partly at Leamington, partly at Redcar on the Yorkshire coast, partly at Bath — to finish the book and publish it in England on the same terms as a native author. Not until the summer of 1860, after an absence nearly twice as long as they had prepared for at the outset, did the Hawthornes set their faces homeward.

On the continent, as in England, different as all the factors were, Hawthorne was torn between the old emotions of delight and disgust — delight with all that was hospitable to the imagination, disgust with all that held him at arm's length. Not even the few days in France were too short for the dichotomy to show itself. "I never knew what a palace was," he wrote in his journal, "till I had a glimpse of the Louvre and the Tuileries; never had my idea of a city gratified till I trod these stately streets." "London," he declared, "is not to be mentioned, nor compared even, with Paris." Yet in almost the same breath he was defining the limits of his appreciation. "Truly, I have no sympathies towards the French people; their eyes do not win me, nor do their glances melt and mingle with mine. But they do grand and beautiful things in the architectural way; and I am grateful for it." The visual magnificence of Napoleon III's Paris was by no means lost upon Hawthorne; but a week, was enough to weary him of a city in which he felt himself so unambiguously a stranger. "Nothing really thrives here," he wrote on his last day, speaking of the trees in the Champs Elysées; "man and vegetables have but an artificial life, like flowers stuck in a little mould, but never taking root. I am quite tired of Paris, and never longed for a home so much."

To Rome his first response was, if anything, still less cordial than this. It was mid-January when the Hawthornes arrived in Rome; and the bleak Italian winter, unmitigated by any real comfort in their living quarters, was too much for the low spirits into which Hawthorne was already sunk. "I have seldom or never," he declared at the end of a fortnight, "spent so wretched a time anywhere"; and indeed, save for an hour or so in the middle of the day, he had passed most of those two weeks shivering disconsolately by the fireside of their barnlike *palazzo*. "Soon, I suppose," he ventured to hope, "warmer weather will come, and perhaps reconcile me to Rome against my will." As much of the city as he did manage to see in these weeks repelled him with peculiar stringency. "I vainly try to get down upon paper," he wrote early in February, "the ugliness, shabbiness, unhome-likeness of a Roman street." Sharp and unwholesome cold, prevailing filth, ruins unpoetized — like those in England — by the soft mists of centuries — such were Hawthorne's first impressions of Rome. During the second week in February came the Carnival, but its standardized hilarities only exasperated his dejection and aggravated his homelessness. "There is very little to be said about the spectacle. Sunshine would have improved it, no doubt; but a person must have very broad sunshine within himself to be joyous on such shallow provocation. . . . Upon my honor, this was all the fun, and I never in my life knew a shallower joke than the Carnival at Rome. . . . The whole affair is not worth this page or two."

Fortunately for Hawthorne this mood was not to last. Once the cold weather began to relent, he found himself more and more in the spirit for seeing sights; and before long he was spending the better part of every day on walks about the city, approaching with his old eagerness and even with a certain piety those central spots of the western world about which his imagination had so long hovered. How could Hawthorne of all men fail to be moved, in the long run, by finding himself under the dome of St. Peter's or the Pantheon,

surveying Rome from the summit of the Pincian Hill,
or wandering among the arches and broken columns of
the Forum? "Rome struck me very disagreeably at
first," he wrote about this time to Ticknor, "but rather
improves upon acquaintance, and has a sort of fascination which will make me reluctant to take final leave
of it." In fact, these spring months of his first stay in
Rome were richer in new impressions, and livelier in
imaginative stimuli, than any previous period of the
same length in Hawthorne's life; and at the end he had
almost forgotten his initial disappointment. The last
entry in his journal before the departure for Florence
is eloquent of what had meanwhile happened.

This evening — it was late in May — Una and I took
a farewell walk in the Pincian Gardens to see the
sunset. . . . When the sun went down, we descended
into the Piazza del Popolo, and thence into the Via
Ripetta, and emerged through a gate to the shore of the
Tiber, along which there is a pleasant walk beneath a
grove of trees. We traversed it once and back again,
looking at the rapid river, which still kept its mud-
puddly aspect even in the clear twilight, and beneath
the brightening moon. The great bell of St. Peter's
tolled with a deep boom, a grand and solemn sound;
the moon gleamed through the branches of the trees
above us; and Una spoke with somewhat alarming
fervor of her love for Rome, and regret at leaving it.
We shall have done the poor child no good office in
bringing her here, if the rest of her life is to be a dream
of this "city of the soul," and an unsatisfied yearning
to come back to it. On the other hand, nothing elevat-
ing and refining can be really injurious, and so I hope
she will always be the better for Rome, even if her
life should be spent where there are no pictures, no
statues, nothing but the dryness and meagerness of a
New England village.

As they left Rome the following morning in their *vettura*, moving along the Flaminian Way, a regiment of French troops passed them, to the accompaniment of military music, marching toward the Porta del Popolo.

On the whole — he observed in his journal — I was not sorry to see the Gauls still pouring into Rome; but after all I begin to find that I have a strange affection for it, and so did we all. . . . It is very singular, the sad embrace with which Rome takes possession of the soul. Though we intend to return in a few months, and for a longer residence than this has been, yet we felt the city pulling at our heartstrings far more than London did, where we shall probably never spend much time again. It may be because the intellect finds a home there more than in any other spot in the world, and wins the heart to stay with it, in spite of a good many things strewn all about to disgust us.

The summer in Florence, though it could not compare with a stay in Rome, Hawthorne was to look back upon as a "peaceful and not uncheerful one." When, after two months at the Casa del Bello, the family moved out to the Villa Montauto, about a mile beyond the city walls, Hawthorne wrote to Fields of his delight in Florence, which he put on interesting grounds:

It is pleasant to feel at last that I am really away from America, — a satisfaction that I never enjoyed as long as I stayed in Liverpool, where it seemed to me that the quintessence of nasal and hand-shaking Yankeedom was continually filtered and sublimated through my consulate, on the way outward and homeward. I first got acquainted with my own countrymen there. At Rome, too, it was not much better. But here in Florence, and in the summer-time, and in this secluded villa, I have escaped out of all my old tracks, and am really remote.

It was not quite literally true that he was really remote from America, since he saw no one more frequently or with more pleasure than the sculptor, Hiram Powers; but Powers, after all, had himself been an expatriate for twenty years, and certainly he was the only important reminder of home in the four months in Florence. Here, for the first time, Hawthorne began really to take pleasure in pictures, — "to find myself capable, at least, of loving one picture better than another"; and here, though he seldom grew weary of visiting the Florentine churches and galleries, he again achieved the tranquillity and comparative seclusion that were necessary to his powers of composition. "I hardly think," he had written during his first week in Tuscany, "there can be a place in the world where life is more delicious for its own simple sake than here." At the end of September, recording a last visit to the Uffizi gallery, "it is not a pleasant thought," he wrote, "that we are so soon to give up this gallery, with little prospect (none, or hardly any, on my part) of ever seeing it again. . . . My memory will often tread there as long as I live. What shall we do in America!" It was with distinct reluctance, a few days later, that he turned his face away from Florence for what he knew was the last time.

Their next short resting place was at Siena, and among the hills of southern Tuscany Hawthorne was visited by emotions of the same order as those he had experienced at Gloucester and Peterborough. "The interest of the old town," he perceived, "would soon be exhausted for the passing traveller, but," he went on, "I can conceive that a thoughtful and shy man might settle down here with the view of making the place a home, and spend many years in a sombre kind of happiness. I should prefer it to Florence as a residence, but it would be terrible without an independent life in one's own mind." A week later, after he had seen the cathedral many times, and taken walks through every corner of Siena, his enthusiasm was undiminished. "It is a fine old town, with every promise of health and vigor in its atmosphere, and really, if I could take root anywhere, I know not but it could as well be here as in another place." But he was wise enough to know the limits of such a feeling. "It would only be a kind of despair, however," he continued, "that would ever make me dream of finding a home in Italy; a sense that I had lost my country through absence or incongruity, and that earth, at any rate, is not an abiding-place."

In spite, however, of the attractions of Florence and Siena, Hawthorne was not sorry to return to Rome. On the seventeenth of October, after four days on the road, they drove along the Cassian Way, across the sunny Campagna, toward the city that was to be their home for seven more months. "I had a quiet, gentle, comfortable pleasure, as if, after many wanderings, I was drawing near Rome, for, now that I have known it once, Rome certainly does draw into itself my heart, as I think even London, or even little Concord itself, or old sleepy Salem, never did and never will." Unhappily, the ensuing winter was not to reënforce this feeling, partly because Hawthorne was now really aging more rapidly than he probably supposed, and partly because the long and dangerous illness of his eldest daughter cast a heavy shadow over his spirits from early in November till late in February. Even before Una fell ill, however, he had given evidence of waning vitality. "I do hate the Roman atmosphere," he complained, a week after they had returned; "indeed, all my pleasure in getting back — all my home-feeling — has already evaporated, and what now impresses me, as before, is the languor of Rome, — its weary pavements, its little life, pressed down by a weight of death." At the end of the winter, this growing fatigue was still more marked; yet even then — and to the very last day of his residence in Rome — Hawthorne's emotions were divided.

I am wearing away listlessly — he wrote toward the end of March, 1859 — these last precious days of my abode in Rome . . . I am weary of Rome, without having seen and known it as I ought; and I shall be glad to get away from it, though no doubt there will be many yearnings to return hereafter, and many regrets that I did not make better use of the opportunities within my grasp . . . In the state of mind in which I now stand towards Rome, there is very little advantage to be gained by staying here longer.

Conflicting in just this way were to be his last emotions on Roman soil. After breakfast on the May morning fixed for their departure, Hawthorne walked again to the Pincian Hill, whence he could see the city, the Borghese grounds, and the dome of St. Peter's, in an earlier sunlight than ever before.

Methought they never looked so beautiful, nor the sky so bright and blue. I saw Soracte on the horizon, and I looked at everything as if for the last time; nor do I wish ever to see any of these objects again, though no place ever took so strong a hold of my being as Rome, nor ever seemed so close to me and so strangely familiar. I seem to know it better than my birthplace, and to have known it longer; and though I have been very miserable there, and languid with the effects of the atmosphere, and disgusted with a thousand things in daily life, still I cannot say I hate it — perhaps might fairly own a love for it. But life being too short for such questionable and troublesome enjoyments, I desire never to set eyes on it again.

A little more than a year in Europe was left to Hawthorne after he had departed from Rome. As the time for returning to America drew near, thoughts of his own country assailed him more and more, and these thoughts too, pleasant as they sometimes were, gave him but little peace. Was he eager to be back again in Concord, restored to the Wayside and his hilltop, from which he had been so unwilling to be torn? Could he not, on the contrary, in what time remained to him for living, be content enough to stay on in England, or on the continent, a permanent exile? In fact, Hawthorne scarcely knew. A year before he had left England, he had confessed to Ticknor that "if it were not for the children, I should consider myself a citizen of the world, and perhaps never come home"; and now he wrote to Fields that "as regards going home I alternate between a longing and a dread." The prospects of the expatriate he had not failed to consider. At Isa Blagden's, in Florence, where he had seen much of the Brownings, he had also met Thomas Adolphus Trollope, who had lived in Italy eighteen years. "It seems a pity to do this," reflected Hawthorne. "It needs the native air to give life a reality; a truth which I do not fail to take home regretfully to myself, though without feeling much inclination to go back to the realities of my own." The case of Hiram Powers had come home to him with even greater force, and in this connection also he had generalized suggestively.

It makes a very unsatisfactory life, thus to spend all the bulk of it in exile. In such a case, we are always deferring the reality of life till a future moment, and, by and by, we have deferred it until there are no future moments; or, if we do go back, we find that life has shifted whatever of reality it had to the country where we deemed ourselves only living temporarily; and so between two stools we come to the ground, and make ourselves a part of one or the other country only by laying our bones in its soil.

Making such reflections as these, he could scarcely fail to be pleasantly stirred, now and then, by the anticipation of being once more in Concord on his own estate. From Geneva, in June, he wrote to his former assistant at the consulate, requesting him to get passages for them on a boat leaving Liverpool during the next month — a sailing that was to be deferred, of course, for another year. But "it makes my heart thrill, half pleasantly, half otherwise," he wrote at the time; "so much nearer does this step seem to bring that home whence I have now been absent six years, and which, when I see it again, may turn out not to be my home any longer." To Henry Bright, his English friend, he wrote from Leamington, the following March, when "The Marble Faun" had just been published.

I begin to be restless (and so do we all) with the anticipation of our approaching departure, and, almost for the first time, I long to be at home. Nothing more can be done or enjoyed till we have breathed our native air again. . . . Our roots are pulled up, and we cannot really live till we stick them into the ground again.

At about the same time he was writing to Ticknor, "For my part, I absolutely long to be at home, and if an earlier voyage would be comfortable, I should certainly prefer it. I shall enjoy nothing, till I have touched my native soil again." A month later, from Bath, he wrote, in much the same vein:

I already begin to count the days that intervene between now and our departure, and we are all restless and feverish with the thought of home. I cannot promise to be contented when I get there, after becoming habituated to constant change; but I mean to try to settle down into a respectable character, and have serious thoughts of going to meeting every Sunday forenoon.

Such was Hawthorne's nostalgia during the last months of his stay in England. He had not felt so sure as this of his yearning for America during the whole of those last two years abroad, nor was he to be sure of it even on the voyage home. "I shall go home, I fear, with a heavy heart, not expecting to be very well contented there," he had written to Fields from Rome a year earlier; and to Ticknor, in May, he had said: "I shall be delighted to see you all again; but I will fairly own that it is not altogether agreeable to think of coming back, after so long an absence as mine has been. I am afraid I have lost my country by staying away too long." Even when writing from Geneva for passages to America, he had realized how reluctant he would be to leave England. Francis Bennoch and

Henry Bright, he was aware, were the only two men in England to whom he would be much grieved to say farewell: "but to the island itself I cannot bear to say that word as a finality. I shall dreamily hope to come back again at some indefinite time; rather foolishly, perhaps, for it will tend to take the substance out of my life in my own land. But this, I suspect, is apt to be the penalty of those who stay abroad and stay too long." From Leamington, in the autumn of 1859, he wrote to Ticknor: "I must confess that I have outlived all feeling of homesickness; but still there are some friends whom I shall be rejoiced to see again — and none more than yourself. I doubt whether I shall ever again be contented to live long in one place, after the constant changes of residence for nearly seven years past." In June, 1860, the voyage home had at last to be made; but even then Hawthorne was far from sure of his desire to return. On the boat, he had as traveling companions Fields himself and Harriet Beecher Stowe, and we have the word of both that Hawthorne said many times — "in his quiet, earnest way" — "I should like to sail on and on forever, and never touch the shore again."

It was while this subtle struggle was going on in Hawthorne's bosom that he wrote "The Marble Faun", and doubtless to this cause we may attribute much that is ambiguous and unsatisfactory in the book. For of all Hawthorne's finished romances it is at once the most ambitious and the least successful. He himself, though he wrote to Ticknor as if he were peculiarly contented with what he had done, is recorded to have said more than once, "The thing is a failure"; and in this harsh judgment we must ourselves, however unwillingly, concur. Not that "The Marble Faun" is a mere failure, a mere commonplace trifle of the sort that does competently what is scarcely worth doing at all. Even in its unsuccess, the book has an irreducible grandeur. Its theme, stated abstractly, is, like all Hawthorne's themes, profoundly serious. The style is Hawthorne's wonderful prose at its ripest and richest — a prose that, for all its tenuity, for all its troubled grace, is as sound and pure as the prose of the great Augustans. It is a perfect vehicle for the use to which Hawthorne here chiefly puts it — for the evocation of that solemn, distantly focussed, unwholesome, ennobled Roman scene that is the last thing we forget about "The Marble Faun." However personal the treatment may be, no city was ever embodied in fiction more grandly than Rome is embodied here; and the imagination of western readers will long inhabit, on Hawthorne's terms, the environs of the Borghese gardens, of St. Peter's, of the Coliseum, of the Campagna, — of all those stately sites upon which the story of Miriam and Donatello enacts itself.

It is for this reason, however, among others, that the book fails of the weightiest effect. Rome, in "The Marble Faun", is not the setting of a drama intimately and necessarily connected with it; it is a background chosen for its picturesque remoteness, a background against which the drama, no matter how incredible in itself, may be acceptably unrolled. It is the old defect of the earlier romances, in an aggravated form. Here, too, Hawthorne was explicit about his purpose.

Italy, as the site of his Romance — he said in the preface — was chiefly valuable to him [the author] as affording a sort of poetic or fairy precinct, where actualities would not be so terribly insisted upon as they are, and must needs be, in America. No author — he went on to say — without a trial, can conceive of the difficulty of writing a romance about a country where there is no shadow, no antiquity, no mystery, no picturesque and gloomy wrong, nor anything but a commonplace prosperity, in broad and simple daylight, as is happily the case with my dear native land.

In this light, the choice of Rome was no doubt a happy inspiration; but Hawthorne's confession is the key to the failure of the book. Miriam herself, early in the tale, says something that recurs oddly, in this connection, to one's mind. "We artists," she remarks to Donatello, when he calls on her in her studio, "purposely exclude sunshine, and all but a partial light, because we think it necessary to put ourselves at odds with Nature before trying to imitate her. That strikes you very strangely, does it not? But we make very pretty pictures sometimes with our artfully arranged lights and shadows." It would be an exaggeration, but one in the spirit of the truth, to say that "The Marble Faun" is little more than an extremely pretty picture.

Miriam and the other three characters of the small cast — Hilda, Kenyon, and Donatello — are men and women of the sort one would expect to find moving in the midst of lights and shadows too artfully arranged. They exist, that is to say, in the most conventional sense. Detach them for a moment from their majestic background, and see how insubstantially they are put together. Donatello, as we know, owes his very exis-

tence, not to Hawthorne's study of human beings, but
to his cogitations about a Greek statue; and a piece of
cunningly chiselled marble, painted too in the fashion
which Hawthorne condemned in sculpture, poor Donatello remains to the end. A good deal of stress is laid
on his resemblance to Praxiteles' Faun, and the mystery
of his ears — are they, or are they not, pointed and
furred? — is touched upon at many points in the book
— of which, indeed, it is the last note to be struck;
but Hawthorne exaggerates our interest in the speculation; Donatello is too artificially contrived as a whole
for the structure of his ears to seem a matter of any
moment. To Miriam's mystery we are, at least in the
end, equally indifferent. According to various rumors,
we are told, she was supposed to be the fugitive daughter and heiress of a great Jewish banker, a German
princess, the lady of an English nobleman, and so on;
but, in effect, it is of little consequence what her origin
was; Miriam herself is a melodramatic shadow with
whom only a faun such as Donatello could fall pas-
sionately in love, and for whose sake it is somewhat
remarkable that even he could commit a great crime.
At the end of the book, in the midst of the Roman Carnival, they both assume pretty costumes and conceal
their identities behind masks; but the costumes and
the masks are as real as their own garments and their
own faces, and conceal nothing that we might know
about them otherwise. Hilda, in spite of the cool colors in which she is painted, has a little spark of true
vitality that makes us remember her longer than the
others; Roman as her setting is, she herself is New
England in one of its genuine incorporations, and

Hawthorne could not fail to impart some reality to her character. Yet even she is real rather by contrast than absolutely; early in the book, we feel it to be an ominous fact that Hilda is a copyist rather than an original painter, and something of the spuriousness of her occupation clings about her to the end; her disappearance from the scene for several chapters is rather an evaporation than an exit, and we should feel that Kenyon, in winning her hand, had been undeservedly deluded by a phantom if he himself were not the weakliest characterized of the whole group.

No single explanation will account for Hawthorne's failure to vitalize the men and women of "The Marble Faun"; but here, as in the earlier books, we may certainly lay part of their defectiveness to that paralyzing fatalism which presides over so much of their conduct, and about which they are themselves so depressingly articulate. In the interview with her spectral model in the Borghese Grove, Miriam cries out against her apparent doom, giving vent to the wish that both of them might have been buried by the crumbling ceilings of the catacombs in which they had so fatefully met.

It were vain to wish it — replies her tormentor — In all that labyrinth of midnight paths, we should have found one another out to live or die together. Our fates cross and are entangled. The threads are twisted into a strong cord, which is dragging us to an evil doom. Could the knots be severed, we might escape. But neither can your slender fingers untie those knots, nor my masculine force break them. We must submit!

To a similar philosophy Miriam herself gives voice, stopping in the antechamber of Kenyon's studio to scrutinize a half-finished bust emerging from the marble block under the stroke of the workman's chisel. "As these busts in the block of marble," she reflects, "so does our individual fate exist in the limestone of time. We fancy that we carve it out; but its ultimate shape is prior to all our action." And Donatello, speaking to Kenyon, reminds us strongly of Hollingsworth. "It is not my will," he says, "but my necessity, to avoid men's eyes." Under such auspices, it would be unduly sanguine to expect that character would develop richly.

Even within these limits, however, "The Marble Faun" might be a book more justly comparable than it is with "The Scarlet Letter" and "The Blithedale Romance." In spite of their dramatic deficiencies, those books are redeemed, as we have seen, by the seriousness and truth of the moral conceptions they develop, and the closeness with which those conceptions are worked out. Even in "The Marble Faun", Hawthorne is struggling — or should we say playing? — with a serious and a related theme. Even here he is at least formally concerned with the problem of personality; the center of the book, indeed, is of course the humanizing of Donatello through his very sin and the suffering that follows it; and the chief secondary interest is the slow moral effect upon Hilda of her first real contact with evil. But it is not enough that such a book should deal with moral problems of this order; everything depends upon the setting they are given, and the fullness of reference with which they are developed. We can believe in Dimmesdale's and in Chillingworth's tragedies because we can believe in their offenses; we can accept Hollingsworth's downfall because his selfishness has been gross and palpable. But the moral drama of "The Marble Faun" is either too abstract or not abstract enough. If the fable had been translated into purely poetic symbols, it might have had a misty and disembodied truth. Actually, it is a group of presumably real men and women we are asked to take an interest in; but we know too little about them, we are put off too wantonly with a frivolous mystification, to believe in the justice or truth of anything that befalls them. The crime that Donatello commits is the fruit of angry and justifiable impulse, not of something radically vicious in his make-up; and how guilty Miriam may be, in her silent complicity, we simply cannot guess, since we know virtually nothing of her history. It is a disengaged, isolated, pictorial guilt we are challenged to take seriously; and against such a concession the imagination rebels. Nor are the consequences of the crime unfolded before us, as in "The Scarlet Letter", swiftly, relentlessly, and lucidly; in the hundreds of pages that follow the great scene of guilt, we learn much about the Italian countryside, about the antiquities of Rome, about wine-making and the Carnival, but extraordinarily little, in proportion, about Donatello himself. What we do learn is finely told; but it has no direction, no relevance, no clear and tragic goal; and at the end Donatello, instead of coming finally to life, is more unreal than ever, so that we consign him to his prison cell with a relief that is in no sense a katharsis.

With "The Marble Faun" we have reached the end of Hawthorne's work as a writer of fiction, save for the four unfinished and imperfect fragments he was to leave behind him at his death. On the basis of this book, we are forced to conclude that his life in Europe, though it enriched his visual memory, did little or nothing fundamentally for his imagination — encouraged him, indeed, in that imaginative irresponsibility which had always been the lurking vice of his creative process. He did well to dread the debilitating effects of exile. Five or six years of it had stolen from him, at least temporarily, the secret of his truest insight. It remains to be seen whether he could yet regain, however precariously, the cunning that his hand had certainly lost.

CHAPTER EIGHT

DISMISSAL

"Enter certain Reapers, properly habited; they join with the nymphs in a graceful dance; towards the end whereof Prospero starts suddenly, and speaks; after which, to a strange, hollow, and confused noise, they heavily vanish."—"The Tempest", Stage direction.

FOR at least a year before his return to America, Hawthorne had given evidence, for the first time in his life, of being in serious ill health; and now, in the four years that were left to him, he was never to be wholly free from physical weariness or distress. In the last year of his life he was to break down miserably, and on the verge of sixty to present all the symptoms of great decrepitude. What ailed him we have no means of knowing, for with quiet tenacity he refused to submit to medical examination or care. But in truth it is peculiarly difficult to believe that the dreary tragedy of Hawthorne's last four years was the accompaniment of a mere physical collapse. Rome, with its evil atmosphere, had no doubt affected his health for the worse; and the strain of Una's illness had certainly told fearfully on his nerves. But a man so robust as Hawthorne had always been does not usually fail rapidly and mysteriously at the age of fifty-six; and, in short, he presented far more the spectacle of a man giving way under the stress of an unstable inner integration than of anything easier to repair. It was as if, at the best, his

effectiveness had been bought at the price of an infinitely delicate adjustment, and as if that adjustment had
finally been deranged, leaving him bewildered, disarmed, vacillating, and at length exhausted. So long as
he remained in Europe, he could accept the conditions of
exile, knowing them to be temporary; and nourish himself, in the mean time, on the sense of being among
scenes to which he could imaginatively relate himself.
Home in America, it would not be so easy to accept
the status of an outsider: was it not for just this reason
that, in spite of all his homesickness, he had never
ceased to dread the necessary return?

An outsider, it is true, Hawthorne had always been
in some degree; but a number of things — his happy marriage and home life, his literary fame, and the hearty
assistance of habit — had combined to reconcile him
thereto in the period of his physical prime and mental
vivacity. Now, the smooth continuity of habit had
been broken; for seven years he had been literally an
exile, and there was nothing to soften for him the
shock of coming home to find himself, with more than
the old acuteness, a virtual stranger among his countrymen. Now, his literary fame was an old story, and
seemed still less than ever, at this juncture, to furnish
a basis on which he could meet seriously with other
Americans. Now, too, he was growing old; and, far
more than in his middle life, the long loneliness, the
chillness, the unmitigated estrangement of his youth,
were returning upon him, and bringing no hopes or
illusions with them. Protected as he might seem to be
by family affections and the esteem of men he respected,
Hawthorne was really haunted by a sense of alienation,

a sense of futility, and a sense of unreality, that were all more poignant and more unbearable than anything he had felt before. Of these things mainly, after four wretched years, he died.

How painful, in any telling, is the record of those four years! The return to the dingy little Wayside itself, on a hot June day; the months of noise and confusion during which the house was being altered and enlarged by carpenters; the disappointment of finding his new tower-study too stifling in summer and too hard to heat properly in winter; the relapse of Una into another serious illness; the distraction and grief of Secession and Civil War; attempts to write worthily in the midst of all this and under the pressure of financial responsibility; excursions with Julian to the North Shore and to West Gouldsborough, Maine, to escape the lifeless summers of Concord, and if possible to restore his vitality; a trip to Washington and its environs, in the second year of the war, undertaken with a similar object; dinners with the embattled celebrities of the Saturday Club, from which he came away more lonely than ever; the constant reminders of England furnished by his journals as he worked over the chapters of "Our Old Home"; the unpleasantness caused by his dedicating the book to Pierce; and, finally, his growing weariness and his humiliating incapacity to write at all; — all this, though it is not the whole story, is so much of it that we can scarcely be surprised by the almost unlightened gloom in which he lived and died.

In England and Italy, Hawthorne had developed a sociability which, though it was certainly not excessive, was for him phenomenal; and it might have been predicted that, on his return to America, this sociability would grow upon him. To Lowell, in fact, that first summer, he seemed "easier in society than formerly"; and it is certainly notable that he was persuaded to belong to the Saturday Club. Actually, he was very quickly to relapse into a passionate need of solitude, a hatred of interruption or social necessities, that were more intense, one might almost say fiercer, than any similar tendencies he had shown before. Over his privacy, now, his wife and children were set on guard; and luckless was the intruder who succeeded in breaking in upon him. Concord was what it had always been: Emerson was still within call; Alcott was Hawthorne's next neighbor; for a year or so, Henry Thoreau was accessible and in tolerable health; and visitors that had never sought out the obscure tale-teller in the Manse would have been glad to catch a mere glimpse of Nathaniel Hawthorne at the Wayside. But the old connections were only perfunctorily resumed, and new ones were avoided with the utmost vigilance. "I have few friends," he wrote to Fields, with a list of names for presentation copies of "Our Old Home"; and it is not easy to feel that the remark was intended as a complaint. Emerson, certainly, was to remember that Hawthorne's "unwillingness and caprice" were partly responsible for his own failure to "conquer a friendship"; and Alcott, whose testimony must be taken with a little irony, was yet more unsuccessful.

During all the time he lived near me — Alcott was later to write — our estates being separated only by a gate and shaded avenue, I seldom caught sight of him; and when I did it was but to lose it the moment he

suspected he was visible; oftenest seen on his hilltop
screened behind the shrubbery and disappearing like
a hare into the bush when surprised. I remember of
his being in my house but twice, and then he was so
ill at ease that he found excuse for leaving politely
forthwith, — "the stove was so hot," "the clock
ticked so loud." Yet he once complained to me of his
wish to meet oftener, and dwelt on the delights of
fellowship, regretting he had so little.

At the Saturday Club, where he might well have
felt a little at ease among men who honored him so
truly as Lowell and Agassiz and Fields and Longfellow
did, Hawthorne appears to have been uncomfortable to
the point of boorishness. To the elder James, who
met him at one of the dinners at Parker's, he seemed
not to be an engaging man personally.

He has the look all the time, to one who doesn't
know him — wrote James to Emerson early in 1861 —
of a rogue who suddenly finds himself in a company of
detectives. But in spite of his rusticity, I felt a sympathy for him amounting to anguish, and couldn't
take my eyes off him all the dinner. . . . It was so
pathetic to see him, contented, sprawling, Concord
owl that he was and always has been, brought blind-
fold into the brilliant daylight, and expected to wink
and be lively like any little dapper Tommy Titmouse or
Jenny Wren. How he buried his eyes in his plate, and
ate with a voracity that no person should dare to ask
him a question. My heart broke for him as that atten-
uated Y kept putting forth his long antennae toward
him, stroking his face, and trying whether his eyes
were shut. . . . It was heavenly to see him persist in
ignoring Y, and shutting his eyes against his spectral
smiles; eating his dinner and doing absolutely nothing
but that, and then going home to his Concord den to

fall on his knees and ask his Heavenly Father why it
was that an owl couldn't remain an owl, and not be
forced into the diversions of a canary.

At home in his Concord den, in fact, after one or
two of these ordeals, Hawthorne pretty consistently
remained.

I cannot come to Boston — he wrote to Fields late in
1862 — to spend more than a day just at present. It
would suit me better to come for a visit when the spring
of next year is a little advanced, and if you renew your
hospitable proposition then, I shall probably be glad to
accept it; though I have now been a hermit so long, that
the thought affects me somewhat as it would to invite
a lobster or a crab to step out of his shell.

Doubtless, this revived and exasperated sense of
estrangement from his fellows would have been strong
enough in any event; certainly it was aggravated by the
approach, the outbreak, and the progress of the Civil
War. Nothing, at this juncture, could have operated
so tellingly to isolate Hawthorne in a moral solitude.
So far as the great struggle had been brought on by the
agitation of reformers and humanitarians, it could
mean less than nothing to Hawthorne, the political
fatalist, the creator of Hollingsworth. So far as it was
animated by a desire to preserve the Union, it could
mean little to a man who had said, "The States are too
various and too extended to form really one country.
New England is quite as large a lump of earth as my
heart can really take in." Yet he could not remain
wholly indifferent to the great seismic throes that were
shaking the entire country; some attitude he had to take,
and this was strangely compounded of bewilderment,

skepticism, and a factitious ferocity. "Are times so terribly bad as people say?" he wrote to Ticknor as from another planet, late in the year of Lincoln's first election. "I have left off reading newspapers, and only know by hearsay that the Union is falling asunder." In May of the following year, he was able to give voice to stronger feelings. "The war, strange to say," he wrote to Bridge, "has had a beneficial effect upon my spirits, which were flagging wofully before it broke out. But it was delightful to share in the heroic sentiment of the time, and to feel that I had a country — a consciousness which seemed to make me young again." In the same letter, however, Hawthorne betrayed the quality of his enthusiasm; he was less inflamed than perplexed.

Meantime (though I approve of the war as much as any man), I don't quite understand what we are fighting for, or what definite result can be expected. If we pummel the South ever so hard, they will love us none the better for it; and even if we subjugate them, our next step should be to cut them adrift. If we are fighting for the annihilation of slavery, to be sure, it may be a wise object, and offers a tangible result, and the only one which is consistent with a future reunion between North and South. . . . Whatever happens next I must say that I rejoice that the old Union is smashed. We never were one people, and never really had a country since the Constitution was formed.

In the purposes of the war, good or bad, Hawthorne had no genuine interest. If he was skeptical about the Union, he was at least as skeptical about emancipation. On this, as on so many matters, he vacillated pitifully. Edward Dicey, who saw him in Washington in the

HAWTHORNE IN 1862

spring of 1862, was mainly struck by this morbid indecision.

So I recollect — he wrote — on the old battlefield of Manassas, in which I strolled in company with Hawthorne, meeting a batch of runaway slaves — weary, footsore, wretched, and helpless beyond conception; we gave them food and wine, some small sums of money, and got them a lift upon a train going Northwards; but not long afterwards, Hawthorne turned to me with the remark, "I am not sure we were doing right after all. How can those poor beings find food and shelter away from home?"

Only against the background of such a Pyrrhonism as this could Hawthorne have written his article, "Chiefly about War Matters", for the *Atlantic*, with its fatigued facetiousness, its insensitiveness to public emotions, its lukewarm and formal loyalty. In this light we are struck rather by the unwholesomeness than by the vigor of the strong expressions he did sometimes use. "I wish," he wrote to Ticknor, for example, "they would push on the war a little more briskly. The excitement had an invigorating effect on me for a time, but it begins to lose its influence." And we are told that, referring to the Southerners, he used to say, "I hope that we shall give them a terrible thrashing, and then kick them out." Manifestly, this is the vehemence, not of deep feeling, but of secret apathy.

In his heart, Hawthorne was all but completely unmoved by the agitation of the period; and this he confessed, indirectly but unmistakably, on every page of "Septimius Felton." Not for nothing is that abortive tale laid in the days of the American Revolution, or its hero credited with an engrossing purpose that bears no relation to the desires of his countrymen. If ever a character was symbolically identified with his creator, Septimius is Hawthorne himself, and this not merely because he lives in the shadow of Hawthorne's own hillside. How does he behave on that April morning when the rattle of musketry fire near at hand announces the outbreak of the Revolution?

Septimius went into his house, and sat in his study for some hours, in that unpleasant state of feeling which a man of brooding thought is apt to experience when the world around him is in a state of intense action, which he finds it impossible to sympathize with. There seemed to be a stream rushing past him, by which, even if he plunged into the midst of it, he could not be wet. He felt himself strangely ajar with the human race, and would have given much either to be in full accord with it, or to be separated from it forever.

When Septimius meditates upon his condition, we may feel sure that we are overhearing something more than an imaginary soliloquy.

I am dissevered — he says — from [the human race]. It is my doom to be only a spectator of life; to look on as one apart from it. Is it not well, therefore, that, sharing none of its pleasures and happiness, I should be free of its fatalities, its brevity? How cold I am now, while this whirlpool of public feeling is eddying around me! It is as if I had not been born of woman!

There had been a time when Hawthorne could attach some substantial value even to the rôle of a spectator; now he was made wretched by what seemed to him the illusoriness of his very hold on life. Again and again, as we catch glimpses of him in these last years, he has the aspect of a man wandering in a miserable dream, laying his hand on shadows, and finally quite wearied by the play. Recall the story that Edward Emerson told Conway, about a call by Hawthorne at the Emerson house one Sunday evening.

Father was away and mother not well, and Edith and I sat alone in the parlor. . . . He was, as I always remember him, kindly, but shy as a wild thing from the woods; and to conceal his embarrassment even with us, children of thirteen and fifteen, took up the stereoscope we had on the table and began looking at the views. He presently asked us of what places they were taken. They represented the Concord Common, the Court House and Town House, and the Milldam, as we call the center of the town where the stores and post-office are. He evidently asked in good faith, and, though he walked through these places on his visits to the post-office and railway station, knew as little about them as the fox that might burrow in his hillside did.

So precarious was his attachment even to his beloved Wayside and the hill behind it, so dreamlike was the whole movement of his life, that he began again to confess a nostalgic longing for England. "It is odd," he wrote to Ticknor, "that I have never felt so earnest a desire to go back to England as now that I have irrevocably planted myself at home . . . It is folly for mortal man to do anything more than pitch a tent." Toward the very end, utterly hopeless of his literary prospects, "If I could but go to England now," he wrote to Fields, "I think that the sea voyage and the

'Old Home' might set me all right." But in his wiser moments, Hawthorne himself must have counted this too an illusion; there is a truer, if a more deadly, ring in the words of a letter to Una from the seashore: "I am not much more discontented than with many other spots in this weary world." Rest, if he was to find it, was at once nearer and farther off than England. Late in the fall of 1863, he showed, in a letter to Fields, that he knew this: "Those verses entitled 'Weariness,' in the last magazine, seem to me profoundly touching. I too am weary, — and begin to look ahead for the Wayside Inn."

Dejected and tormented as Hawthorne was by such emotions and reflections, he could scarcely have survived for many years the homecoming of 1860; but doubtless the process was hastened by the necessity he felt himself under to go on accumulating money for his family, and by his painful inability to write with the old fluency and success. Nothing in his life is more distressing to contemplate than the baffled literary struggles of these years, the repetition of false starts, the blunderings into blind alleys, the frivolous concluding of projects undertaken seriously, the final failure to get beyond the threshold of a book. It was not as if Hawthorne, like many authors, had always and characteristically floundered about from book to book, producing a little of value at the price of a vast diffusion of effort; almost from the beginning he had written swiftly, confidently, thriftily. In these last years, he was to stumble along like a confused beginner. And in the place of his old pleasure in composition he was to experience continual vexation. Early in 1861, he wrote, in a new vein, to Ticknor: "I spend two or three hours a day in my sky-parlor, and duly spread a quire of paper on my desk; but no very important result has followed, thus far. Perhaps, however, I shall have a new Romance ready, by the time New England becomes a separate nation — a consummation I rather hope for than otherwise." "The war continues to interrupt my literary industry," he wrote querulously a few months later; "and I am afraid it will be long before Romances are in request again, even if I could write one. I wish I could turn my hand to any useful labor." So bitterly against the grain as this was "Dr. Grimshawe's Secret" written, so far as we can judge, during the unhappy months of 1861.

Wearied finally by the futility of attempting imaginative composition, Hawthorne turned, in 1862, to the lighter task of revamping passages from his English journals for a series of *Atlantic* travel articles, later collected in the volume "Our Old Home." In the preface to this volume, he confessed his emotions at the time. Of all this English material, he explained, he had hoped to make a substantial work of fiction.

Of course, I should not mention this abortive project, only that it has been utterly thrown aside and will never now be accomplished. The Present, the Immediate, the Actual, has proved too potent for me. It takes away not only my scanty faculty, but even my desire for imaginative composition, and leaves me sadly content to scatter a thousand peaceful fantasies upon the hurricane that is sweeping us all along with it, possibly, into a Limbo where our nation and its polity may be as literally the fragments of a shattered dream as my unwritten Romance.

On such terms, he could hardly fail to be disheartened even about the travel essays, and in fact he took little or no satisfaction in their production. "I hope you will like it," he wrote to Fields of one of the early essays, "for the subject seemed interesting to me when I was on the spot, but I always feel a singular despondency and heaviness of heart in reopening those old journals now." Toward the close of 1862, he wrote: "I am delighted at what you tell me about the kind appreciation of my articles, for I feel rather gloomy about them myself"; and in February of the following year: "Heaven sees fit to visit me with an unshakable conviction that all this series of articles is good for nothing." In April, as the series drew near to its conclusion, "I don't think," he decided, "the public will bear any more of this sort of thing." Finally, when the volume itself was to be published in the summer of 1863, and the ticklish question of dedicating it to Pierce had to be discussed, Hawthorne confessed himself as being of three minds about the matter — first, that the tribute was owing to Pierce for having sent him to England originally; second, that it might well be paid to Francis Bennoch, his best English friend; "thirdly, I am not convinced that it is worth while to inscribe it to anybody."

Meanwhile, at some indeterminate time, Hawthorne had forced himself to make another attempt at the writing of romance; and now, giving up the English subject as a hopeless one, he had written, on a theme suggested to him by Thoreau years before, "Septimius Felton." This, however, had proved almost as abortive as the earlier tale; and it was in a mood of desperate levity that Hawthorne had terminated, rather than finished, the book. In its raw and sketchy condition, "Septim-ius" was unfit for anything but posthumous publication; yet even now something of the sort Hawthorne felt himself obliged to undertake, and, at Fields' suggestion, he set himself, toward the end of 1863, to the writing of a serial for the *Atlantic*, to be based on a similar theme, approached from another angle. By this time, ill health and low spirits were conspiring to make such work virtually impossible. "I can't tell you when to expect an instalment of the Romance, if ever," he wrote to Fields. "There is something preternatural in my reluc-tance to begin. I linger at the threshold, and have a perception of very disagreeable phantasms to be encoun-tered if I enter." As the fall wore on, this frustration continued. "I don't see much probability," he ad-mitted, "of my having the first chapter of the Romance ready so soon as you want it. There are two or three chapters ready to be written, but I am not yet robust enough to begin, and I feel as if I should never carry it through." In the same letter, having to complain of money anxieties, he declared: "If it were not for these troublesome necessities, I doubt whether you would ever see so much as the first chapter of the new Romance."

Finally, in December, the first chapter of "The Dol-liver Romance" was in a state to be taken to Fields; and Hawthorne, on his way to Concord, New Hamp-shire, for the funeral of Mrs. Pierce, left it with his publisher in Boston. Returning two days later, he spent the night with Mr. and Mrs. Fields, and the latter recorded that Hawthorne "has already written the first chapter of a new romance, but he thought so little

of the work himself as to make it impossible for him to
continue until Mr. Fields had read it and expressed
his sincere admiration for the work. This has given
him better heart to go on with it." The encouragement
was to be of little avail. "I am not quite up to writing
yet," he wrote in January, 1864, "but shall make an
effort as soon as I see any hope of success. . . . Seriously
my mind has, for the present, lost its temper and its fine
edge, and I have an instinct that I had better keep quiet."
At length, in February, the last word had to be said.

I hardly know — he wrote on the 25th — what to
say to the public about this abortive Romance, though
I know pretty well what the case will be. I shall never
finish it. Yet it is not quite pleasant for an author to
announce himself, or to be announced, as finally broken
down as to his literary faculty. It is a pity that I let
you put this work in your programme for the year,
for I had always a presentiment that it would fail us
at the pinch. Say to the public what you think best,
and as little as possible. . . . Say anything you like,
in short, though I really don't believe that the public
will care what you say or whether you say anything.
. . . I cannot finish it unless a great change comes
over me; and if I make too great an effort to do so, it
will be my death; not that I should care much for that,
if I could fight the battle through and win it, thus
ending a life of much smoulder and scanty fire in a blaze
of glory. But I should smother myself in mud of my
own making. . . . I am not low-spirited, nor fanciful, nor freakish, but look what seem to be realities in
the face, and am ready to take whatever may come.

With these tragic sentences, the literary life of Hawthorne came to an end. He was to outlive his own
powers but a few weeks.

It goes without saying that nothing Hawthorne wrote during these four years can be criticized as one would criticize a finished performance. To this generalization, "Our Old Home" is but an apparent exception. It was not really written, it was at the most elaborately revised, at Concord; page by page, it is based on the journals kept in England, and the passages are not infrequent in which the alterations are of the merest detail. It is, in spite of Hawthorne's own contempt for it, a beautiful book. It is the most substantial monument we have to his uncommon skill as an essayist; less delicately personal and less subtly atmospheric than "The Old Manse" and "The Custom-House", the essays in "Our Old Home" are richer than either in extrinsic fact, blended of more intricate — perhaps more interesting — emotions, and of course more imposing in their very mass. Supplemented by his journals, the book demonstrates that Hawthorne, if he had not been a romancer, might easily have been a great memorialist or a great travel writer: the descriptions of Leigh Hunt, of Delia Bacon, of the Lord Mayors' dinners in Liverpool and London, illustrate the one; such chapters as that on the Burns country or that on Old Boston illustrate the other. Observation of the most accomplished, the most nicely disciplined sort, is at work in both directions; and always it is integrated, enriched, and made significant by the presence of an important personal unity lying behind it. No book that Hawthorne wrote is, on its own terms, more perfect than "Our Old Home."

Of all his work from the beginning, on the other hand, the four romantic fragments — "The Ancestral

Footstep" and "Dr. Grimshawe's Secret" (two versions of a single tale) and "Septimius Felton" and "The Dolliver Romance" (similarly related) — are the most sorrily imperfect portions. It will not do to subject them to criticism; at the best, as works of literary art, they but exemplify, for the pathologist, the implicit weaknesses of a creative faculty never before so unhappily off its guard. It is not that they are, or could be, destitute of literary value. There are passages of energetic writing, glimpses of dramatic truth, both in the bloody-footstep cycle and in "Septimius"; and "The Dolliver Romance", strangely enough in view of the state that produced it, has, more than any of the others, much of the old duskiness of atmosphere and delicacy of mood that had never been so exquisitely mingled since "The Seven Gables." Grandsir Dolliver, though we see but little of him, has some of the minor and melancholy interest, frail as it is dramatically, that Hepzibah began by having. Beyond this, it is impossible to go. "The Ancestral Footstep" and "Grimshawe" are not only faltering and inchoate as they stand; they suggest that no amount of re-working would have given them serious interest. The plot around which they both stagger — the attempt of an American to regain an ancestral heritage in England — is too tame, too tediously complicated, too close to jejune melodrama, to be capable of fine development. There is plenty of romantic machinery; the tale is full of old graveyards, mysterious keys, graybeards in black mantles, secret chambers, old family documents, and revealed identities; but all this is unredeemed by any central interest in a human problem or a vital conflict of characters. The people do not believe in themselves, and we cannot believe in them. Even Redclyffe, the leading character in "Grimshawe", never decides what he intends to do about his prospects in England; and his indecision destroys not only him but the whole story. It must have been through some sense of this radical emptiness in his plot that Hawthorne, with a gesture of ironic levity, ended the book with that mocking scene in which a coffer, opened by an occult silver key, proves to be full of nothing but locks of golden hair.

The plot of "Grimshawe" is intrinsically meretricious; the plot of "Septimius" could have been treated justly only in a short tale of the type represented by "Ethan Brand": it is enervated and rendered silly by being spun out to two hundred pages. In itself, the idea of a man devoting his time to the search for an elixir of immortality has a certain narrow and abstract importance; but it does not lend itself to treatment on a canvas occupied by many characters or enlivened by many incidents. Yet Hawthorne attempted mistakenly to work on such a canvas — to invent a group of characters and a longish series of incidents — and the result is disaster. We might readily accept the provisional truth of Septimius himself as a man; we cannot accept the others, except Sybil Dacy, even on such terms, for they bear no relation to the constricted drama. Robert Hagburn is soon disposed of for just this reason, and Rose Garfield, who begins by being Septimius' sweetheart, has so little place in the story that she is easily transformed, at a certain point, into his sister. Sybil Dacy alone is relevant to what happens, and she is by definition too fantastic and too insubstantial to appear as frequently as she must, in a story on such a scale, without destroying the illusion. As for the incidents, most of them were obviously invented in despair, and as if, since something had to happen, it might as well have been this. Save for one or two, such as the duel on the hillside, they have no separate vigor and no cumulative force. Again, as in "Grimshawe", Hawthorne must have been conscious of this as he neared the end: Septimius' potent elixir, on which he has labored so long and from which he has hoped so much, proves to be only an unusually pleasant poison, and even that, so bitterly does the author deride him in Sybil's action, he is not allowed to drink, but must watch it partly drunk by her and the rest spilled on the floor. What began as an allegorical tragedy ends as a limping farce.

As works of art, the four fragments are all but utter failures; as biographical documents, they have no little interest. So far as a distinction can be made between their plots and their themes, the two themes that organize them, and that are uncertainly intertwisted in "Septimius", remind us at least of the unity of Hawthorne's experience and the essential integrity of his imagination. Both, that is to say, are developments of the old theme of pride and isolation. The conflict in Redclyffe's mind — or, in "The Ancestral Footstep", in Middleton's — is the conflict between his quasi-colonial pride in being an American and the centralizing pull of his desire to regain his English heritage. More than half of "Grimshawe", and all of "The Ancestral Footstep", take place in England; and the effect of this is to give both Middleton and Redclyffe quite as much the

aspect of outsiders as, in their different settings, Hester
Prynne and Hepzibah and Hollingsworth have. Unim-
peded by a melodramatic plot, and developed to a tragic
conclusion, the theme might well have had as much
austerity as the theme of "The Scarlet Letter" or
"Blithedale." It sprang, as we have seen, directly
from Hawthorne's personal experience; and, if raised
to the impersonal plane, might have been the basis
for a warmer and grander book than any other, with
one exception, that Hawthorne wrote. So much cannot be said for the theme of "Septimius", essentially
adaptable as it was to the conditions of a short tale;
but it too, and indeed more plainly than the other, is
a recurrence of the old motive. Septimius, in his search
for the elixir of immortality, is but another Rappaccini, another Ethan Brand, another Hollingsworth;
he is a selfish egotist, aiming at a goal beyond the powers or the desires of ordinary humanity, and his aim
cuts him off from all relations with his fellowmen. He
himself feels this in that dialogue with Rose Garfield
while she is still his sweetheart. What he has been
saying has borne upon his desire for mutual sympathy —

. . . but even while he spoke, there was something
that dragged upon his tongue; for he felt that the solitary pursuit in which he was engaged carried him apart
from the sympathy of which he spoke, and that he
was concentrating his efforts and interest entirely upon
himself, and that the more he succeeded the more
remotely he should be carried away, and that his final
triumph would be the complete seclusion of himself
from all that breathed, — the converting him, from an
interested actor, into a cold and disconnected spectator
of all mankind's warm and sympathetic life.

In the end, he is not so much destroyed as discomfited, and the fable thus lacks the solemnity of "Ethan Brand"; but it was produced by the same spiritual experience. If Hawthorne failed again to embody his whole vision, he had but fallen behind the bright mistress as he poetized — *"come all'ultimo suo ciascuno artista."*

Less than three months after the breakdown of "Dolliver", Hawthorne lay dead in a hotel room in Plymouth, New Hampshire. During all that time, and doubtless for weeks before, he had known that death was upon him; and though he had been consoled rather than alarmed by that knowledge, he had been haunted by a dread of dying at the Wayside in the heart of his family. No effort to postpone the end had seemed to him worth making, and he had made none; but he had left no stone unturned to insure his being away from home when the end came. Deeper than anything else in his nature lay the intense longing for solitude; and, now that the last loneliness was at hand, he could not bear to have it mitigated even by the human realities that were closest to him. No doubt he would have preferred to die, not only on an unfamiliar spot, but wholly in the midst of strangers; that, in his reduced condition, would not have been possible, and in fact he had reached Plymouth after a few days of driving through the country from Boston in the company of Franklin Pierce. But there is a grave and fitting symbolism, for a life spent in such incorrigible isolation, in the fact that he should have died, accompanied by a discredited ex-president, in a meaningless little room in

a White Mountain hotel with which he had no other
affiliations. No place is more identified with him, to
the fancy, than the dismal chamber under the eaves
in which he spent his solitary youth; second to that,
those who cherish Hawthorne's memory will retain
the impression of that room in the Pemigewasset House
where, during the night of May 18, 1864, he died
tranquilly in his sleep, having evidently not stirred
since he lost consciousness. Such a dismissal from anxiety and chagrin he had looked forward to so desirously
that the imagination rests upon the event without distress. Two years earlier, at the Wayside, he had discussed with Dicey the spiritualist creed that existence
recommences, under another form, the moment after
death. "Ah," Hawthorne had said, half laughing,
half seriously, "I hope there will be a break. A couple
of thousand years or so of sleep is the least that I can
do with before I begin life again."

At the funeral in Concord, a few days later, "in a
pomp of sunshine and verdure and gentle winds",
the clergyman who officiated — the same who had
married Hawthorne and his wife — made something
of the theme that Hawthorne had done more justice
than other writers to all shades of life, had shown a
sympathy with the guilty passions in human nature,
and had been, like Jesus, the friend of sinners. Emerson, who was among the pallbearers, had a more searching insight than this into the drama just ended. "I
thought," he wrote in his journal the next day, "there
was a tragic element in the event that might be more
fully rendered, — in the painful solitude of the man,
which, I suppose, could not longer be endured, and

he died of it." Indeed, he had not done justice to many shades of life, or shown much sympathy with human evil in most of its tangible forms; but he had done the ultimate justice to one highly serious experience, and had bodied forth the consequences that follow upon the first of the sins. There was a tragic element in his life as well as in his death; it was the tragedy of every life in which the self is not brought into the right relation with what lies beyond it; the essential tragedy of pride. But the whole drama had been acted out on the noblest level; there had been no element of meanness or paltriness or vulgarity in it; and it has a high and durable significance. The best that Hawthorne wrote is the reflection of his tragic adventure, and it will not soon be forgotten. "His memory has great allies." It is more certain now than ever that he is among the greatest of American writers: it is at least as certain as it ever was that he is among the greatest of Americans.

CHRONOLOGY

CHRONOLOGY

1804. Hawthorne born on Union Street, Salem, July 4.

1808. Captain Nathaniel Hathorne dies in Surinam.
Family moves to Manning household on Herbert Street.

1816–1820. Life at Raymond, Maine.

1820–1821. Studying and working for William Manning in Salem.

1821–1825. At Bowdoin College, Brunswick, Maine.

1825–1837. "The chamber under the eaves." Herbert Street, Salem.

1828. "Fanshawe."

1829. Hawthorne begins writing for "The Token."

1836. Hawthorne edits "The American Magazine of Useful and Entertaining Knowledge."

1837. "Twice-Told Tales." Hawthorne visits Bridge at Augusta, July and August.

1838. Hawthorne meets Sophia Peabody, and is secretly engaged to her. At North Adams, July and August.

1839–1841. Hawthorne a Measurer at the Boston Customhouse.

1841. At Brook Farm, April to November.

1842. Hawthorne married to Sophia Peabody in Boston, July 9.

1842–1845. At the Manse in Concord.

1846–1849. Hawthorne a Surveyor at the Salem Customhouse.

1846. "Mosses from an Old Manse."

1849–1850. Hawthorne dismissed from surveyorship, June, 1849. Death of Madame Hathorne, July, 1849. "The Scarlet Letter" published, April, 1850.

1850–1851. At Lenox. "The House of the Seven Gables" published, March, 1851. "The Snow Image" and "A Wonder Book", 1851.

1851–1852. At West Newton, November to May.

1852–1853. At the Wayside, Concord. "The Blithedale Romance" and "Life of Franklin Pierce", 1852. "Tanglewood Tales", 1853.

1853–1857. Hawthorne at the Liverpool Consulate.

1858–1859. Residence in Rome and Florence. Travel in France and Switzerland.

1859–1860. Second residence in England. At Redcar in Yorkshire, and at Leamington in Warwickshire. "The Marble Faun" published, 1860.

1860. Return to the Wayside in Concord, June.

1862. Visit in Washington, March. At West Gouldsborough, Maine, with Julian, August.

1863. "Our Old Home."

1864. Trip to New York and Philadelphia with Ticknor, March. Hawthorne dies at Plymouth, New Hampshire, May 19.

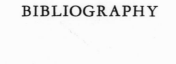

BIBLIOGRAPHY

BIBLIOGRAPHY

Alcott, A. Bronson. "Concord Days." Boston, 1873.
Bridge, Horatio. "Personal Recollections of Nathaniel Hawthorne." New York, 1893.
Browne, Nina E. "A Bibliography of Nathaniel Hawthorne." Boston, 1905.
Chandler, Elizabeth L. "A Study of the Sources of the Tales and Romances Written by Nathaniel Hawthorne before 1853." (Smith College Studies in Modern Languages) Northampton, 1926.
Conway, M. D. "Emerson at Home and Abroad." Boston, 1882.
"Life of Nathaniel Hawthorne." New York, 1890.
Dhaleine, L. "Hawthorne, sa vie et son œuvre." Paris, 1905.
Dicey, Edward. "Nathaniel Hawthorne." *Macmillan's Magazine.* July, 1864.
Fields, J. T. "Yesterdays with Authors." Boston, 1871.
Goodrich, Samuel Griswold. "Recollections of a Lifetime." New York, 1856.
Hawthorne, Julian. "Hawthorne and his Circle." New York, 1903.
"Nathaniel Hawthorne and his Wife." Boston, 1885.
Hoar, Elizabeth. "Mrs. Samuel Ripley. A Sketch." Philadelphia, 1888.
Howe, Julia Ward. "Two Glimpses of Hawthorne." *The Critic.* June 18, 1881.
Howe, M. A. DeWolfe. "Memories of a Hostess." Boston, 1922.

James, Henry. "Nathaniel Hawthorne." (English Men of Letters) London, 1880.

Jepson, G. E. "Hawthorne in the Boston Custom-House." *Bookman.* August, 1904.

Lathrop, G. P. "A Study of Hawthorne." Boston, 1876.

Lathrop, R. H. "Memories of Hawthorne." Boston, 1897.

"Letters of Hawthorne to W. D. Ticknor." Carteret Book Club. Newark, 1910.

Longfellow, Samuel. "Life of Henry Wadsworth Longfellow." Boston, 1886.

"Final Memorials of Henry Wadsworth Longfellow." Boston, 1887.

"Love Letters of Nathaniel Hawthorne." Privately printed for the Society of the Dofobs. Chicago, 1907.

Morris, Lloyd. "The Rebellious Puritan: Portrait of Mr. Hawthorne." New York, 1927.

Pickard, S. T. "Hawthorne's First Diary." Boston, 1897.

Poe, E. A. Two Reviews of "Twice-Told Tales." Volume XI of "The Complete Works of Edgar Allan Poe," edited by James A. Harrison. New York, 1902.

Reed, A. L. "Self-Portraiture in the Works of Nathaniel Hawthorne." *Studies in Philology.* January, 1926.

Stoddard, R. H. "Recollections, Personal and Literary." New York, 1903.

Swift, Lindsay. "Brook Farm: Its Members, Scholars, and Visitors." New York, 1900.

Ticknor, Caroline. "Hawthorne and his Publishers." Boston, 1913.

Trollope, Anthony. "The Genius of Nathaniel Hawthorne." *North American Review.* September, 1879.

Woodberry, G. E. "Nathaniel Hawthorne." (American Men of Letter Series) Boston, 1902.

INDEX

INDEX

ALBANY, N. Y., 42

Alcott, Amos Bronson, at Brook Farm, 97; Hawthorne buys Wayside from, 175; a neighbor of Hawthorne's, 267; on Hawthorne's unsociability, 267–268; 114

Allegory, exaggerated devotion to, 126–128

Allen, William, President of Bowdoin College, 19–20, 27

Allen, William, at Brook Farm, 103

Allingham, William, Hawthorne's impression of, 239

American Magazine of Useful and Entertaining Knowledge, as editor of, 52

"Ancestral Footstep, The", composition of, 279–281; analysis of, 282–283

Atlantic Monthly, The, 271, 275, 277

"Artist of the Beautiful, The", theme of, 132–133

BALZAC, HONORÉ DE, 182

Bancroft, George, 33; secures appointment as Measurer for Hawthorne, 84; praises him, 85; as Secretary of the Navy befriends him, 146

Bancroft, Mrs. George, a letter from Sumner to, 146

Bath, England, residence at, 245

Benjamin, Park, praises Hawthorne's early tales, 53

Bennoch, Francis, reluctance to bid farewell to, 255–256; possibility of dedicating "Our Old Home" to, 276

"Biographical Stories for Children", 103

"Birthmark, The", selfish search for perfection as theme of, 135–137

Blagden, Isa, H. spends evening at villa of, 253

"Blithedale Romance, The", quoted from, 105; composition of, 175; analysis of, 196–201; quotation from preface of, 208–209; limitations of, 209–219

Blodgett's, Mrs., boarding-house, stay at, 238

Boston, residence in, 84–95; as setting for "The Scarlet Letter", 210–211

Bowdoin College, commencement at, 3; a student at, 19–26

Bradford, George, description of Hawthorne at Brook Farm by, 102

Bridge, Horatio, classmate at Bowdoin, 5, 24–26; assists H. in publishing "Twice-Told Tales", 53–54; entertains Hawthorne at Augusta, 73–76; letters to, 50, 160–161, 162–163, 167, 229, 241, 270

Bright, Henry, letter to, 254; reluctance to bid farewell to, 256

Brook Farm, a colonist at, 95–106

Browning, Elizabeth Barrett, 253

Browning, Robert, 144; acquaintance with, 253

Bryant, William Cullen, 33

Buffalo, N. Y., 42

Burley, Susan, meetings at the house of, 80

Bunyan, John, 10, 15, 129, 220–221

"CANTERBURY PILGRIMS, THE", autobiography in, 68–69

Casa del Bello, residence in, 245, 249

"Celestial Railroad, The", satire in, 129–131

Channing, Ellery, acquaintance with, 114–116; 175–176

Cheever, George B., 4

Chester, England, interest in, 233

Date Due